# Microsoft®

# Excel 2000

## Illustrated Introductory Edition

# Microsoft®
# Excel 2000
## Illustrated Introductory Edition

Tara Lynn O'Keefe
Elizabeth Eisner Reding

**APPROVED COURSEWARE**

ONE MAIN STREET, CAMBRIDGE, MA 02142

Australia • Canada • Denmark • Japan • Mexico • New Zealand • Philippines
Puerto Rico • Singapore • South Africa • Spain • United Kingdom • United States

## Microsoft Excel 2000—Illustrated Introductory Edition is published by Course Technology

| | |
|---|---|
| Senior Product Manager: | Kathryn Schooling |
| Product Managers: | Jennifer A. Duffy, Rebecca VanEsselstine |
| Associate Product Manager: | Emily Heberlein |
| Production Editors: | Elena Montillo, Jennifer Goguen |
| Developmental Editors: | Rachel Biheller Bunin, India Koopman |
| Marketing Manager: | Karen Bartlett |
| Editorial Assistant: | Stacie Parillo |
| Composition House: | GEX Publishing Services |
| QA Manuscript Reviewers: | Jeff Schwartz, John Freitas, Jon Greacen, Matt Carroll |
| Text Designer: | Joseph Lee, Joseph Lee Designs |
| Cover Designer: | Doug Goodman, Doug Goodman Designs |

**For more information contact:**

Course Technology
One Main Street
Cambridge, MA  02142

Or find us on the World Wide Web at: www.course.com

**Disclaimer**
Course Technology reserves the right to revise this publication and make changes from time to time in its content without notice.

ISBN 0-7600-6062-2

Printed in the United States of America

7 8 9 BM 04 03 02

# The Illustrated Series Offers the Entire Package for your Microsoft Office 2000 Needs

## Office 2000 MOUS Certification Coverage

The Illustrated Series offers a growing number of Microsoft-approved titles that cover the objectives required to pass the Office 2000 MOUS exams. After studying with any of the approved Illustrated titles (see list on inside cover), you will have mastered the Core and Expert skills necessary to pass any Office 2000 MOUS exam with flying colors. In addition, **Excel 2000 MOUS Certification Objectives** at the end of the book map to where specific MOUS skills can be found in each lesson and where students can find additional practice.

## Helpful New Features

The Illustrated Series responded to Customer Feedback by adding a **Project Files list** at the back of the book for easy reference, Changing the red font in the Steps to green for easier reading, and Adding New Conceptual lessons to units to give students the extra information they need when learning Office 2000.

## New Exciting Case and Innovative On-Line Companion

There is an exciting new case study used throughout our textbooks, a fictitious company called MediaLoft, designed to be "real-world" in nature by introducing the kinds of activities that students will encounter when working with Microsoft Office 2000. The **MediaLoft Web site**, available at www.course.com/illustrated/medialoft, is an innovative Student Online Companion which enhances and augments the printed page by bringing students onto the Web for a dynamic and continually updated learning experience. The MediaLoft site mirrors the case study used throughout the book, creating a real-world intranet site for this chain of bookstore cafés. This Companion is used to complete the WebWorks exercise in each unit of this book, and to allow students to become familiar with the business application of an intranet site.

# Enhance Any Illustrated Text with these Exciting Products!

## Course CBT

Enhance your students' Office 2000 classroom learning experience with self-paced computer-based training on CD-ROM. Course CBT engages students with interactive multimedia and hands-on simulations that reinforce and complement the concepts and skills covered in the textbook. All the content is aligned with the MOUS (Microsoft Office User Specialist) program, making it a great preparation tool for the certification exams. Course CBT also includes extensive pre- and post-assessments that test students' mastery of skills.

## Course Assessment

How well do your students *really* know Microsoft Office? Course Assessment is a performance-based testing program that measures students' proficiency in Microsoft Office 2000. Previously known as SAM, Course Assessment is available for Office 2000 in either a live or simulated environment. You can use Course Assessment to place students into or out of courses, monitor their performance throughout a course, and help prepare them for the MOUS certification exams.

# Create Your Ideal Course Package with CourseKits™

If one book doesn't offer all the coverage you need, create a course package that does. With Course Technology's CourseKits—our mix-and-match approach to selecting texts—you have the freedom to combine products from more than one series. When you choose any two or more Course Technology products for one course, we'll discount the price and package them together so your students can pick up one convenient bundle at the bookstore.

For more information about any of these offerings or other Course Technology products, contact your sales representative or visit our web site at:

## www.course.com

# Preface

**W**elcome to *Microsoft Excel 2000—Illustrated Introductory Edition*. This highly visual book offers users a hands-on introduction to aspects of Microsoft Excel 2000 and also serves as an excellent reference for future use. If you would like additional coverage of Microsoft Excel 2000, we also offer *Microsoft Excel 2000—Illustrated Second Course*, a logical continuation of the Introductory Edition.

## ► Organization and Coverage

This text contains eight units that cover basic through intermediate Excel skills. In these units, students learn how to build, edit, and format worksheets and charts, work with formulas and functions, and manage workbooks.

## ► About this Approach

What makes the Illustrated approach so effective at teaching software skills? It's quite simple. Each skill is presented on two facing pages, with the step-by-step instructions on the left page, and large screen illustrations on the right. Students can focus on a single skill without having to turn the page. This unique design makes information extremely accessible and easy to absorb, and provides a great reference for after the course is over. This hands-on approach also makes it ideal for both self-paced or instructor-led classes.

Each lesson, or "information display," contains the following elements:

---

Each 2-page spread focuses on a single skill.

Clear step-by-step directions explain how to complete the specific task, with what students are to type in green. When students follow the numbered steps, they quickly learn how each procedure is performed and what the results will be.

Concise text that introduces the basic principles discussed in the lesson. Procedures are easier to learn when concepts fit into a framework.

---

### Excel 2000

# Controlling Page Breaks and Page Numbering

The vertical and horizontal dashed lines in worksheets indicate page breaks. Excel automatically inserts a page break when your worksheet data doesn't fit on one page. These page breaks are dynamic, which means they adjust automatically when you insert or delete rows and columns and when you change column widths or row heights. Everything to the left of the first vertical dashed line and above the first horizontal dashed line is printed on the first page. You can override the automatic breaks by choosing the Page Break command on the Insert menu. Table F-2 describes the different types of page breaks you can use. Jim wants another report displaying no more than half the hourly workers on each page. To accomplish this, he must insert a manual page break.

### Steps

1. Click cell **A16**, click **Insert** on the menu bar, then click **Page Break**
   A dashed line appears between rows 15 and 16, indicating a horizontal page break. See Figure F-13. After you set page breaks, it's a good idea to preview each page.

2. Preview the worksheet, then click **Zoom**
   Notice that the status bar reads "Page 1 of 4" and that the data for the employees up through Charles Gallagher appears on the first page. Jim decides to place the date in the footer.

   **QuickTip**
   To insert the page number in a header or footer section yourself, click in the Header or Footer dialog box.

3. While in the Print Preview window, click **Setup**, click the **Header/Footer** tab, click **Custom Footer**, click the **Right section** box, click the **Date button**

4. Click the **Left section** box, type your name, then click **OK**
   Your name, the page number, and the date, appear in the Footer preview area.

   **QuickTip**
   To remove a manual page break, select any cell directly below or to the right of the page break, click Insert on the menu bar, then click Remove Page Break.

5. In the Page Setup dialog box, click **OK**, and, still in Print Preview, check to make sure all the pages show your name and the page numbers, click **Print**, then click **OK**

6. Click **View** on the menu bar, click **Custom Views**, click **Add**, type **Half N Half**, then click **OK**
   Your new custom view has the page breaks and all current print settings.

7. Click **Insert** on the menu bar, then click **Remove Page Break**

8. Save the workbook

TABLE F-2: **Page break options**

| Type of page break | where to position cell pointer |
|---|---|
| Both horizontal and vertical page breaks | Select the cell below and to the right of the gridline where you want the breaks to occur |
| Only a horizontal page break | Select the cell in column A that is directly below the gridline where you want the page to break |
| Only a vertical page break | Select a cell in row 1 that is to the right of the gridline where you want the page to break |

---

Hints as well as trouble-shooting advice, right where you need it — next to the step itself.

Quickly accessible summaries of key terms, toolbar buttons, or keyboard alternatives connected with the lesson material. Students can refer easily to this information when working on their own projects at a later time.

Every lesson features large-size, full-color representations of what the students' screen should look like after completing the numbered steps.

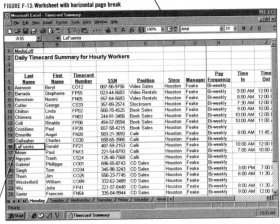

FIGURE F-13: Worksheet with horizontal page break

Dashed line indicates horizontal break after row 15

### Using Page Break Preview

By clicking View on the menu bar, then clicking Page Break Preview, or clicking Page Break Preview in the Print Preview window, you can view and change page breaks manually. (If you see a dialog box asking if you want help, just click OK to close it.) Simply drag the page break lines to the desired location. See Figure F-14. To exit Page Break Preview, click View on the menu bar then click Normal.

FIGURE F-14: Page Break Preview window

Cell pointer in cell A16

Drag page break lines to change page breaks

MANAGING WORKBOOKS AND PREPARING THEM FOR THE WEB  EXCEL F-13 ◄

Clues to Use boxes provide concise information that either expands on one component of the major lesson skill or describes an independent task that is in some way related to the major lesson skill.

The page numbers are designed like a road map. Excel indicates the Excel section, F indicates the sixth unit, and 13 indicates the page within the unit.

# Other Features

The two-page lesson format featured in this book provides the new user with a powerful learning experience. Additionally, this book contains the following features:

### ▶ MOUS Certification Coverage

Each unit opener has a ⌐MOUS⌐ next to it to indicate where Microsoft Office User Specialist (MOUS) skills are covered. In addition, there is a MOUS appendix which contains a grid that maps to where specific Core Excel MOUS skills can be found in each lesson and where students can find additional practice. This textbook thoroughly prepares students to learn the skills needed to pass the Excel 2000 MOUS exam. *Microsoft Excel—Illustrated Complete*, 0-7600-6064-9, teaches students the Expert skills needed for the Excel 2000 Expert MOUS exam.

### ▶ Real-World Case

The case study used throughout the textbook, a fictitious company called MediaLoft, is designed to be "'real-world" in nature and introduces the kinds of activities that students will encounter when working with Microsoft Excel 2000. With a real-world case, the process of solving problems will be more meaningful to students. Students can also enhance their skills by completing the Web Works exercises in each unit by going to the innovative Student Online Companion, available at **www.course.com/illustrated/medialoft**. The MediaLoft site mirrors the case study by acting as the company's intranet site, further allowing students to become familiar with applicable business scenarios.

### ▶ End of Unit Material

Each unit concludes with a Concepts Review that tests students' understanding of what they learned in the unit. The Concepts Review is followed by a Skills Review, which provides students with additional hands-on practice of the skills. The Skills Review is followed by Independent Challenges, which pose case problems for students to solve. At least one Independent Challenge in each unit asks students to use the World Wide Web to solve the problem as indicated by a Web Work icon. The Visual Workshops that follow the Independent Challenges help students develop critical thinking skills. Students are shown completed Web pages or screens and are asked to recreate them from scratch.

# Instructor's Resource Kit

The Instructor's Resource Kit is Course Technology's way of putting the resources and information needed to teach and learn effectively into your hands. With an integrated array of teaching and learning tools that offers you and your students a broad range of technology-based instructional options, we believe this kit represents the highest quality and most cutting edge resources available to instructors today. Many of these resources are available at www.course.com. The resources available with this book are:

**MediaLoft Web site**   Available at **www.course.com/illustrated/medialoft**, this innovative Student Online Companion enhances and augments the printed page by bringing students onto the Web for a dynamic and continually updated learning experience. The MediaLoft site mirrors the case study used throughout the book, creating a real-world intranet site for this fictitious company, a national chain of bookstore cafés. This Companion is used to complete the WebWorks exercise in each unit of this book, and to allow students to become familiar with the business application of an intranet site.

**Instructor's Manual**   Available as an electronic file, the Instructor's Manual is quality-assurance tested and includes unit overviews, detailed lecture topics for each unit with teaching tips, an Upgrader's Guide, solutions to all lessons and end-of-unit material, and extra Independent Challenges. The Instructor's Manual is available on the Instructor's Resource Kit CD-ROM, or you can download it from **www.course.com**.

**Course Test Manager**   Designed by Course Technology, this Windows-based testing software helps instructors design, administer, and print tests and pre-tests. A full-featured program, Course Test Manager also has an online testing component that allows students to take tests at the computer and have their exams automatically graded.

**Course Faculty Online Companion**   You can browse this textbook's password-protected site to obtain the Instructor's Manual, Solution Files, Project Files, and any updates to the text. Contact your Customer Service Representative for the site address and password.

**Project Files**   Project Files contain all of the data that students will use to complete the lessons and end-of-unit material. A Readme file includes instructions for using the files. Adopters of this text are granted the right to install the Project Files on any standalone computer or network. The Project Files are available on the Instructor's Resource Kit CD-ROM, the Review Pack, and can also be downloaded from www.course.com.

**Solution Files**   Solution Files contain every file students are asked to create or modify in the lessons and end-of-unit material. A Help file on the Instructor's Resource Kit includes information for using the Solution Files.

**Figure Files**   Figure files contain all the figures from the book in bitmap format. Use the figure files to create transparency masters or in a PowerPoint presentation.

**WebCT**   WebCT is a tool used to create Web-based educational environments and also uses WWW browsers as the interface for the course-building environment. The site is hosted on your school campus, allowing complete control over the information. WebCT has its own internal communication system, offering internal e-mail, a Bulletin Board, and a Chat room.

Course Technology offers pre-existing supplemental information to help in your WebCT class creation, such as a suggested Syllabus, Lecture Notes, Figures in the Book / Course Presenter, Student Downloads, and Test Banks in which you can schedule an exam, create reports, and more.

# Brief Contents

Exciting New Features and Products    V
Preface    VI

**Excel 2000**

Getting Started with Excel 2000 .......................................EXCEL A-1

Building and Editing Worksheets .....................................EXCEL B-1

Formatting a Worksheet....................................................EXCEL C-1

Working with Charts ........................................................EXCEL D-1

Working with Formulas and Functions...............................EXCEL E-1

Managing Workbooks and Preparing Them for the Web..........EXCEL F-1

Automating Worksheet Tasks ...........................................EXCEL G-1

Using Lists.......................................................................EXCEL H-1

**Excel 2000 MOUS Certification Objectives**    1
**Project Files**    7
**Glossary**    9
**Index**    13

# Contents

Exciting New Features and Products    V
Preface    VI

## Excel 2000

### Getting Started with Excel 2000    EXCEL A-1

Defining Spreadsheet Software......................................................EXCEL A-2
Starting Excel 2000 .....................................................................EXCEL A-4
Viewing the Excel Window...........................................................EXCEL A-6
   *Personalized toolbars and menus in Excel 2000* .........................EXCEL A-7
Opening and Saving a Workbook  ................................................EXCEL A-8
Entering Labels and Values...........................................................EXCEL A-10
   *Navigating a worksheet* .............................................................EXCEL A-11
Previewing and Printing a Worksheet ..........................................EXCEL A-12
   *Using Zoom in Print Preview* ....................................................EXCEL A-12
Getting Help ................................................................................EXCEL A-14
   *Changing the Office Assistant* ....................................................EXCEL A-14
Closing a Workbook and Exiting Excel ........................................EXCEL A-16
Concepts Review .........................................................................EXCEL A-18
Skills Review ..............................................................................EXCEL A-20
Independent Challenges ...............................................................EXCEL A-21
Visual Workshop..........................................................................EXCEL A-24

### Building and Editing Worksheets    EXCEL B-1

Planning and Designing a Worksheet ...........................................EXCEL B-2
Editing Cell Entries and Working with Ranges.............................EXCEL B-4
   *Using range names in a workbook*...............................................EXCEL B-5
Entering Formulas  ......................................................................EXCEL B-6
   *Order of precedence in Excel formulas* ......................................EXCEL B-7
Introducing Excel Functions  .......................................................EXCEL B-8
   *Using the MIN and MAX functions* ............................................EXCEL B-9

## Contents

Copying and Moving Cell Entries .................................................. EXCEL B-10
  *Using the Office Clipboard* .................................................. EXCEL B-11
Understanding Relative and Absolute Cell References ............. EXCEL B-12
  *Using a mixed reference* .................................................. EXCEL B-12
Copying Formulas with Relative Cell References ..................... EXCEL B-14
  *Filling cells with sequential text or values* .................... EXCEL B-14
Copying Formulas with Absolute Cell References .................... EXCEL B-16
  *Copying and moving using named ranges* ...................... EXCEL B-17
Naming and Moving a Sheet ................................................... EXCEL B-18
  *Moving and copying worksheets* .................................. EXCEL B-19
Concepts Review ................................................................... EXCEL B-20
Skills Review ........................................................................ EXCEL B-21
Independent Challenges ......................................................... EXCEL B-22
Visual Workshop ................................................................... EXCEL B-24

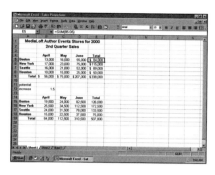

## Formatting a Worksheet

EXCEL C-1

Formatting Values ................................................................. EXCEL C-2
  *Using the Format Painter* .............................................. EXCEL C-3
Using Fonts and Font Sizes .................................................... EXCEL C-4
  *Using the Formatting toolbar to change fonts and font sizes* ....... EXCEL C-4
Changing Attributes and Alignment of Labels ........................ EXCEL C-6
  *Using AutoFormat* ...................................................... EXCEL C-7
Adjusting Column Widths ...................................................... EXCEL C-8
  *Specifying row height* .................................................. EXCEL C-8
Inserting and Deleting Rows and Columns ............................. EXCEL C-10
  *Using dummy columns and rows* ................................. EXCEL C-11
Applying Colors, Patterns, and Borders ................................. EXCEL C-12
  *Using color to organize a worksheet* ........................... EXCEL C-12
Using Conditional Formatting ................................................ EXCEL C-14
  *Deleting conditional formatting* .................................. EXCEL C-15
Checking Spelling ................................................................ EXCEL C-16
  *Modifying the spell checker* ........................................ EXCEL C-16

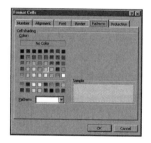

Concepts Review .................................................EXCEL C-18

Skills Review .....................................................EXCEL C-19

Independent Challenges .......................................EXCEL C-21

Visual Workshop ................................................EXCEL C-24

## Working with Charts
EXCEL D-1

Planning and Designing a Chart ............................EXCEL D-2

Creating a Chart ................................................EXCEL D-4

Moving and Resizing a Chart ...............................EXCEL D-6

*Identifying chart objects* .................................EXCEL D-7

Editing a Chart .................................................EXCEL D-8

*Rotating a chart*............................................EXCEL D-8

Formatting a Chart ............................................EXCEL D-10

Enhancing a Chart ............................................EXCEL D-12

*Changing text font and alignment in charts*............EXCEL D-12

Annotating and Drawing on a Chart .......................EXCEL D-14

*Exploding a pie slice* ....................................EXCEL D-15

Previewing and Printing a Chart ...........................EXCEL D-16

*Using the Page Setup dialog box for a chart* ..........EXCEL D-16

Concepts Review ...............................................EXCEL D-18

Skills Review ....................................................EXCEL D-20

Independent Challenges .......................................EXCEL D-22

Visual Workshop................................................EXCEL D-24

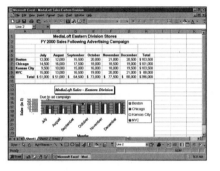

## Working with Formulas and Functions
EXCEL E-1

Creating a Formula with Several Operators ..............EXCEL E-2

*Using Paste Special to paste formulas and values and to perform calculations*................................EXCEL E-3

Using Names in a Formula ...................................EXCEL E-4

*Producing a list of names*................................EXCEL E-5

Generating Multiple Totals with AutoSum ...............EXCEL E-6

*Quick calculations with AutoCalculate*..................EXCEL E-7

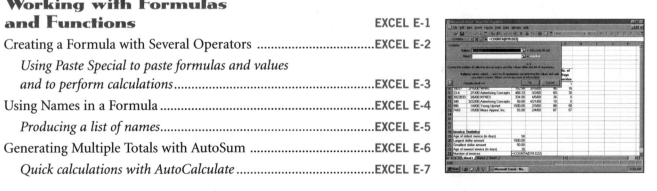

# Contents

Using Dates in Calculations .........................................EXCEL E-8

   *Using date functions* ...........................................EXCEL E-8

   *Custom number and date formats*...........................EXCEL E-9

Building a Conditional Formula with the IF Function .............EXCEL E-10

   *Inserting and deleting selected cells* .....................EXCEL E-11

Using Statistical Functions .........................................EXCEL E-12

   *Using the Formula Palette to enter and edit formulas* .............EXCEL E-13

Calculating Payments with the PMT Function......................EXCEL E-14

   *Calculating future value with the FV function* .......................EXCEL E-15

Displaying and Printing Formula Contents ......................EXCEL E-16

   *Setting margins and alignment when printing part of a worksheet* .....................................EXCEL E-17

Concepts Review ....................................................EXCEL E-18

Skills Review .........................................................EXCEL E-19

Independent Challenges .............................................EXCEL E-20

Visual Workshop ....................................................EXCEL E-24

## Managing Workbooks and Preparing Them for the Web       EXCEL F-1

Freezing Columns and Rows .......................................EXCEL F-2

   *Splitting the worksheet into multiple panes*...................EXCEL F-3

Inserting and Deleting Worksheets ...............................EXCEL F-4

   *Specifying headers and footers* ...............................EXCEL F-5

Consolidating Data with 3-D References...........................EXCEL F-6

   *Consolidating data from different workbooks using linking* ........EXCEL F-7

Hiding and Protecting Worksheet Areas ..........................EXCEL F-8

   *Changing workbook properties* .................................EXCEL F-9

Saving Custom Views of a Worksheet .............................EXCEL F-10

   *Using a workspace* ...............................................EXCEL F-11

Controlling Page Breaks and Page Numbering ..........................EXCEL F-12

   *Using Page Break Preview* .....................................EXCEL F-13

Creating a Hyperlink between Excel Files ....................EXCEL F-14

   *Using hyperlinks to navigate large worksheets*.....................EXCEL F-14

   *Inserting a picture* ...........................................EXCEL F-15

Saving an Excel file as an HTML Document........................EXCEL F-16

   *Send a workbook via e-mail* ................................EXCEL F-17

Concepts Review ........................................................EXCEL F-18

Skills Review ...........................................................EXCEL F-19

Independent Challenges .............................................EXCEL F-20

Visual Workshop ......................................................EXCEL F-24

## Automating Worksheet Tasks

                                                    EXCEL G-1

Planning a Macro .....................................................EXCEL G-2

   *Macros and viruses* .........................................EXCEL G-3

Recording a Macro ....................................................EXCEL G-4

   *Using templates to create a workbook* .......................EXCEL G-5

Running a Macro ......................................................EXCEL G-6

Editing a Macro........................................................EXCEL G-8

   *Adding comments to code* ...................................EXCEL G-9

Using Shortcut Keys with Macros ................................EXCEL G-10

Using the Personal Macro Workbook ...........................EXCEL G-12

   *Working with the Personal Macro Workbook* ...............EXCEL G-13

Adding a Macro as a Menu Item .................................EXCEL G-14

Creating a Toolbar for Macros .....................................EXCEL G-16

Concepts Review.......................................................EXCEL G-18

Skills Review ...........................................................EXCEL G-20

Independent Challenges .............................................EXCEL G-21

Visual Workshop......................................................EXCEL G-24

## Using Lists

                                                    EXCEL H-1

Planning a List ........................................................EXCEL H-2

   *Lists versus databases* ......................................EXCEL H-3

Creating a List.........................................................EXCEL H-4

   *Maintaining the quality of information in a list* .......EXCEL H-5

Adding Records with the Data Form.............................EXCEL H-6

## Contents

Finding Records ................................................................EXCEL H-8

   *Using wildcards to fine-tune your search* ...................EXCEL H-9

Deleting Records.............................................................EXCEL H-10

   *Advantage of deleting records from the worksheet* ..................EXCEL H-11

Sorting a List by One Field.............................................EXCEL H-12

   *Rotating and indenting to improve label appearance*...............EXCEL H-13

Sorting a List by Multiple Fields ..................................EXCEL H-14

   *Specifying a custom sort order*.....................................EXCEL H-15

Printing a List .................................................................EXCEL H-16

   *Setting a print area* ......................................................EXCEL H-17

Concepts Review............................................................EXCEL H-18

Skills Review ..................................................................EXCEL H-19

Independent Challenges .................................................EXCEL H-20

Visual Workshop.............................................................EXCEL H-24

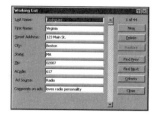

**Excel 2000 MOUS Certification Objectives**     1

**Project Files**     7

**Glossary**     9

**Index**     13

# Getting
## Started with Excel 2000

### Objectives

► **Define spreadsheet software**
► **Start Excel 2000**
► **View the Excel window**
⌐MOUS⌐ ► **Open and save a workbook**
⌐MOUS⌐ ► **Enter labels and values**
⌐MOUS⌐ ► **Preview and print a worksheet**
⌐MOUS⌐ ► **Get Help**
► **Close a workbook and exit Excel**

In this unit, you will learn how to start Microsoft Excel 2000 and use different elements of the Excel window. You will also learn how to open and save existing files, enter data in a worksheet, and use the extensive Help system. ✐ Jim Fernandez is the office manager at MediaLoft, a nationwide chain of bookstore cafés selling books, CDs, and videos. MediaLoft cafés also sell coffee and pastries to customers. Jim uses Excel to analyze a worksheet that summarizes budget information for the MediaLoft Café in the New York City store.

# Defining Spreadsheet Software

Microsoft Excel is an electronic spreadsheet program that runs on Windows computers. You use an **electronic spreadsheet** to perform numeric calculations rapidly and accurately. See Table A-1 for common ways spreadsheets are used in business. The electronic spreadsheet that you produce when using Excel is also referred to as a **worksheet**. Excel helps Jim produce professional-looking documents that can be updated automatically so they always have accurate information. Figure A-1 shows a budget worksheet that Jim created using pencil and paper, while Figure A-2 shows the same worksheet Jim created using Excel.

## The advantages of using Excel include:

### Enter data quickly and accurately

With Excel, you can enter information faster and more accurately than when using the pencil-and-paper method. For example, in the MediaLoft NYC Café budget, certain expenses such as rent, cleaning supplies, and products supplied on a yearly plan (coffee, creamers, sweeteners) remain constant for the year. You can copy the expenses that don't change from quarter to quarter, and then use Excel to calculate Total Expenses and Net Income for each quarter by simply supplying the data and formulas.

### Recalculate data easily

Fixing typing errors or updating data using Excel is easy, and the results of a changed entry are recalculated automatically. For example, if you receive updated expense figures for Quarter 4, you simply enter the new numbers and Excel recalculates the worksheet.

### Perform a what-if analysis

One of the most powerful decision-making features of Excel is the ability to change data and then quickly view the recalculated results. Anytime you use a worksheet to answer the question "what if," you are performing a **what-if analysis.** For instance, if the advertising budget for a quarter is increased to $3,600, you can enter the new figure into the worksheet and immediately see the impact on the overall budget.

### Change the appearance of information

Excel provides powerful features for enhancing a spreadsheet so that information is visually appealing and easy to understand. You can use boldface type and shade text headings or numbers to add emphasis to key data in the worksheet.

### Create charts

Excel makes it easy to create charts based on information in a worksheet. With Excel, charts are automatically updated as data changes. The worksheet in Figure A-2 includes a pie chart that graphically shows the distribution of the MediaLoft NYC Café's budget expenses for the year 2000.

### Share information with other users

Because everyone at MediaLoft is now using Microsoft Office, it's easy to share worksheet data among colleagues. For example, you can complete the MediaLoft budget that your manager started creating in Excel. Simply access the files you need or want to share through the network or from a disk, and then make any changes or additions.

### Create new worksheets from existing ones quickly

It's easy to take an existing Excel worksheet and quickly modify it to create a new one. When you are ready to create next year's budget, you can open the file for this year's budget, save it with a new file name, and use the existing data as a starting point.

**FIGURE A-1:** Traditional paper worksheet

## MediaLoft NYC Café Budget

|  | Qtr1 | Qtr 2 | Qtr 3 | Qtr 4 | Total |
|---|---|---|---|---|---|
| Net Sales | 48,000 | 76,000 | 64,000 | 80,000 | 268,000 |
| Expenses |  |  |  |  |  |
| Salary | 13,000 | 13,000 | 13,000 | 13,000 | 52,000 |
| Rent | 3,500 | 3,500 | 3,500 | 3,500 | 14,000 |
| Advertising | 3,600 | 8,000 | 16,000 | 20,000 | 47,600 |
| Cleaners | 1,500 | 1,500 | 1,500 | 1,500 | 6,000 |
| Pastries | 2,500 | 2,500 | 2,500 | 2,500 | 10,000 |
| Milk/Cream | 1,000 | 1,000 | 1,000 | 1,000 | 4,000 |
| Coffee/Tea | 4,250 | 4,250 | 4,250 | 4,250 | 17,000 |
| Sweeteners | 300 | 300 | 300 | 300 | 1,200 |
| Total Expenses | 29,650 | 34,050 | 42,050 | 46,050 | 151,800 |
| Net Income | 18,350 | 41,950 | 21,950 | 33,950 | 116,200 |

**FIGURE A-2:** Excel worksheet

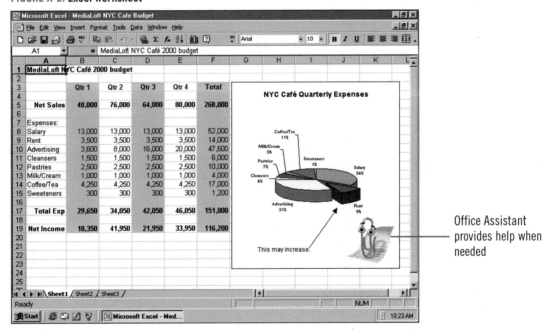

Office Assistant provides help when needed

**TABLE A-1:** Common business uses for spreadsheets

| spreadsheets are used to: | by: |
|---|---|
| **Maintain values** | Calculating numbers |
| **Represent values visually** | Creating charts based on worksheet figures |
| **Create consecutively numbered pages using multiple workbook sheets** | Printing reports containing workbook sheets |
| **Organize data** | Sorting data in ascending or descending order |
| **Analyze data** | Creating data summaries and short-lists using PivotTables or AutoFilters |
| **Create what-if data scenarios** | Using variable values to investigate and sample different outcomes |

# Starting Excel 2000

To start any Windows program, you use the Start button on the taskbar. A slightly different procedure might be required for computers on a network and those that use Windows-enhancing utilities. If you need assistance, ask your instructor or technical support person. ✐ Jim is ready to begin work on the budget for the MediaLoft Café in New York City. He begins by starting Excel.

## Steps

**1.** Point to the **Start button** ▤ Start on the taskbar

The Start button is on the left side of the taskbar and is used to start programs on your computer.

**2.** Click ▤ Start

Microsoft Excel is located in the Programs group, which is at the top of the Start menu, as shown in Figure A-3.

**Trouble?**

If you don't see the Microsoft Excel icon, consult your instructor or technical support person.

**3.** Point to **Programs**

All the programs on your computer, including Microsoft Excel, are listed in this area of the Start menu. See Figure A-4. Your program list might look different depending on the programs installed on your computer.

**4.** Click the **Microsoft Excel program icon** on the Programs menu

Excel opens and a blank worksheet appears. In the next lesson, you will familiarize yourself with the elements of the Excel worksheet window.

**FIGURE A-3: Start menu**

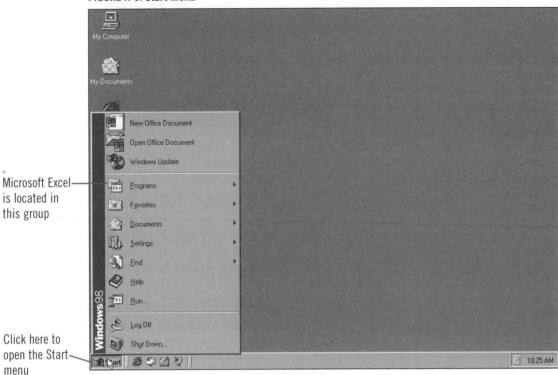

Microsoft Excel is located in this group

Click here to open the Start menu

**FIGURE A-4: Programs list**

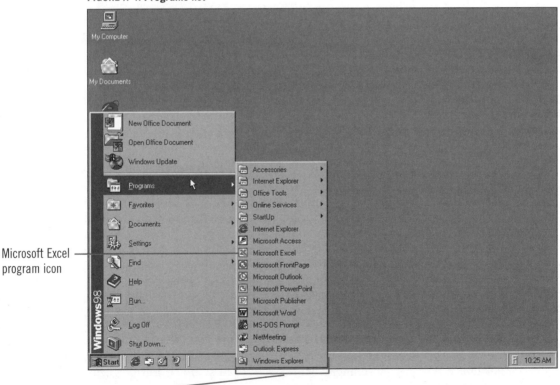

Microsoft Excel program icon

Your list of programs might vary

# Viewing the Excel Window

Excel 2000

When you start Excel, the **worksheet window** appears on your screen. The worksheet window includes the tools that enable you to create and work with worksheets. Jim needs to familiarize himself with the Excel worksheet window and its elements before he starts working with the budget worksheet. Compare the descriptions below to Figure A-5.

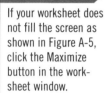

**Trouble?**

If your worksheet does not fill the screen as shown in Figure A-5, click the Maximize button in the worksheet window.

The **worksheet window** contains a grid of columns and rows. Columns are labeled alphabetically (A, B, C, etc.) and rows are labeled numerically (1, 2, 3, etc.). The worksheet window displays only a tiny fraction of the whole worksheet, which has a total of 256 columns and 65,536 rows. The intersection of a column and a row is a **cell**. Cells can contain text, numbers, formulas, or a combination of all three. Every cell has its own unique location or **cell address**, which is identified by the coordinates of the intersecting column and row. For example, the cell address of the cell in the upper-left corner of a worksheet is A1.

The **cell pointer** is a dark rectangle that highlights or outlines the cell you are working in. This cell is called the **active cell**. In Figure A-5, the cell pointer is located at A1, so A1 is the active cell. To activate a different cell, just click any other cell or press the arrow keys on your keyboard to move the cell pointer elsewhere.

The **title bar** displays the program name (Microsoft Excel) and the filename of the open worksheet (in this case the default filename, Book1). As shown in Figure A-5, the title bar also contains a control menu box, a Close button, and resizing buttons, which are common to all Windows programs.

The **menu bar** contains menus from which you choose Excel commands. As with all Windows programs, you can choose a menu command by clicking it with the mouse or by pressing [Alt] plus the underlined letter in the menu name. When you click a menu, a short list of commonly used commands may appear at first; you can wait or click the double arrows at the bottom of the menu to see expanded menus.

The **name box** displays the active cell address. In Figure A-5, "A1" appears in the name box, indicating that A1 is the active cell.

The **formula bar** allows you to enter or edit data in the worksheet.

The **toolbars** contain buttons for frequently used Excel commands. The **Standard toolbar** is located just below the left edge of the menu bar and contains buttons that effect operations within the worksheet. The **Formatting toolbar**—to the right of the Standard toolbar—contains buttons that change the worksheet's appearance. Each button contains a graphic representation of its function. For instance, the face of the Printing button contains a printer. To choose a button, simply click it with the left mouse button. Not all the buttons on the Standard and Formatting toolbars are visible on the screen. To view other toolbar buttons, click the More Buttons button [≈] at the right end of each toolbar to display a list of additional buttons. Throughout the lessons in this book, you will need to remember to click the More Buttons button if a button you are instructed to click is not visible on your screen. When you use a button from the More Buttons list, Excel adds it to your visible toolbar. That's why each user's toolbars look unique. Be sure to read the Clues to Use in this lesson to learn more about working with Excel's toolbars.

**Sheet tabs** below the worksheet grid let you keep your work in collections called **workbooks**. Each workbook contains three worksheets by default and can contain a maximum of 255 sheets. **Sheet tabs** can be given meaningful names. **Sheet tab scrolling buttons** help you move from one sheet to another.

The **status bar** is located at the bottom of the Excel window. The left side of the status bar provides a brief description of the active command or task in progress. The right side of the status bar shows the status of important keys such as [Caps Lock] and [Num Lock].

**FIGURE A-5: Excel worksheet window elements**

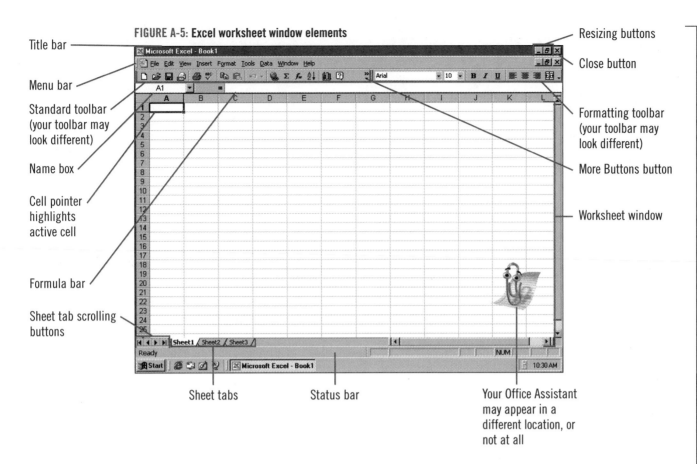

Title bar

Menu bar

Standard toolbar
(your toolbar may
look different)

Name box

Cell pointer
highlights
active cell

Formula bar

Sheet tab scrolling
buttons

Resizing buttons

Close button

Formatting toolbar
(your toolbar may
look different)

More Buttons button

Worksheet window

Sheet tabs

Status bar

Your Office Assistant
may appear in a
different location, or
not at all

## Personalized toolbars and menus in Excel 2000

Excel toolbars and menus modify themselves to
your working style. The Standard and Formatting
toolbars you see when you first start Excel include
the most frequently used buttons. To locate a button
not visible on a toolbar, click the **More Buttons
button** 🔧 on that toolbar to see the list of additional toolbar buttons. As you work, Excel promotes
the buttons you use to the visible toolbars, and
demotes the buttons you don't use to the More
Buttons list. Similarly, Excel menus adjust to your
work habits, so that the commands you use most
often automatically appear on the shortened menus.
Click the double arrow at the bottom of a menu to
view additional menu commands. You can return
toolbars and menus to their default settings by clicking Reset my usage data on the Options tab of the
Customize dialog box, as shown in Figure A-6.
Resetting your usage data erases changes made automatically to your menus and toolbars. It does not
affect the options you customize.

**FIGURE A-6: Customize dialog box**

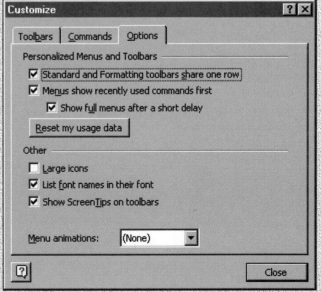

**Excel 2000**

# Opening and Saving a Workbook

Sometimes it's more efficient to create a new worksheet by modifying one that already exists. This saves you from having to retype information that can be reused from previous work. Throughout this book, you will create new worksheets by opening a file from your Project Disk, using the Save As command to create a copy of the file with a new name, and then modifying the new file by following the lesson steps. Use the Save command to store changes made to an existing file. It is a good idea to save your work every 15 minutes or before printing. Saving the files with new names keeps your original Project Disk files intact, in case you have to start the lesson over again or you wish to repeat an exercise. ✐ Jim wants to complete the New York City MediaLoft Café budget that a member of the accounting staff has been working on. Jim opens the budget workbook and then uses the Save As command to create a copy with a new name.

**1.** Insert your Project Disk in the appropriate disk drive

**2.** Click the **Open button** 🖼 on the Standard toolbar
The Open dialog box opens. See Figure A-7.

**3.** Click the **Look in list arrow,** then click the **drive that contains your Project Disk**
A list of the files on your Project Disk appears in the Open dialog box.

**QuickTip**

You could also double-click the filename in the Open dialog box to open the file.

**4.** Click the file **EX A-1,** then click **Open**
The file EX A-1 opens.

**5.** Click **File** on the menu bar, then click **Save As**
The Save As dialog box opens with the drive containing your Project Disk displayed in the Save in list box. You should save all your files to your Project Disk, unless instructed otherwise.

**QuickTip**

You can click 💾 or use the shortcut key [Ctrl][S] to save a workbook using the same filename.

**6.** In the File name text box, select the current file name (if necessary), type **MediaLoft Cafe Budget,** as shown in Figure A-8, then click **Save**
Both the Save As dialog box and the file EX A-1 close, and a duplicate file named MediaLoft Café Budget opens, as shown in Figure A-9. The Office Assistant may or may not appear on your screen. As you will learn, toolbars and menus change as you work with Excel. It is a good idea to return toolbars and menus to their default settings when you begin these lessons.

**7.** Click **Tools** on the menu bar, click **Customize,** make sure the Options tab in the Customize dialog box is displayed, click **Reset my usage data** to restore the default settings, click **Yes** in the alert box or dialog balloon, then click **Close**

**FIGURE A-7: Open dialog box**

Click to display a list of available drives and folders

Your folder may differ

Your files and folders display here

The selected filename will appear here

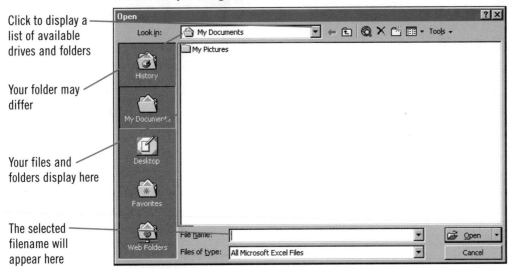

**FIGURE A-8: Save As dialog box**

Current drive or folder (yours may differ)

Your list of files might be different

Type the new filename here

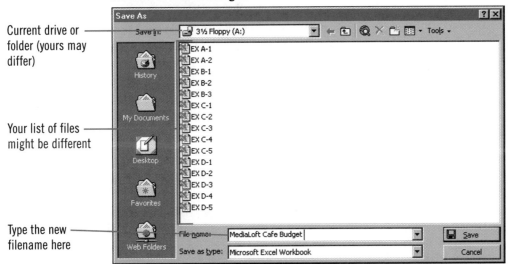

**FIGURE A-9: MediaLoft Cafe Budget workbook**

Because toolbars adapt as you work, your toolbars may not match the figures

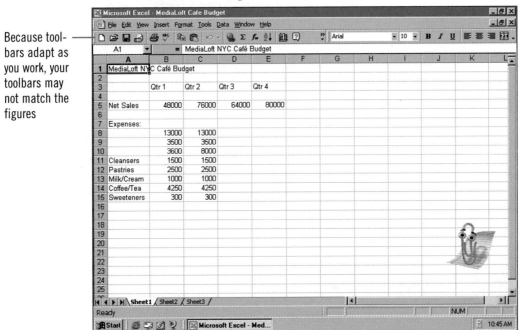

# Entering Labels and Values

Labels are used to identify the data in the rows and columns of a worksheet. They also make your worksheet more readable and understandable. You should try to enter all labels in your worksheet before entering the data. Labels can contain text and numerical information not used in calculations, such as dates, times, or addresses. Labels are left-aligned by default. **Values**, which include numbers, formulas, and functions, are used in calculations. Excel recognizes an entry as a value when it is a number or begins with special symbols: +, -, =, @, #, or $. All values are right-aligned by default. When a cell contains both text and numbers it is not a valid formula; Excel recognizes the entry as a label. Jim needs to enter labels identifying the rest of the expense categories, and the values for Qtr 3 and Qtr 4 into the MediaLoft Café Budget worksheet.

## Steps 1234

**1.** Click cell **A8** to make it the active cell
Notice that the cell address A8 appears in the name box. As you work, the mouse pointer has a variety of appearances, depending on where it is and what Excel is doing. Table A-2 lists and identifies some mouse pointers. The labels in cells A1:A15 identify the expenses.

### Trouble?

If you notice a mistake in a cell entry after it has been confirmed, double-click the cell, use [Backspace] or [Delete] to make your corrections, then press [Enter]. You can also click Edit on the menu bar, point to Clear, then click Contents to remove a cell's contents.

**2.** Type **Salary**, as shown in Figure A-10, then click the **Enter button** 🔲 on the formula bar
The label is entered in cell A8 and its contents display in the formula bar. You can also confirm a cell entry by pressing [Enter], pressing [Tab], or by pressing one of the arrow keys on the keyboard. If a label does not fit in a cell, Excel displays the remaining characters in the next cell to the right as long as it is empty. Otherwise, the label is **truncated**, or cut off.

**3.** Click cell **A9**, type **Rent**, press [**Enter**] to complete the entry and move the cell pointer to cell A10, type **Advertising** in cell A10, then press [**Enter**]
The remaining expense values have to be added to the worksheet.

**4.** Click cell **D8**, press and hold the left mouse button, drag the ✚ pointer to cell **E8** then down to cell **E15**, then release the mouse button
Two or more selected cells is called a **range**. The active cell is still cell D8, the cells in the range are shaded in purple. Since entries often cover multiple columns and rows, selecting a range makes working with data entry easier.

### QuickTip

To enter a number that will not be used as part of a calculation, such as a telephone number, type an apostrophe (') before the number.

**5.** Type **13000**, press [**Enter**], type **3500** in cell D9, press [**Enter**], type **16000** in cell D10, press [**Enter**], type **1500** in cell D11, press [**Enter**], type **2500** in cell D12, press [**Enter**], type **1000** in cell D13, press [**Enter**], type **4250** in cell D14, press [**Enter**], type **300** in cell D15, then press [**Enter**]
All the values in the Qtr 3 column have been added. The cell pointer is now in cell E8.

**6.** Using Figure A-11 as a guide, type the remaining values for cells E8 through E15
Before confirming a cell entry you can click the Cancel button on the formula bar or press [Esc] to cancel or delete the entry.

**7.** Type your name in cell **A17**, then click the **Save button** 🔲 on the Standard toolbar
Your name identifies the worksheet as yours when it is printed.

TABLE A-2: Commonly used pointers

| name | pointer | use to |
|---|---|---|
| **Normal or Cross** | ✚ | Select a cell or range; indicates Ready mode |
| **I-beam** | I | Edit contents of formula bar |
| **Select** | ⌖ | Select objects and commands |

**FIGURE A-10:** Worksheet with initial label entered

Name box ——

Cancel button ——

Enter button ——

Formula bar ——

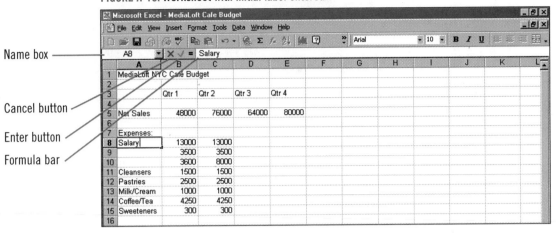

**FIGURE A-11:** Worksheet with new labels and values

Type these values ——

Labels entered ——

Values entered ——

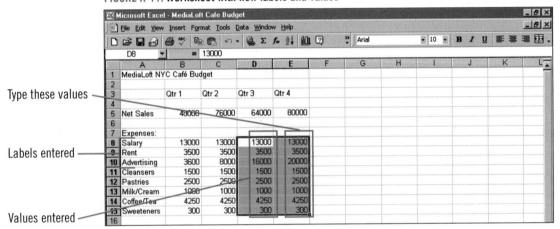

## Navigating a worksheet

With over a million cells available to you, it is important to know how to move around, or **navigate**, a worksheet. You can use the arrow keys on the keyboard ([↑], [↓], [←], [→]) to move a cell or two at a time, or [Page Up] or [Page Down] to move a screenful at a time. To move a screen to the left press [Alt] [Page Up]; to move a screen

to the right press [Alt] [Page Down]. You can also simply use your mouse pointer to click the desired cell. If the desired cell is not visible in the worksheet window, use the scroll bars or the Go To command to move the location into view. To return to the first active cell in a worksheet, click cell A1, or press [Ctrl][Home].

# Previewing and Printing a Worksheet

When a worksheet is completed, you may want to print it to have a paper copy to reference, file, or give to others. You can also print a worksheet that is not complete to review your work when you are not at a computer. Before you print a worksheet, you should save any changes. That way, if anything happens to the file as it is being sent to the printer, you will have your latest work saved to your disk. Then you should preview it to make sure it will fit on a page the way you want. When you preview a worksheet, you see a copy of the worksheet exactly as it will appear on paper. Table A-3 provides additional printing tips.  Jim is finished entering the labels and values into the MediaLoft Café budget. Since he already saved his changes, he previews and prints a copy of the worksheet to review on the way home.

### 1. Make sure the printer is on and contains paper
If a file is sent to print and the printer is off, an error message appears.

**Trouble?**

If is not visible on your Standard toolbar, click the More Buttons button to view additional toolbar buttons.

### 2. Click the **Print Preview button** on the Standard toolbar
A miniature version of the worksheet appears on the screen, as shown in Figure A-13. If there were more than one page, you could click the Next button or the Previous button to move between pages. You can also enlarge the image by clicking the Zoom button.

### 3. Click **Print**
The Print dialog box opens, as shown in Figure A-14. To print, you could also click File on the menu bar, then click Print Preview.

### 4. Make sure that the **Active Sheet(s) option button** is selected and that **1** appears in the Number of copies text box
Adjusting the value in the Number of copies text box enables you to print multiple copies. You could also print the selected range, the values you just entered, by clicking the Selection option button.

### 5. Click **OK**
The Printing dialog box appears briefly while the file is sent to the printer. Note that the dialog box contains a Cancel button. You can use it to cancel the print job provided you can catch it before the file is sent to the printer.

## CLUES TO USE

### Using Zoom in Print Preview
When you are in the Print Preview window, you can enlarge the image by clicking the Zoom button. You can also position the mouse pointer over a specific part of the worksheet page, then click it to view that section of the page. Figure A-12 shows a magnified section of a document. While the image is zoomed in, use the scroll bars to view different sections of the page.

**FIGURE A-12: Enlarging the preview using Zoom**

Microsoft Excel - MediaLoft Cafe Budget

| Next | Previous | Zoom | Print... | Setup... | Margins | Page Break Preview | Close | Help |

MediaLoft NYC Café Budget

|  | Qtr 1 | Qtr 2 | Qtr 3 | Qtr 4 |
|---|---|---|---|---|
| Net Sales | 48000 | 76000 | 64000 | 80000 |
| Expenses: |  |  |  |  |
| Salary | 13000 | 13000 | 13000 | 13000 |
| Rent | 3500 | 3500 | 3500 | 3500 |
| Advertising | 3600 | 8000 | 16000 | 20000 |
| Cleansers | 1500 | 1500 | 1500 | 1500 |
| Pastries | 2500 | 2500 | 2500 | 2500 |
| Milk/Cream | 1000 | 1000 | 1000 | 1000 |
| Coffee/Tea | 4250 | 4250 | 4250 | 4250 |
| Sweeteners | 300 | 300 | 300 | 300 |

**FIGURE A-13: Print Preview screen**

Move to another page

Enlarge the screen image

Print the worksheet

Change print options

Return to worksheet

Mouse pointer enlarges section of sheet when clicked

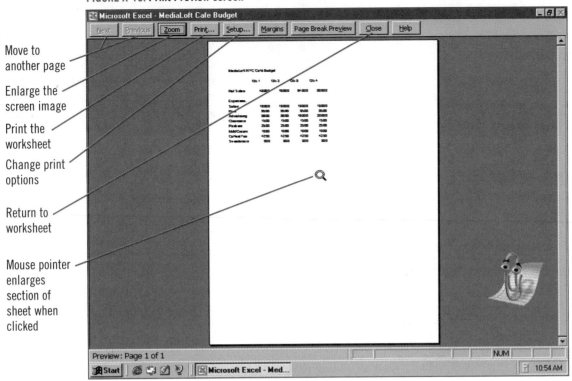

**FIGURE A-14: Print dialog box**

Your printer may differ

Indicates the number of copies to be printed

Prints the current worksheet

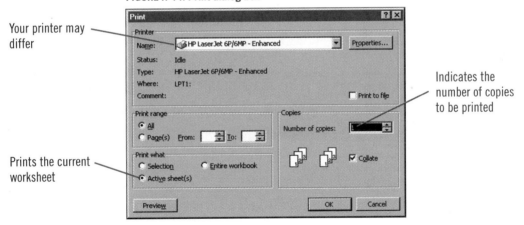

**TABLE A-3: Worksheet printing tips**

| before you print | recommendation |
|---|---|
| Save your work | Make sure your work is saved to a disk |
| Check the printer | Make sure that the printer is turned on and is online, that it has paper, and that there are no error messages or warning signals |
| Preview the worksheet | Check the formatted image for page breaks, page setup (vertical or horizontal), and overall appearance of the worksheet |
| Check the printer selection | Use the Printer setup command in the Print dialog box to verify that the correct printer is selected |
| Check the Print what options | Verify that you are printing either the active sheet, the entire workbook, or just a selected range |

# Getting Help

Excel features an extensive **Help system** that gives you immediate access to definitions, explanations, and useful tips. The animated Office Assistant provides help in two ways. You can type a keyword to search on, or access a question and answer format to research your help topic. The Office Assistant provides **ScreenTips** (indicated by a light bulb) on the current action you are performing. You can click the light bulb to access further information in the form of a dialog box that you can resize and refer to as you work. In addition, you can press [F1] at any time to get immediate help. ▰▰▰ Jim wants to find out more about ranges so he can work more efficiently with them. He knows he can find more information using the animated Office Assistant.

## Steps

> **1.** Click the **Microsoft Excel Help button** 🔃 on the Standard toolbar
>
> An Office Assistant dialog box opens. You can get information by typing a word to search on in the query box, or by typing a question. If the text within the query box is already selected, any typed text will automatically replace what is highlighted. The Office Assistant provides help based on text typed in the query box.

**QuickTip**

If it's displayed, you can also click the Office Assistant to access Help.

**2.** Type **Define a range**

See Figure A-16.

**3.** Click **Search**

The Office Assistant searches for relevant topics from the help files in Excel and then displays the results.

**QuickTip**

Clicking the Print button in the Microsoft Excel Help window prints the information.

> **4.** Click **See More** if necessary, click **Name cells in a workbook**, then click **Name a cell or a range of cells** in the Microsoft Excel Help window
>
> A Help window containing information about ranges opens. See Figure A-17.

**5.** Read the text, then click the **Close button** on the Help window title bar

The Help window closes and you return to your worksheet.

**6.** Right-click the **Office Assistant**, then click **Hide**

The Office Assistant is no longer visible on the worksheet.

### Changing the Office Assistant

The default Office Assistant character is Clippit, but there are others from which you can choose. To change the appearance of the Office Assistant, right-click the Office Assistant, then click Choose Assistant. Click the Gallery tab, click the Back and Next buttons until you find an Assistant you want to use, then click OK. (You may need to insert your Microsoft Office 2000 CD to perform this task.) Each Office Assistant makes its own unique sounds and can be animated by right-clicking its window and clicking Animate! Figure A-15 shows the Office Assistant dialog box.

**FIGURE A-15: Office Assistant dialog box**

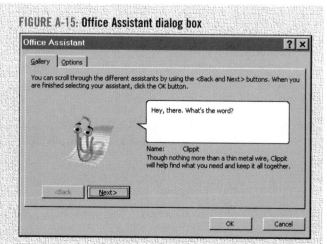

**FIGURE A-16: Office Assistant**

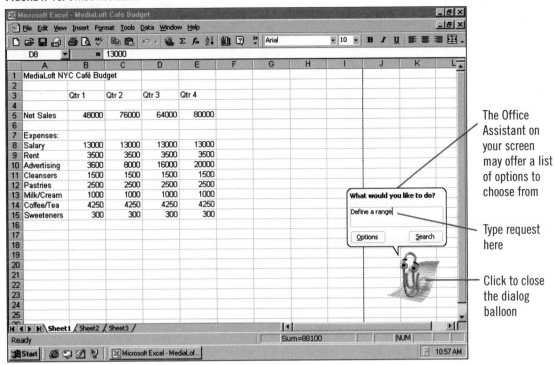

The Office Assistant on your screen may offer a list of options to choose from

Type request here

Click to close the dialog balloon

**FIGURE A-17: Help window**

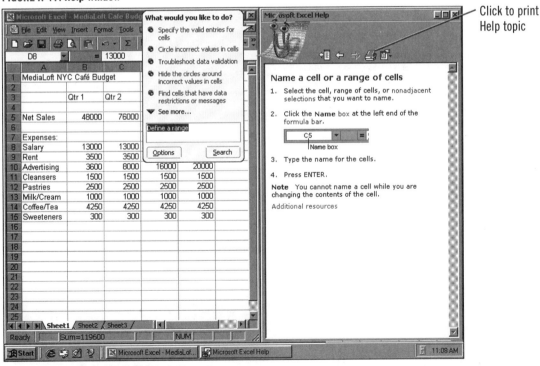

Click to print Help topic

Excel 2000

# Closing a Workbook and Exiting Excel

When you have finished working you need to save the file and close it. When you have completed all your work in Excel you need to exit the program. You can exit Excel by clicking Exit on the File menu.  Since Jim has completed his work on the MediaLoft Café budget, he is finished using Excel for the day. He closes the workbook and then exits Excel.

## Steps

**QuickTip**

You could also click the workbook Close button instead of clicking the File menu.

**1.** Click **File** on the menu bar

The File menu opens. See Figure A-18.

**2.** Click **Close**

Excel closes the workbook and asks if you want to save your changes; if you have made any changes be sure to save them.

**Trouble?**

To exit Excel and close several files at once, click Exit on the File menu. Excel will prompt you to save changes to each open workbook before exiting.

**3.** Click **File** on the menu bar, then click **Exit**

You could also click the program Close button to exit the program. Excel closes and you return to the desktop. Memory is now freed up for other computing tasks.

FIGURE A-18: **Closing a workbook using the File menu**

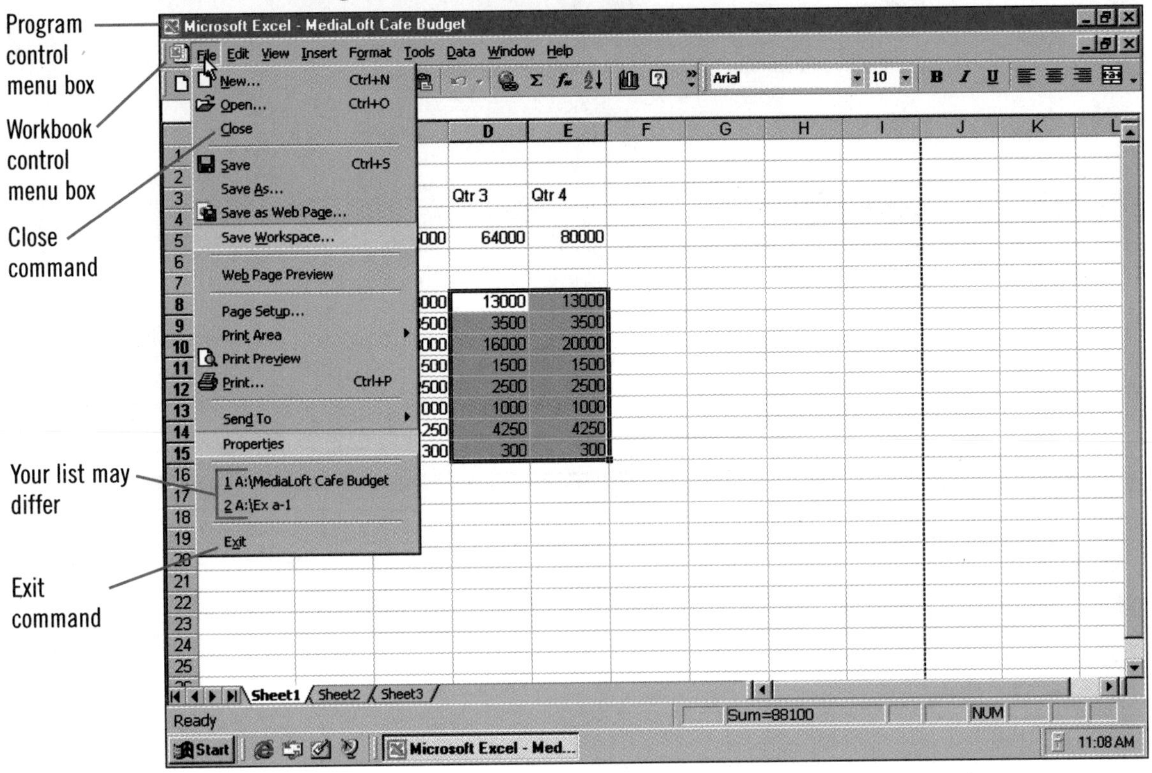

Program control menu box

Workbook control menu box

Close command

Your list may differ

Exit command

| Microsoft Excel - MediaLoft Cafe Budget |
| File Edit View Insert Format Tools Data Window Help |

New...          Ctrl+N
Open...         Ctrl+O
Close

Save            Ctrl+S
Save As...
Save as Web Page...
Save Workspace...

Web Page Preview

Page Setup...
Print Area
Print Preview
Print...         Ctrl+P

Send To
Properties

1 A:\MediaLoft Cafe Budget
2 A:\Ex a-1

Exit

Arial        10    B  I  U

|   | D | E | F | G | H | I | J | K | L |
|---|---|---|---|---|---|---|---|---|---|
| 3 | Qtr 3 | Qtr 4 | | | | | | | |
| 5 | 64000 | 80000 | | | | | | | |
| 8 | 13000 | 13000 | | | | | | | |
| 9 | 3500 | 3500 | | | | | | | |
| 10 | 16000 | 20000 | | | | | | | |
| 11 | 1500 | 1500 | | | | | | | |
| 12 | 2500 | 2500 | | | | | | | |
| 13 | 1000 | 1000 | | | | | | | |
| 14 | 4250 | 4250 | | | | | | | |
| 15 | 300 | 300 | | | | | | | |

Sheet1  Sheet2  Sheet3

Ready                          Sum=88100          NUM

Start    Microsoft Excel - Med...                  11:08 AM

Excel 2000

# Practice

## ► Concepts Review

Label the elements of the Excel worksheet window shown in Figure A-19.

FIGURE A-19

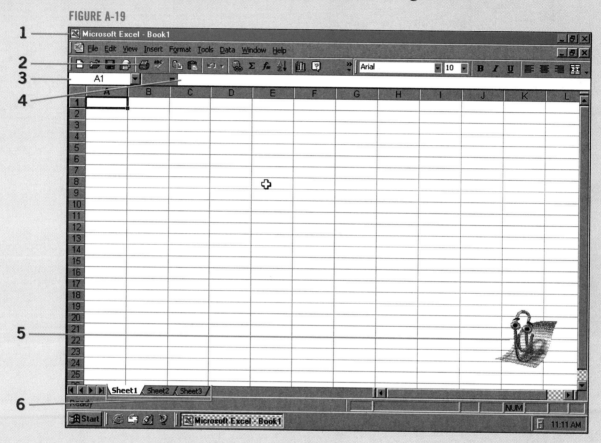

Match each term with the statement that describes it.

7. Cell pointer
8. Button
9. Worksheet window
10. Name box
11. Cell
12. Workbook

a. Area that contains a grid of columns and rows
b. The intersection of a column and row
c. Graphic symbol that depicts a task or function
d. Collection of worksheets
e. Rectangle indicating the active cell
f. Displays the active cell address

**Select the best answer from the list of choices.**

13. **An electronic spreadsheet can perform all of the following tasks, *except***
    a. Display information visually.
    b. Calculate data accurately.
    c. Plan worksheet objectives.
    d. Recalculate updated information.

14. **Each of the following is true about labels, *except***
    a. They are left-aligned by default.
    b. They are not used in calculations.
    c. They are right-aligned by default.
    d. They can include numerical information.

15. **Each of the following is true about values, *except***
    a. They can include labels.
    b. They are right-aligned by default.
    c. They are used in calculations.
    d. They can include formulas.

16. **What symbol is typed before a number to make the number a label?**
    a. "
    b. !
    c. '
    d. ;

17. **You can get Excel Help any of the following ways, *except***
    a. Clicking Help on the menu bar.
    b. Pressing [F1].
    c. Clicking 🔲.
    d. Minimizing the program window.

18. **Each key(s) can be used to confirm cell entries, *except***
    a. [Enter].
    b. [Tab].
    c. [Esc].
    d. [Shift][Enter].

19. **Which button is used to preview a worksheet?**
    a. 🔲
    b. 🔲
    c. 🔲
    d. 🔲

**20. Which feature is used to enlarge a print preview view?**
- **a.** Magnify
- **b.** Enlarge
- **c.** Amplify
- **d.** Zoom

**21. Each of the following is true about the Office Assistant, *except***
- **a.** It provides tips based on your work habits.
- **b.** It provides help using a question and answer format.
- **c.** You can change the appearance of the Office Assistant.
- **d.** It can complete certain tasks for you.

# ▶ Skills Review

**1. Start Excel 2000.**
- **a.** Point to Programs in the Start menu.
- **b.** Click the Microsoft Excel program icon.

**2. View the Excel window.**
- **a.** Identify as many elements in the Excel worksheet window as you can without referring to the unit material.

**3. Open and save a workbook.**
- **a.** Open the workbook EX A-2 from your Project Disk by clicking the Open button.
- **b.** Save the workbook as "Totally Together Fashions" by clicking File on the menu bar, then clicking Save As.

**4. Enter labels and values.**
- **a.** Enter the labels shown in Figure A-20, the Totally Together Fashions worksheet.
- **b.** Enter values shown in Figure A-20.
- **c.** Type the label "New Data" in cell A2, then clear the cell contents in A2 using the Edit menu.
- **d.** Type your name in cell A10.
- **e.** Save the workbook by clicking the Save button.

FIGURE A-20

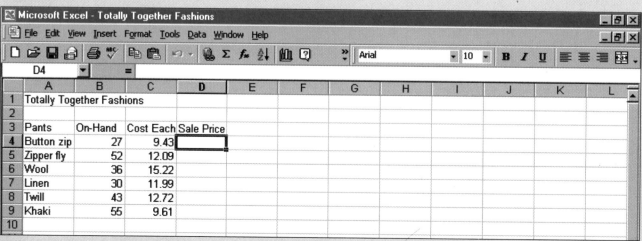

5. **Preview and print a worksheet.**
   a. Click the Print Preview button.
   b. Use the Zoom button to see more of your worksheet.
   c. Print one copy of the worksheet.

6. **Get Help.**
   a. Click the Office Assistant button if the Assistant is not displayed.
   b. Ask the Office Assistant for information about changing the Excel Office Assistant.
   c. Print information offered by the Office Assistant using the Print topic command on the Options menu.
   d. Close the Help window.

7. **Close a workbook and exit Excel.**
   a. Click File on the menu bar, then click Close.
   b. If asked if you want to save the worksheet, click No.
   c. If necessary, close any other worksheets you might have opened.
   d. Click File on the menu bar, then click Exit.

# ► Independent Challenges

**1.** The Excel Help feature provides definitions, explanations, procedures, and other helpful information. It also provides examples and demonstrations to show you how Excel features work. Topics include elements such as the active cell, status bar, buttons, and dialog boxes, as well as detailed information about Excel commands and options.

To complete this independent challenge:

a. Start Excel and open a new workbook.
b. Click the Office Assistant.
c. Type a question that will give you information about opening and saving a workbook. (*Hint*: You may have to ask the Office Assistant more than one question.)
d. Print the information.
e. Return to your workbook when you are finished.
f. Exit Excel.

Excel 2000

**2.** Spreadsheet software has many uses that can affect the way work is done. Some examples of how Excel can be used are discussed in the beginning of this unit. Use your own personal or business experiences to come up with five examples of how Excel could be used in a business setting.

To complete this independent challenge:

**a.** Start Excel.

**b.** Open a new workbook.

**c.** Think of five business tasks that you could complete more efficiently by using an Excel worksheet.

**d.** Sketch a sample of each worksheet. See Figure A-21, a sample payroll worksheet, as a guide.

**e.** Open a new workbook and save it as "Sample Payroll" on your Project Disk.

**f.** Give your worksheet a title in cell A1, type your name in cell B1.

**g.** Enter the labels shown in Figure A-21.

**h.** Enter sample data for Hours Worked and Hourly Wage in the worksheet.

**i.** Save your work, then preview and print the worksheet.

**j.** Close the worksheet and exit Excel.

FIGURE A-21

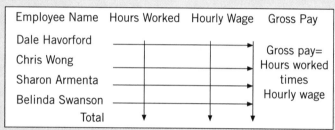

**3.** You are the office manager for Christine's Car Parts, a small auto parts supplier. Although the company is just three years old, it is expanding rapidly, and you are continually looking for ways to make your job easier. Last year you began using Excel to manage and maintain data on inventory and sales, which has greatly helped you to track information accurately and efficiently. The owner of the company has just approved your request to hire an assistant. This person will need to learn how to use Excel. Create a short training document that your new assistant can use as a reference while becoming familiar with Excel.

To complete this independent challenge:

**a.** Draw a sketch of the Excel worksheet window and label the key elements, such as toolbars, title bar, formula bar, scroll bars, etc.

**b.** For each labeled element, write a short description of its use.

**c.** List three ways to get Help in Excel. (*Hint*: Use the Office Assistant to learn all of the ways to get Help in Excel.)

**d.** Create a sketch for three of the following spreadsheet uses: accounts payable schedule, accounts receivable, payroll, list of inventory items, employee benefits data, income statement, cash flow report, or balance sheet. (*Hint*: Make up data for these sketches.)

**e.** Start Excel.

**f.** Create a new workbook and enter the values and labels for a sample spreadsheet. Make sure you have labels in column A. Enter a title for the worksheet and put your name in cell A1.

**g.** Select the range which includes the column labels.

**h.** Use the Print dialog box to print the selected range.

**i.** Preview the entire worksheet.

**j.** Save the workbook as "Christine's Car Parts" on your Project Disk, and then exit Excel.

**4.** To make smart buying decisions, you can use the World Wide Web to gather the most up-to-date information available. MediaLoft employees have access to the Web through the company's intranet. An **intranet** is a group of connected networks owned by a company or organization that is used for internal purposes. Intranets use Internet software to handle the data communications, such as e-mail and Web pages, within an organization. These pages often provide company-wide information. As with all intranets, the MediaLoft intranet limits access to MediaLoft employees.

Imagine that your supervisor at MediaLoft has just given you approval for buying a new computer. Cost is not an issue, and you need to provide a list of hardware and software requirements. You use Excel to create a worksheet using data found on the World Wide Web to support your purchase decision.

To complete this independent challenge:

**a.** Start Excel, open a new workbook and save it on your Project Disk as "New Computer Data."

**b.** List the features you want your ideal computer to contain (e.g. CD-ROM drive, etc.).

**c.** Connect to the Internet, go to the MediaLoft intranet site at http://www.course.com/illustrated/MediaLoft, then click the Research Center link.

**d.** Use any of the links to computer companies provided at the Research Center to compile your data.

**e.** Compile data for the components you want. When you find a system that meets your needs, include that in your list. Be sure to identify the system's key features, such as the processor chip, hard drive capacity, RAM, and monitor size. List any extra/upgrade items you want to purchase.

**f.** When you are finished gathering data, disconnect from the Internet.

**g.** Make sure all components are listed and totaled. Include any tax and shipping costs the manufacturer charges.

**h.** Indicate on the worksheet your final purchase decision. Enter your name in one of the cells.

**i.** Save, preview, and then print your worksheet.

**j.** Close and exit Excel.

Excel 2000

# ▶ Visual Workshop

Create a worksheet similar to Figure A-22 using the skills you learned in this unit. Save the workbook as "Carrie's Camera and Darkroom" on your Project Disk. Type your name in cell A11, then preview and print the worksheet.

FIGURE A-22

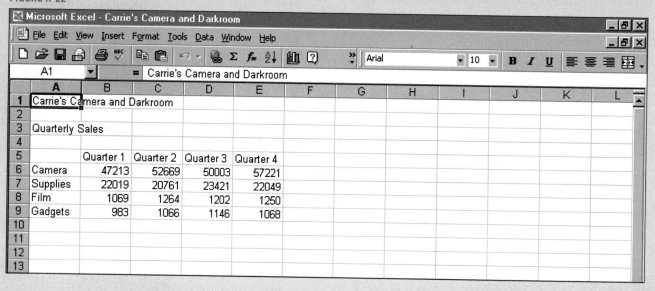

# Building
## and Editing Worksheets

### Objectives

- ▶ **Plan and design a worksheet**
- MOUS ▶ **Edit cell entries and work with ranges**
- MOUS ▶ **Enter formulas**
- MOUS ▶ **Introduce Excel functions**
- MOUS ▶ **Copy and move cell entries**
- MOUS ▶ **Understand relative and absolute cell references**
- MOUS ▶ **Copy formulas with relative cell references**
- MOUS ▶ **Copy formulas with absolute cell references**
- MOUS ▶ **Name and move a sheet**

Using your understanding of the basics of Excel, you can now plan and build your own worksheets. When you build a worksheet, you enter text, values, and formulas into worksheet cells. Once you create a worksheet, you can save it in a workbook file and then print it. ✎━━ Jim Fernandez has received a request from the Marketing department for a forecast of this summer's author events and an estimate of the average number of author appearances. Marketing hopes that the number of appearances will increase 20% over last year's figures. Jim needs to create a worksheet that summarizes appearances for last year and forecasts the summer appearances for this year.

# Planning and Designing a Worksheet

Before you start entering data into a worksheet, you need to know the purpose and approximate layout of the worksheet. You should also familiarize yourself with the mouse pointers you will encounter; refer to Table B-1.  MediaLoft encourages authors to come to stores and sign their books. These author events are great for sales. Jim wants to forecast MediaLoft's 2001 summer author appearances. The goal, already identified by the Marketing department, is to increase the year 2000 signings by 20%. Using the planning guidelines below, work with Jim as he plans this worksheet.

## Details

**In planning and designing a worksheet it is important to:**

### Determine the purpose of the worksheet and give it a meaningful title
Jim needs to forecast summer appearances for 2001. Jim titles the worksheet "Summer 2001 MediaLoft Author Events Forecast."

### Determine your worksheet's desired results, or "output"
Jim needs to begin scheduling author events and will use these forecasts to determine staffing and budget needs if the number of author events increases by 20%. He also wants to calculate the average number of author events since the Marketing department uses this information for corporate promotions.

### Collect all the information, or "input", that will produce the results you want
Jim gathers together the number of author events that occurred at four stores during the 2000 summer season, which runs from June through August.

### Determine the calculations, or formulas, necessary to achieve the desired results
First, Jim needs to total the number of events at each of the selected stores during each month of the summer of 2000. Then he needs to add these totals together to determine the grand total of summer appearances. Because he needs to determine the goal for the 2001 season, the 2000 monthly totals and grand total are multiplied by 1.2 to calculate the projected 20% increase for the 2001 summer season. He'll use the Paste Function to select the Average function, which will determine the average number of appearances for the Marketing department.

### Sketch on paper how you want the worksheet to look; identify where to place the labels and values
Jim decides to put store locations in rows and the months in columns. He enters the data in his sketch and indicates where the monthly totals and the grand total should go. Below the totals, he writes out the formula for determining a 20% increase in appearances for 2000. He also includes a label for the location of the average number of events calculations. Jim's sketch of his worksheet is shown in Figure B-1.

### Create the worksheet
Jim enters the labels first to establish the structure of the worksheet. He then enters the values—the data about the events—into his worksheet. Finally, he enters the formulas necessary to calculate totals, averages, and forecasts. These values and formulas will be used to calculate the necessary output. The worksheet Jim creates is shown in Figure B-2.

**FIGURE B-1:** Worksheet sketch showing labels, values, and calculations

## Summer 2001 MediaLoft Author Events Forecast

|  | June | July | August | Total | Average |
|---|---|---|---|---|---|
| Boston | 15 | 10 | 23 |  |  |
| New York | 14 | 10 | 12 |  |  |
| Seattle | 12 | 13 | 6 |  |  |
| San Diego | 10 | 24 | 15 |  |  |
| Total | June Total | July Total | August Total | Grand Total |  |
| 20% rise | Total X 1.2 |  |  |  |  |

**FIGURE B-2:** Jim's forecasting worksheet

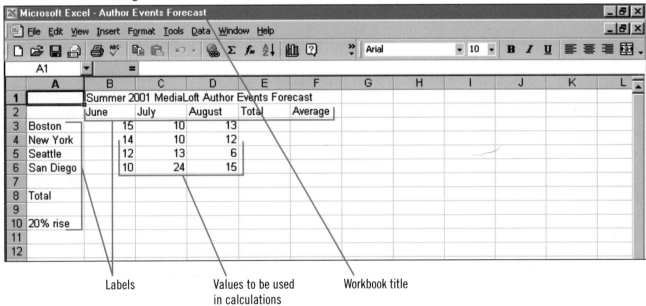

Labels

Values to be used
in calculations

Workbook title

**TABLE B-1:** Commonly used pointers

| name | pointer | use to |
|---|---|---|
| Normal | ✛ | Select a cell or range; indicates Ready mode |
| Copy | ▷ | Create a duplicate of the selected cell(s) |
| Fill handle | ✛ | Create an alphanumeric series in a range |
| I-beam | I | Edit contents of formula bar |
| Move | ▷ | Change the location of the selected cell(s) |

# Editing Cell Entries and Working with Ranges

You can change the contents of any cell at any time. To edit the contents of a cell, you first select the cell you want to edit. Then you have three options: you can click the formula bar, double-click the selected cell, or press [F2]. This puts Excel into Edit mode. To make sure you are in Edit mode, look at the **mode indicator** on the far left side of the status bar. After planning and creating his worksheet, Jim notices that he entered the wrong value for the August Seattle events, and that Houston should be entered instead of San Diego. He fixes the event figures, replaces the San Diego label, and corrects the value for July's Houston events.

**Steps**

1. Start Excel, click **Tools** on the menu bar, click **Customize**, click the **Options tab** in the Customize dialog box, click **Reset my usage data** to restore the default settings, click **Yes,** then click **Close**

2. Open the workbook **EX B-1** from your Project Disk, then save it as **Author Events Forecast**

3. Click cell **D5**
   This cell contains August Seattle events, which you want to change to reflect the correct numbers for the year 2000.

4. Click to **the right of 6** in the formula bar
   Excel goes into Edit mode, and the mode indicator on the status bar displays "Edit." A blinking vertical line called the **insertion point** appears in the formula bar, and if you move the mouse pointer to the formula bar, the pointer changes to I, which is used for editing. See Figure B-3.

5. Press **[Backspace]**, type **11**, then click the **Enter button** on the formula bar
   The value in cell D5 is changed or edited from 6 to 11. Additional modifications can also be made using the [F2] key.

6. Click cell **A6**, then press **[F2]**
   Excel is in Edit mode again, and the insertion point is in the cell.

**QuickTip**

The Redo command reverses the action of the Undo command. Click the Redo button on the Standard toolbar if you change your mind after an undo.

7. Press **[Backspace]** nine times, type **Houston,** then press **[Enter]**
   The label changes to Houston. If you make a mistake, you can either click the Cancel button on the formula bar *before* accepting the cell entry, or click the Undo button on the Standard toolbar if you notice the mistake *after* you have accepted the cell entry. The Undo button allows you to reverse up to 16 previous actions, one at a time.

8. Double-click cell **C6**
   Double-clicking a cell also puts Excel into Edit mode with the insertion point in the cell.

9. Press **[Delete]** twice, then type **14**
   The number of book signings for July in Houston has been corrected. See Figure B-4.

10. Click to confirm the entry, then click the **Save button** on the Standard toolbar

FIGURE B-3: Worksheet in Edit mode

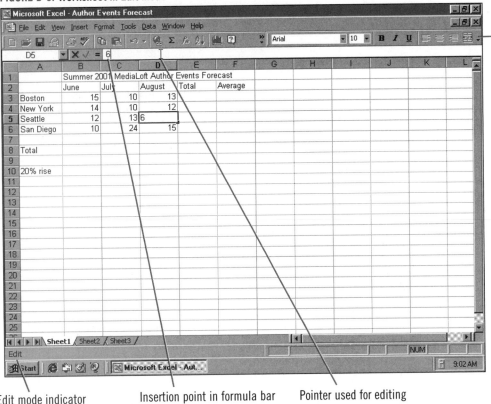

Your toolbars
may not
match the
toolbars in
the figures

Edit mode indicator    Insertion point in formula bar    Pointer used for editing

FIGURE B-4: Edited worksheet

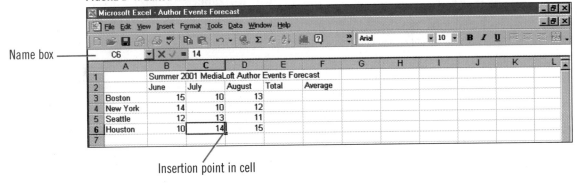

Name box

Insertion point in cell

## Using range names in a workbook

Any group of cells (two or more) is called a range. To select a range, click the first cell and drag to the last cell you want to include in the range. The range address is defined by noting the first and last cells in the range separated by a colon, for example A8:B16. Once you select a range, the easiest way to give it a name is by clicking the name box and typing in a name. Range names—meaningful English names— are usually easier to remember than cell addresses. You can use a range

name in a formula (for example, Income-Expenses) or to move around the workbook more quickly. Simply click the name box list arrow, then click the name of the range you want to go to. The cell pointer moves immediately to select that range. To clear the name from a range, click Insert on the menu bar, point to Name, then click Define. Select the range name you want to delete from the Define Name dialog box, click Delete, then click OK.

**Excel 2000**

# Entering Formulas

You use formulas to perform numeric calculations such as adding, multiplying, and averaging. Formulas in an Excel worksheet usually start with the formula prefix—the equal sign (=) and contain cell addresses and range names. Arithmetic formulas use one or more arithmetic operators to perform calculations; see Table B-2. Using a cell address or range name in a formula is called cell referencing. If you change a value in a cell, any formula containing that cell reference will be automatically recalculated using the new value. In formulas using more than one arithmetic operator, Excel uses the order of precedence rules to determine which operation to perform first. Jim needs to total the values for the monthly author events for June, July, and August, and forecast what the 20% increase in appearances will be. He performs these calculations using formulas.

## Steps

**1.** Click cell **B8**
This is the cell where you want to enter the calculation that totals the June events.

**2.** Type = (the equal sign)
Placing an equal sign at the beginning of an entry tells Excel that a formula is about to be entered, rather than a label or a value. "Enter" appears on the status bar. The total number of June events is equal to the sum of the values in cells B3, B4, B5, and B6.

**Trouble?**

If the formula instead of the result appears in the cell after you click ☑, make sure you began the formula with = (the equal sign).

**3.** Type **b3+b4+b5+b6**, then click the **Enter button** ☑ on the formula bar
Notice that the result of 51 appears in cell B8, and the formula appears in the formula bar. Also, Excel is not case-sensitive: it doesn't matter if you type upper or lower-case characters when you enter cell addresses. See Figure B-5.

**4.** Click cell **C8**, type **=c3+c4+c5+c6**, press [**Tab**]; in cell **D8**, type **=d3+d4+d5+d6**, then press [**Enter**]
The total appearances for July, 47, and for August, 51, appear in cells C8 and D8 respectively.

**5.** Click cell **B10**, type **=B8*1.2**, then click ☑
To calculate the 20% increase, you multiply the total by 1.2. The formula in cell B10 multiplies the total events for June, cell B8, by 1.2. The result of 61.2 appears in cell B10 and is the projected value for an increase of 20% over the 51 June events. Now you need to calculate the 20% increase for July and August. You can use the pointing method, by which you specify cell references in a formula by selecting the desired cell with your mouse instead of typing its cell reference into the formula. Pointing is a preferred method because it eliminates typing errors.

**QuickTip**

Press [Esc] to turn off a moving border.

**6.** Click cell **C10**, type **=**, then click cell **C8**
When you click cell C8, a moving border surrounds the cell. This moving border—as well as the mode indicator—indicates the cell that is copied in this operation. Moving borders can display around a single cell or a range of cells.

**7.** Type ***1.2**, then press [**Tab**]
The calculated value 56.4 appears in cell C10.

**8.** In cell **D10**, type **=**, click cell **D8**, type ***1.2**, then click ☑
Compare your results with Figure B-6.

**9.** Click the **Save button** 🖫 on the Standard toolbar

**FIGURE B-5:** Worksheet showing formula and result

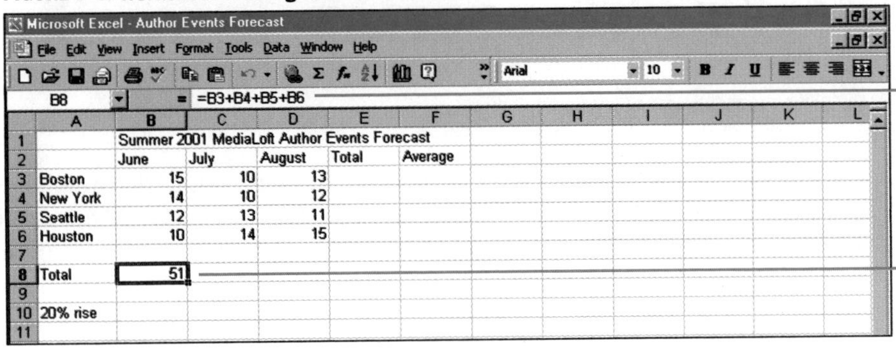

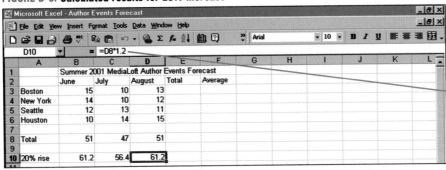

Formula in formula bar

Calculated result in cell

**FIGURE B-6:** Calculated results for 20% increase

Formula calculates 20% increase over value in cell D8 and displays result in cell D10

**TABLE B-2:** Excel arithmetic operators

| operator | purpose | example |
|---|---|---|
| + | Addition | =A5+A7 |
| − | Subtraction or negation | =A5-10 |
| * | Multiplication | =A5*A7 |
| / | Division | =A5/A7 |
| % | Percent | =35% |
| ^ (caret) | Exponent | =6^2 (same as 6*6) |

CLUES TO USE

## Order of precedence in Excel formulas

A formula can include several mathematical operations. When you work with formulas that have more than one operator, the order of precedence is very important. If a formula contains two or more operators, such as 4 + .55/4000 * 25, the computer performs the calculations in a particular sequence based on these rules: Operations inside parentheses are calculated before any other operations. Exponents are calculated next, then any multiplication and division—from left to right. Finally, addition and subtraction is calculated from left to right. In the example 4 + .55/4000 * 25, Excel performs the arithmetic operations by first dividing 4000 into .55, then multiplying the result by 25, then adding 4. You can change the order of calculations by using parentheses. For example, in the formula (4+.55)/4000 * 25, Excel would first add 4 and .55, then divide that amount by 4000, then finally multiply by 25.

## Excel 2000

# Introducing Excel Functions

Functions are predefined worksheet formulas that enable you to do complex calculations easily. Like formulas, functions always begin with the formula prefix = (the equal sign). You can enter functions manually, or you can use the Paste Function to select the function you need from a list. Jim uses the SUM function to calculate the grand totals in his worksheet and the AVERAGE function to calculate the average number of author events per store.

**1.** Click cell **E3**

This is the cell where you want to display the total of all author events in Boston for June, July, and August. You use **AutoSum** to create the totals. By default, AutoSum sets up the SUM function to add the values in the cells above the cell pointer. If there are one or fewer values in the cells above the cell pointer, AutoSum adds the values in the cells to the left of the cell pointer—in this case, the values in cells B3, C3, and D3.

**Trouble?**

If you don't see Σ on your toolbar, click the More Buttons button 🔀 on the Standard toolbar.

**2.** Click the **AutoSum button** Σ on the Standard toolbar, then click the **Enter button** ☑ on the formula bar

The formula =SUM(B3:D3) appears in the formula bar. The result, 38, appears in cell E3. The information inside the parentheses is the **argument**, or the information to be used in calculating a result of the function. An argument can be a value, a range of cells, text, or another function.

**3.** Click cell **E4**, click Σ , then click ☑

The values for the Boston and New York events are now totaled.

**4.** Click cell **E5**, then click Σ

By default, AutoSum sets up a function to add the two values in the cells above the active cell, as you can see by the formula in the formula bar. You can override the current selection by manually selecting the correct range for this argument.

**5.** Click cell **B5**, drag to cell **D5** to select the range **B5:D5**, then click ☑

As you drag, the argument in the SUM function changes to reflect the selected range, and a ScreenTip appears telling you the size of the range by row and column.

**6.** Click cell **E6**, type **=SUM(** , point to cell **B6**, drag to cell **D6**, press **[Enter]**, click cell **E8**, type **=SUM(** , point to cell **B8**, drag to cell **D8**, press **[Enter]**, click cell **E10**, type **=SUM(** , point to cell **B10**, drag to cell **D10**, then click ☑ to confirm the entry

See Figure B-7 to verify your results. Now the Paste Function can be used to select the function needed to calculate the average number of author events.

**Trouble?**

If the Office Assistant opens, click No, don't provide help now.

**7.** Click cell **F3**, then click the **Paste Function button** 🔧 on the Standard toolbar

The Paste Function dialog box opens. See Table B-3 for frequently used functions. The function needed to calculate averages—named AVERAGE—is included in the Most Recently Used function category.

**QuickTip**

Modify a function's range by clicking the Collapse dialog box button, defining the range with your mouse, then clicking the Expand dialog box button to return to the Paste Function window.

**8.** Click **AVERAGE** in the Function name list box, click **OK**, the AVERAGE dialog box opens; type **B3:D3** in the Number 1 text box, as shown in Figure B-8, then click **OK**

**9.** Click cell **F4**, click 🔧, verify that **AVERAGE** is selected, click **OK**, type **B4:D4**, click **OK**, click cell **F5**, click 🔧, click **AVERAGE**, click **OK**, type **B5:D5**, click **OK**, click cell **F6**, click 🔧, click **AVERAGE**, click **OK**, type **B6:D6**, then click **OK**

The result in Boston (cell F3) is 12.6667; the result in New York (cell F4) is 12; the result in Seattle (cell F5) is 12; and the result in Houston (cell F6) is 13, giving you the averages for all four stores.

**FIGURE B-7: Worksheet with SUM functions entered**

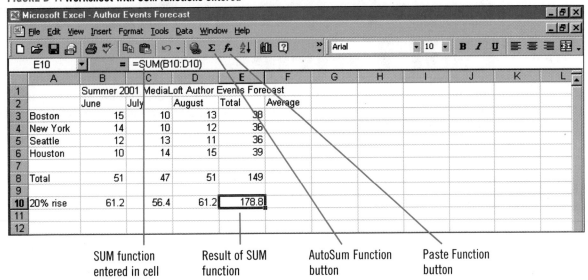

|  | SUM function entered in cell | Result of SUM function | AutoSum Function button | Paste Function button |

**FIGURE B-8: Using the Paste Function to create a formula**

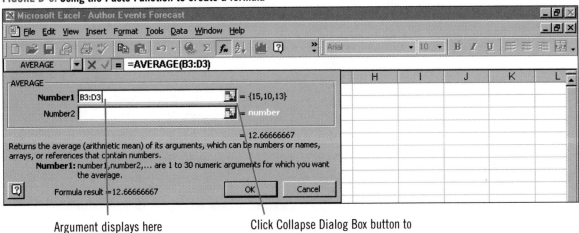

Argument displays here

Click Collapse Dialog Box button to define an argument using your mouse

**TABLE B-3: Frequently used functions**

| function | description |
|---|---|
| SUM(*argument*) | Calculates the sum of the arguments |
| AVERAGE(*argument*) | Calculates the average of the arguments |
| MAX(*argument*) | Displays the largest value among the arguments |
| MIN(*argument*) | Displays the smallest value among the arguments |
| COUNT(*argument*) | Calculates the number of values in the arguments |

## Using the MIN and MAX functions

Other commonly used functions include MIN and MAX. You use the MIN function to calculate the minimum or smallest value in a selected range; the MAX function calculates the maximum or largest value in a selected range. The MAX function is included in the Most Frequently Used function category in the Paste Function dialog box, while the MIN function can be found in the Statistical category. Like AVERAGE, MIN and MAX are preceded by an equal sign and the argument includes a range.

# Copying and Moving Cell Entries

Using the Cut, Copy, and Paste buttons or the Excel drag-and-drop feature, you can copy or move information from one cell or range in your worksheet to another. You can also cut, copy, and paste data from one worksheet to another to make corrections, and add information using the Office Clipboard, which can store up to 12 items. ✎ Jim needs to include the 2001 forecast for spring and fall author events in his Author Events Forecast workbook. He's already entered the spring report in Sheet2 and will finish entering the labels and data for the fall report. Jim copies information from the spring report to the fall report.

**Steps** 1234

1. Click **Sheet 2** of the Author Events Forecast workbook
   To work more efficiently, existing labels can be copied from one range to another and from one sheet to another. You see that the store names have to be corrected in cells A6:A7.

**QuickTip**

The Cut button ✂ removes the selected information from the worksheet and places it on the Office Clipboard.

2. Click **Sheet 1**, select the range **A5:A6**, then click the **Copy button** 📋 on the Standard toolbar
   The selected range (A5:A6) is copied to the **Office Clipboard**, a temporary storage file that holds the selected information you copy or cut. A moving border surrounds the selected range until you press [Esc] or copy additional information to the Clipboard. To copy the most recent item copied to the Clipboard to a new location, you click a new cell and then use the Paste command.

**Trouble?**

If the Clipboard toolbar does not open, click View on the menu bar, point to toolbars, then click Clipboard.

3. Click **Sheet 2**, select the range **A6:A7**, click the **Paste button** 📋 on the Standard toolbar, select the range **A4:A9**, then click 📋
   The Clipboard toolbar opens when you copy a selection to the already occupied Clipboard. You can use the Clipboard toolbar to copy, cut, store, and paste up to 12 items.

**QuickTip**

To use the pop-up menu, right-click, click Copy, click the target cell, right-click, then click Paste to paste the last item copied to the Clipboard.

4. Click cell **A13**, place the pointer on the last 📋 on the Clipboard toolbar, the contents of range A4:A9 display in a ScreenTip, click 📋 to paste the contents in cell A13, then close the Clipboard toolbar
   The item is copied into the range A13:A18. When pasting an item from the Clipboard into the worksheet, you only need to specify the top left cell of the range where you want the selection to go. The moving border remains active. Now you can use the drag-and-drop technique to copy the Total label, which does not copy the contents to the Clipboard.

5. Click cell **E3**, position the pointer on any edge of the cell until the pointer changes to ⬉, then press and hold down **[Ctrl]**
   The pointer changes to the copy pointer ⬉⁺. When you copy cells, the original data remains in the original cell. When you move cells, the original data does *not* remain in the original cell.

6. While still pressing **[Ctrl]**, press and hold the **left mouse button**, drag the cell contents to cell **E12**, release the mouse button, then release **[Ctrl]**
   As you drag, an outline of the cell moves with the pointer, as shown in Figure B-9, and a ScreenTip appears tracking the current position of the item as you move it. When you release the mouse button, the Total label appears in cell E12. You now decide to move the worksheet title over to the left. To use drag and drop to move data to a new cell, do not press [Ctrl].

**Trouble?**

When you drag and drop into occupied cells, Excel asks if you want to replace the existing cells. Click OK to replace the contents with the cell you are moving.

7. Click cell **C1**, position the pointer on the edge of the cell until it changes to ⬉, then drag the cell contents to **A1**
   Once the labels are copied, you can easily enter the fall events data into the range B13:D16.

8. Using the information shown in Figure B-10, enter the author events data for the fall into the range B13:D16
   Compare your worksheet to Figure B-10.

FIGURE B-9: **Using drag and drop to copy information**

Copy button

Paste button

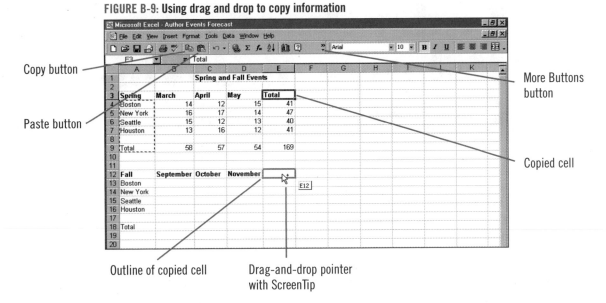

More Buttons button

Copied cell

Outline of copied cell

Drag-and-drop pointer with ScreenTip

FIGURE B-10: **Worksheet with Fall author event data entered**

Sum of selected range displays in status bar

## Using the Office Clipboard

The Office Clipboard lets you copy and paste multiple items such as text, images, tables, or Excel ranges within or between the Microsoft Office applications. The Office Clipboard can hold up to 12 items copied or cut from any Office program. The Clipboard toolbar, shown in Figure B-11, displays the items stored on the Office Clipboard. You choose whether to delete the first item from the Clipboard when you copy the thirteenth item. The collected items remain in the Office Clipboard and are available to you until you close all open Office applications.

FIGURE B-11: **The Office Clipboard**

# Understanding Relative and Absolute Cell References

Like a label or value, an existing formula can be copied to a new location. This enables you to work efficiently by copying a working formula to multiple locations. When copied, a cell reference within a formula is automatically copied *relative* to its new location. This is called a **relative reference**. You can, however, choose to copy a cell reference with an absolute reference or a mixed reference. An **absolute reference** always cites a specific cell when the formula is copied.  Jim often copies existing worksheet formulas and makes use of many types of cell references.

### Use relative references when cell relationships remain unchanged

When Excel copies a formula, all the cell references change to reflect the new location automatically. Each copied formula is identical to the original, except that the column or row is adjusted for its new location. The outlined cells in Figure B-12 contain formulas that contain relative references. For example, the formula in cell E5 is =SUM(B5:D5). When copied to cell E6, the resulting formula is =SUM(B6:D6). The original formula was copied from row 5 to row 6 within the same column, so the cell referenced in the copied formula increased by one row.

### Use an absolute cell reference when one relationship changes

In most cases, you will use relative cell references—the default. Sometimes, however, this is not what is needed. In some cases, you'll want to reference a specific cell, even when copying a formula. You create absolute references by placing a $ (dollar sign) before both the column letter and row number for a cell's address using the [F4] function key (on the keyboard). Figure B-13 displays the formulas used in Figure B-11. Notice that each formula in range B15:D18 contains both a relative and absolute reference. By using an absolute reference when referring to cell $B$12 in a formula, Excel keeps that cell reference (representing the potential increase) constant when copying that formula.

### Using a mixed reference

When copying formulas, the alternative to changing a cell reference relative to its new location and referring to a specific cell location as an absolute reference, is a mixed reference. A mixed reference contains both a relative and absolute reference. When copied, the mixed reference C$14 changes the column relative to its new location but prevents the row from changing.

In the mixed reference $C14, the column would not change but the row would be updated relative to its location. Like the absolute reference, a mixed reference can be created using the [F4] function key. With each press of the [F4] key, you cycle through all the possible combinations of relative, absolute, and mixed references ($C$14, C$14, $C14, C14).

**FIGURE B-12: Location of relative references**

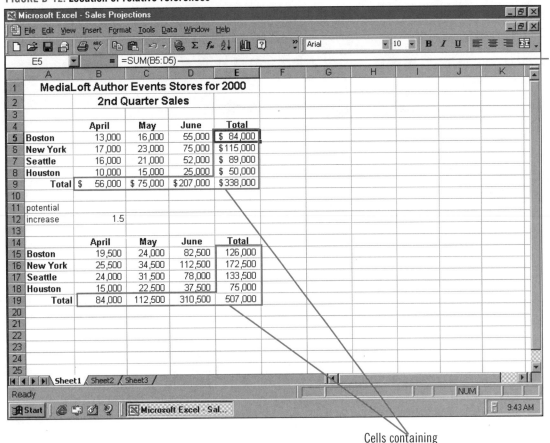

Formula containing relative references

Cells containing relative references

**FIGURE B-13: Absolute and relative reference formulas**

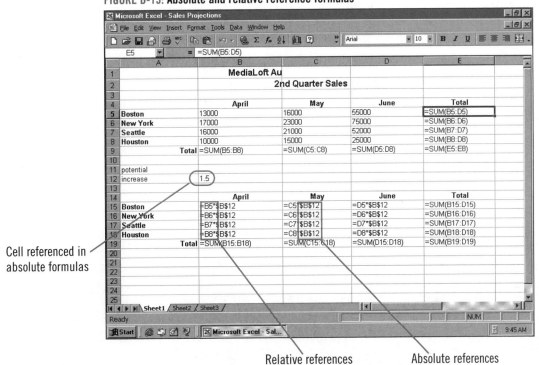

Cell referenced in absolute formulas

Relative references

Absolute references

**Excel 2000**

# Copying Formulas with Relative Cell References

Copying and moving formulas allows you to reuse formulas you've already created. Copying formulas, rather than retyping them, is faster and helps to prevent typing errors. ✎ Jim wants to copy the formulas that total the appearances by region and by month from the spring to the fall. He can use Copy and Paste commands and the Fill Right method to copy this information.

**Steps**

1. Click cell **E4**, then click the **Copy button** 🖺 on the Standard toolbar
   The formula for calculating the total number of spring Boston author events is copied to the Clipboard. Notice that the formula =SUM(B4:D4) displays in the formula bar.

**QuickTip**

Click Edit on the menu bar, then click Paste Special to specify components of the copied cell or range prior to pasting. You can selectively copy formulas, values, comments, validation, and formatting attributes, as well as transpose cells or paste the contents as a link.

2. Click cell **E13**, then click the **Paste button** 🖺 on the Standard toolbar
   The formula from cell E4 is copied into cell E13, where the new result of 39 appears. Notice in the formula bar that the cell references have changed, so that the range B13:D13 appears in the formula. This formula contains **relative cell references** which tell Excel to copy the formula to a new cell, but to substitute new cell references so that the relationship of the cells to the formula in its new location remains unchanged. In this case, Excel adjusted the formula so cells D13, C13, and B13—the three cell references immediately to the left of E13—replaced cells D4, C4, and B4, the three cell references to the left of E4.
   Notice that the bottom right corner of the active cell contains a small square, called the **fill handle.** You can use the fill handle to copy labels, formulas, and values. You use the fill handle to copy the formula in cell E13 to cells E14, E15, and E16.

3. Position the pointer over the **fill handle** until it changes to **+**, press the **left mouse button**, then drag the fill handle to select the range **E13:E16**
   See Figure B-14.

**QuickTip**

As you drag the fill handle, the contents of the last filled cell appear in the name box.

4. Release the mouse button
   Once you release the mouse button, the fill handle copies the formula from the active cell (E13) and pastes it into each cell of the selected range. Again, because the formula uses relative cell references, cells E14 through E16 correctly display the totals for the fall author events.

5. Click cell **B9**, click **Edit** on the menu bar, then click **Copy**

**Trouble?**

If the Clipboard toolbar opens, click the Close button. If the Office Assistant appears, right-click it, then click Hide.

6. Click cell **B18**, click **Edit** on the menu bar, then click **Paste**
   See Figure B-15. The formula for calculating the September events appears in the formula bar. You can use the Fill Right command to copy the formula from cell B18 to cells C18, D18, and E18.

7. Select the range **B18:E18**

8. Click **Edit** on the menu bar, point to **Fill**, then click **Right**
   The rest of the totals are filled in correctly. Compare your worksheet to Figure B-16.

9. Click the **Save button** 🖫 on the Standard toolbar

**CLUES TO USE**

### Filling cells with sequential text or values

Often, we fill cells with sequential text: months of the year, days of the week, years, and text plus a number (Quarter 1, Quarter 2, . . . ). You can easily fill cells using sequences by dragging the fill handle. As you drag the fill handle, Excel automatically extends the existing sequence. (The contents of the last filled cell appears in the name box.) Use the Fill Series command on the Edit menu to examine all of the available fill series options.

**FIGURE B-14: Selected range using the fill handle**

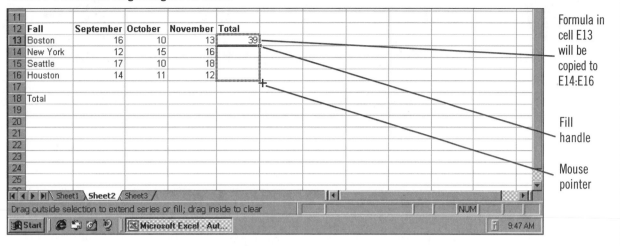

Formula in cell E13 will be copied to E14:E16

Fill handle

Mouse pointer

**FIGURE B-15: Worksheet with copied formula**

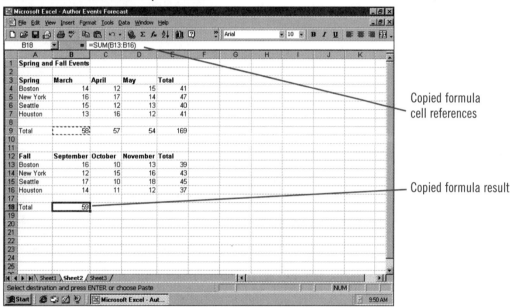

Copied formula cell references

Copied formula result

**FIGURE B-16: Completed worksheet with all formulas copied**

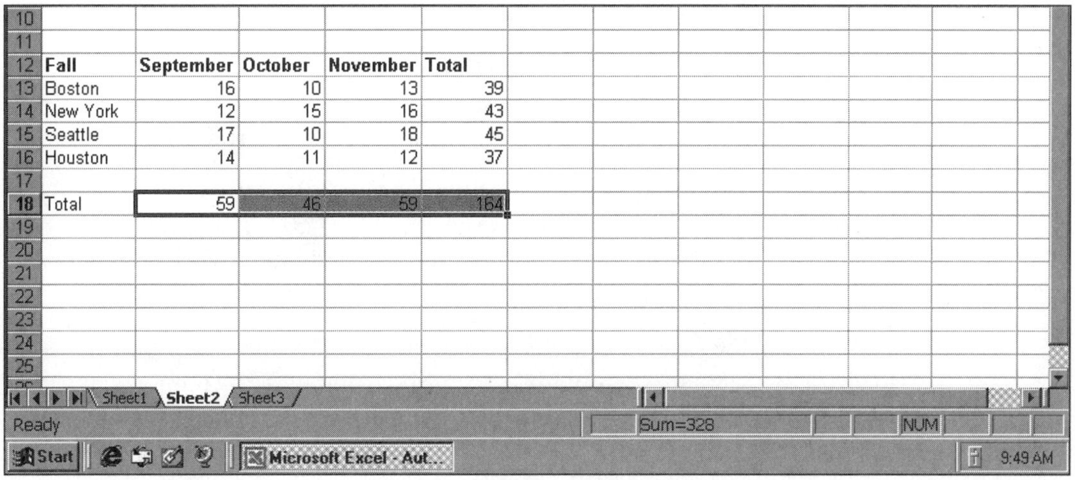

| | Fall | September | October | November | Total | | | | | |
|---|---|---|---|---|---|---|---|---|---|---|
| 13 | Boston | 16 | 10 | 13 | 39 | | | | | |
| 14 | New York | 12 | 15 | 16 | 43 | | | | | |
| 15 | Seattle | 17 | 10 | 18 | 45 | | | | | |
| 16 | Houston | 14 | 11 | 12 | 37 | | | | | |
| 17 | | | | | | | | | | |
| 18 | Total | 59 | 46 | 59 | 164 | | | | | |

Ready

Sum=328

# Copying Formulas with Absolute Cell References

When copying formulas, you might want a cell reference to always refer to a particular cell address. In such an instance, you would use an **absolute cell reference**. An absolute cell reference always refers to a specific cell address when the formula is copied. You identify an absolute reference by placing a dollar sign ($) before the row letter and column number of the address (for example $A$1). The staff in the Marketing department hopes the number of author events will increase by 20% over last year's figures. Jim decides to add a column that calculates a possible increase in the number of spring events in 2001. He wants to do a what-if analysis and recalculate the spreadsheet several times, changing the percentage that the number of appearances might increase each time.

**1.** Click cell **G1**, type **Change**, then press [→]

You can store the increase factor that will be used in the what-if analysis in cell H1.

**2.** Type **1.1**, then press [**Enter**]

The value in cell H1 represents a 10% increase in author events.

**3.** Click cell **G3**, type **What if?**, then press [**Enter**]

Now you create a formula that references a specific address: cell H1.

**4.** In cell **G4**, type **=E4*H1**, then click the **Enter button** 🔲 on the formula bar

The result of 45.1 appears in cell G4. This value represents the total spring events for Boston if there is a 10% increase. To determine the value for the remaining stores, you copy the formula in cell G4 to the range G5:G7.

**QuickTip**

Before you copy or move a formula, check to see if you need to use an absolute cell reference.

**5.** Drag the fill handle to select the range **G4:G7**

The resulting values in the range G5:G7 are all zeros. When you copy the formula it adjusts so the formula in cell G5 is =E5*H2. Since there is no value in cell H2, the result is 0, an error. You need to use an absolute reference in the formula to keep the formula from adjusting. That way, cell H1 will always be referenced. You can change the relative cell reference to an absolute cell reference using [F4].

**6.** Click cell **G4**, press [**F2**] to change to Edit mode, then press [**F4**]

When you press [F2], the **range finder** outlines the equation's arguments in blue and green. When you press [F4], dollar signs appear, changing the H1 cell reference to an absolute reference. See Figure B-17.

**7.** Click the **Enter button** 🔲 on the formula bar

The formula correctly contains an absolute cell reference and the value remains unchanged at 45.1. The fill handle can be used to copy the corrected formula in cell G4 to G5:G7.

**8.** Drag the fill handle to select the range **G4:G7**

The correct values for a 10% increase display in cells G4:G7. You complete the what-if analysis by changing the value in cell H1 from 1.1 to 1.25 to indicate a 25% increase in events.

**9.** Click cell **H1**, type **1.25**, then click 🔲

The values in the range G4:G7 change to reflect the 25% increase. Compare your worksheet to Figure B-18. Since events only occur in whole numbers, the numbers' appearance can be changed later.

FIGURE B-17: Absolute cell reference in cell G4

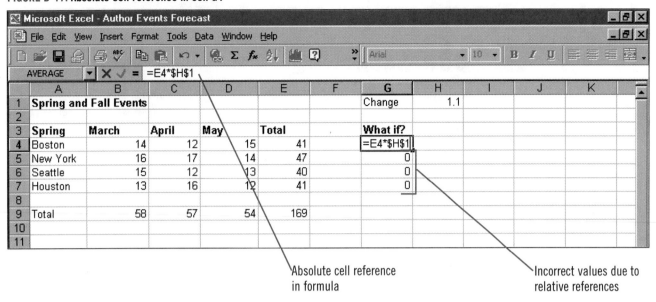

Absolute cell reference in formula

Incorrect values due to relative references

FIGURE B-18: Worksheet with what-if value

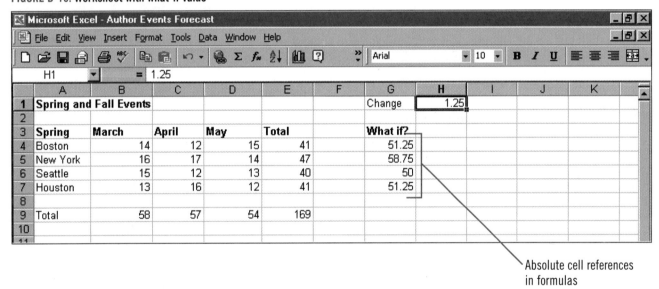

Absolute cell references in formulas

## Copying and moving using named ranges

You can give a range of cells an easy-to-remember meaningful name, such as "2001 Sales." If you move the named range, its name moves with it. Like any range, a named range can be referenced absolutely in a formula by using the $ symbol. To copy or move a named range, you can "go to" it quickly by clicking the name box list arrow and selecting its name.

# Naming and Moving a Sheet

Each workbook initially contains three worksheets named Sheet1, Sheet2, and Sheet3. When the workbook is opened, the first worksheet is the active sheet. To move from sheet to sheet, click the desired sheet tab located at the bottom of the worksheet window. Sheet tab scrolling buttons, located to the left of the sheet tabs, allow rapid movement among the sheets. To make it easier to identify the sheets in a workbook, you can rename each sheet and then organize them in a logical way. The name appears on the sheet tab. For instance, sheets within a single workbook could be named for individual salespeople to better track performance goals, and the sheets can be moved so they appear in alphabetical order. ✎ Jim wants to be able to easily identify the actual author events and the forecast sheets. He decides to name two sheets in his workbook, then changes their order.

1. **Click the Sheet1 tab**

   Sheet1 becomes active; this is the worksheet that contains the summer information you compiled for the Marketing department. Its tab moves to the front, and the tab for Sheet2 moves to the background.

2. **Click the Sheet2 tab**

   Sheet2, containing the spring and fall data, becomes active. Once you have confirmed which sheet is which, you can rename Sheet1 so it has a name that you can easily remember.

3. **Double-click the Sheet1 tab**

   The Sheet1 text becomes selected with the default sheet name ("Sheet1") selected. You could also click Format in the menu bar, point to Sheet, then click Rename to select the sheet name.

4. **Type Summer, then press [Enter]**

   See Figure B-19. The new name automatically replaces the default name in the tab. Worksheet names can have up to 31 characters, including spaces and punctuation.

5. **Double-click the Sheet2 tab, then rename this sheet Spring-Fall**

   Jim decides to rearrange the order of the sheets, so that Summer comes after Spring-Fall.

6. **Click the Summer sheet tab, then drag it to the right of the Spring-Fall sheet tab**

   As you drag, the pointer changes to ⬚, the sheet relocation pointer. See Figure B-20. The first sheet in the workbook is now the Spring-Fall sheet. When there are multiple sheets in a workbook, the navigation buttons can be used to scroll through the sheet tabs. Click the leftmost navigation button to display the first sheet tab; click the rightmost navigation button to display the last sheet tab. The left and right buttons move one sheet in their respective directions.

7. **Type your name in cell A12, click File on the menu bar, click Print, click the Entire workbook option button, then click the Preview button**

   The Preview screen opens. Each worksheet is displayed on a separate page. You can preview the workbook sheets by clicking the Next and Previous buttons.

8. **Click the Print button on the Preview toolbar**

9. **Save and close the workbook, then exit Excel**

**FIGURE B-19: Renamed sheet in workbook**

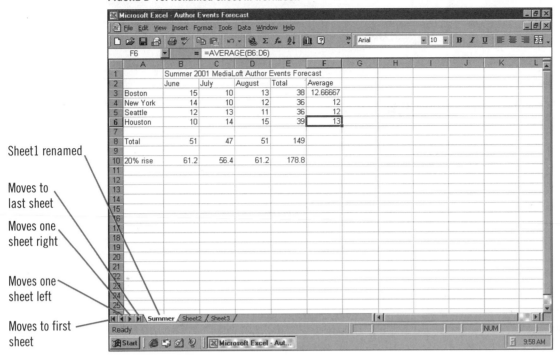

Sheet1 renamed

Moves to
last sheet

Moves one
sheet right

Moves one
sheet left

Moves to first
sheet

**FIGURE B-20: Moving Summer after Spring-Fall sheet**

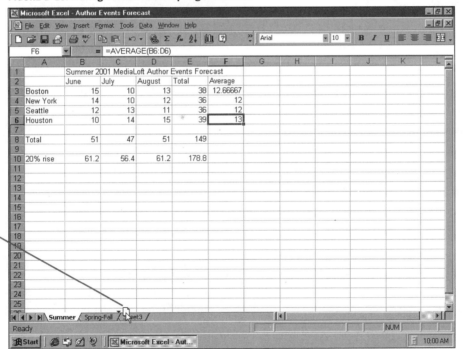

Sheet relocation
pointer

## Moving and copying worksheets

There are times when you may want to move or copy sheets. To move sheets within the current workbook, drag the selected sheet tab along the row of sheet tabs to the new location. To copy, simply press CTRL as you drag the sheet tab and release the mouse button before you release CTRL. Although you have to be careful and carefully check the calculations when doing so, moving and copying worksheets to new workbooks is a relatively simple operation. You must have the workbook that you are copying to, as well as the workbook that you are copying from, open. Select the sheet to copy or move, click File on the menu bar, click Edit, then click Move or Copy sheet. Complete the information in the Move or Copy dialog box. Be sure to click the Create a Copy check box if you are copying rather than moving the worksheet.

# Practice

## ▶ Concepts Review

Label each element of the Excel worksheet window shown in Figure B-20.

**FIGURE B-21**

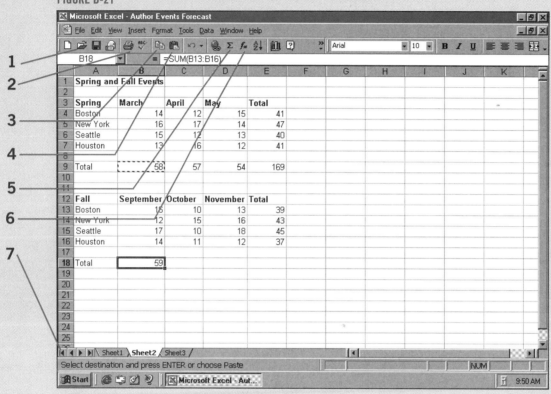

Match the term or button with the statement that describes it.

8. Range
9. Function
10. 📋
11. 📋
12. Formula

a. A predefined formula that provides a shortcut for commonly used calculations
b. A cell entry that performs a calculation in an Excel worksheet
c. A specified group of cells, which can include the entire worksheet
d. Used to copy cells
e. Used to paste cells

Select the best answer from the list of choices.

13. What type of cell reference changes when it is copied?
   a. Absolute
   b. Circular
   c. Looping
   d. Relative

14. What character is used to make a reference absolute?
   a. &
   b. ^
   c. $
   d. @

15. Which button is used to enter data in a cell?

a. [icon]    c. [icon]

b. [icon]    d. [icon]

## ► Skills Review

1. **Edit cell entries and work with ranges.**
   a. Start Excel, open the workbook EX B-2 from your Project Disk and save it as "Office Furnishings."
   b. Change the quantity of Tables to 25.
   c. Change the price of each of the Desks to 250.
   d. Change the quantity of Easels to 17.
   e. Name the range B2:B5 "Quantity" and name the range C2:C5 "Price."
   f. Type your name in cell A20, then save and preview the worksheet.

2. **Enter formulas.**
   a. Click cell B6, then enter the formula B2+B3+B4+B5.
   b. Save your work, then preview the data in the Office Furnishings worksheet.

3. **Introduce Excel functions.**
   a. Type the label "Min Price" in cell A8.
   b. Click cell C8; enter the function MIN(C2:C5).
   c. Type the label "Max Price" in cell A9.
   d. Create a formula in cell C9 that determines the maximum price.
   e. Save your work, then preview the data.

4. **Copy and move cell entries.**
   a. Select the range A1:C6, then copy the range to cell A12.
   b. Use drag and drop to copy the range D1:E1 to cell D12.
   c. Save your work, then preview the worksheet.

5. **Copy formulas with relative cell references.**
   a. Click cell D2, then create a formula that multiplies B2 and C2.
   b. Copy the formula in D2 into cells D3:D5.
   c. Copy the formula in D2 into cells D13:D16.
   d. Save and preview the worksheet.

6. **Copy formulas with absolute cell references.**
   a. Click cell G2 and type the value 1.375.
   b. Click cell E2, then create a formula containing an absolute reference that multiplies D2 and G2.
   c. Use the Office Clipboard to copy the formula in E2 into cells E3:E5.
   d. Use the Office Clipboard to copy the formula in E2 into cells E13:E16.
   e. Change the amount in cell G2 to 2.873.
   f. Save the worksheet.

7. **Name and move a sheet.**
   a. Name the Sheet1 tab "Furniture."
   b. Move the Furniture sheet so it comes after Sheet3.
   c. Name the Sheet2 tab "Supplies."
   d. Move the Supplies sheet after the Furniture sheet.
   e. Save, preview, print and close the workbook, then exit Excel.

# ► Independent Challenges

**1.** You are the box-office manager for Brazil Nuts, a popular jazz band. Your responsibilities include tracking seasonal ticket sales for the band's concerts and anticipating ticket sales for the next season. Brazil Nuts sells four types of tickets: reserved seating, general admission, senior citizen tickets, and student tickets.

The 2000–2001 season includes five scheduled concerts: Spring Hop, Summer Blast, Fall Leaves, Winter Snuggle, and Early Thaw. You will plan and build a worksheet that tracks the sales of each of the four ticket types for all five concerts. To complete this independent challenge:

**a.** Think about the results you want to see, the information you need to build into these worksheets, and what types of calculations must be performed.

**b.** Sketch sample worksheets on a piece of paper to indicate how the information should be laid out. What information should go in the columns? In the rows?

**c.** Start Excel, open a new workbook and save it as "Brazil Nuts" on your Project Disk.

**d.** Plan and build a worksheet that tracks the sales of each of the four ticket types for all five concerts. Build the worksheets by entering a title, row labels, column headings, and formulas.

**e.** Enter your own sales data, but assume the following: the Brazil Nuts sold 1000 tickets during the season; reserved seating was the most popular ticket type for all of the shows except for Winter Snuggle; no concert sold more than 20 student tickets.

**f.** Calculate the total ticket sales for each concert, the total sales for each of the four ticket types, and the total sales for all tickets. Name the worksheet "Sales Data."

**g.** Copy the Sales Data worksheet and name the copied worksheet "5% Increase." Modify this worksheet in the workbook so that it reflects a 5% increase in sales of all ticket types.

**h.** Use named ranges to make the worksheet easier to use. (*Hint*: If your columns are too narrow, position the cell pointer in the column you want to widen. To widen the column, click Format on the menu bar, click Column, click Width, choose a new column width, and then click OK.)

**i.** Type your name in a worksheet cell.

**j.** Save your work, preview and print the worksheets, then close the workbook and exit Excel.

**2.** You have been promoted to computer lab manager at Learn-It-All, a local computer training center. It is your responsibility to make sure there are enough computers for students during scheduled classes. Currently, you have five classrooms: four with IBM PCs and one with Macintoshes. Classes are scheduled Monday, Wednesday, and Friday in two-hour increments from 9 a.m. to 5 p.m. (the lab closes at 7 p.m.), and each room can currently accommodate 35 computers.

You plan and build a worksheet that tracks the number of students who can currently use available computers per two-hour class. You create your enrollment data, but assume that current enrollment averages at 80% of each room's daily capacity. Using an additional worksheet, you show the impact of an enrollment increase of 20%.

To complete this independent challenge:

**a.** Think about how to construct these worksheets to create the desired output.

**b.** Sketch sample paper worksheets to indicate how the information should be laid out.

**c.** Start Excel, open a new workbook and save it as "Learn-it-All" on your Project Disk.

**d.** Build the worksheets by entering a title, row labels, column headings, and formulas. Use named ranges to make the worksheets easier to use, and rename the sheets to identify their contents easily.

**e.** Use separate sheets for actual enrollment and projected changes.

**f.** Name each sheet so you know what's on it.

**g.** Type your name in a worksheet cell.

**h.** Save your work, preview and print the worksheets, then close the workbook and exit Excel.

**3.** The Beautiful You Salon is a small but growing beauty salon that has hired you to organize its accounting records using Excel. The store hopes to track its supplies using Excel once its accounting records are under control. Before you were hired, one of the bookkeepers entered expenses in a workbook, but the analysis was never completed.

To complete this independent challenge:

**a.** Start Excel, open the workbook EX B-3 and save it as "Beautiful You Finances" on your Project Disk. The worksheet includes labels for functions such as the Average, Maximum, and Minimum amounts of each of the expenses in the worksheet.

**b.** Think about what information would be important for the bookkeeping staff to know.

**c.** Use the existing worksheet to create a list of the types of functions and formulas you will use, and the cells where they will be located. Indicate where you will have named ranges.

**d.** Create your sketch using the existing worksheet as a foundation. Your worksheet should use range names in its formulas and functions.

**e.** Rename Sheet1 "Expenses."

**f.** Type your name in a worksheet cell.

**g.** Save your work, then preview and print the worksheet.

**h.** Close the workbook and exit Excel.

**4.** MediaLoft offers eligible employees a variety of mutual fund options in their 401(k) plan. These mutual funds are posted on MediaLoft's intranet site. As a newly eligible MediaLoft employee, you need to determine which mutual funds you want to invest in.

To complete this independent challenge:

**a.** Start Excel, open a new workbook and save it on your Project Disk as "Mutual Fund Data."

**b.** Connect to the Internet and go to the MediaLoft intranet site at http://www.course.com/illustrated/MediaLoft, click the link for the Human Resources page, then click the Employee Benefits link.

**c.** Copy the available mutual fund data from the intranet site to Sheet1 of your workbook.

**d.** Disconnect from the Internet.

**e.** Name Sheet1 "Current Funds."

**f.** On Sheet2, assume this year's annual contribution to your mutual funds will be $10,000. Name this sheet "Investment."

**g.** Choose no more than 4 of the listed mutual funds for your investment, and decide on a percentage for each fund in your contribution.

**h.** Create formulas that multiply those percentages by the total contribution ($10,000). (*Hint:* Use an absolute reference to determine the dollar amount for each mutual fund.)

**i.** Assume that MediaLoft will match your contribution at a rate of 50¢ to your $1. Create formulas that determine how much your total annual investment will be, including the MediaLoft matching funds.

**j.** Type your name in a worksheet cell.

**k.** Preview, then print the Investment worksheet.

**l.** Save and print your work.

**m.** Exit Excel.

# ► Visual Workshop

Create a worksheet similar to Figure B-22 using the skills you learned in this unit. Save the workbook as "Annual Budget" on your Project Disk. Type your name in cell A13, then preview and print the worksheet. (Your toolbars may look different from those shown in the figure.)

**FIGURE B-22**

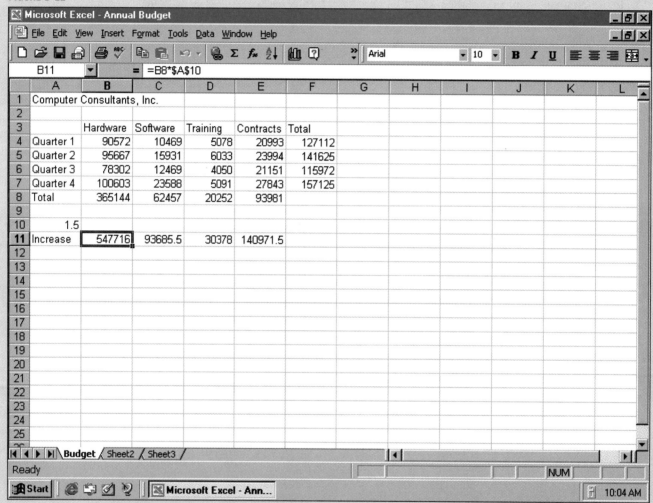

# Formatting

## a Worksheet

### Objectives

- ▶ **Format values**
- ▶ **Use fonts and font sizes**
- ▶ **Change attributes and alignment of labels**
- ▶ **Adjust column widths**
- ▶ **Insert and delete rows and columns**
- ▶ **Apply colors, patterns, and borders**
- ▶ **Use conditional formatting**
- ▶ **Check spelling**

You use Excel's formatting features for a variety of reasons: to make a worksheet more attractive, to make it easier to read, or to emphasize key data. You do this by using colors and different fonts for the cell contents, adjusting column widths, and inserting and deleting columns and rows. The marketing managers at MediaLoft have asked Jim Fernandez to create a workbook that tracks advertising expenses for all MediaLoft stores. Jim has prepared a worksheet for the New York City store containing this information, which can be adapted later for the other stores. Now he uses formatting techniques to make the worksheet easier to read and to call attention to important data.

# Formatting Values

**Formatting** determines how labels and values appear in cells; it does not alter the data in any way. To format a cell, first select it, then apply the formatting. Cells and ranges can be formatted before or after data is entered. If you enter a value in a cell and the cell appears to display the data incorrectly, adjust the cell's format to display the value correctly. ✎ The Marketing department has requested that Jim begin by tracking the New York City store's advertising expenses. Jim developed a worksheet that tracks advertising invoices. He entered all the information and now wants to format some of the labels and values. Because some of the changes might also affect column widths, Jim makes all his formatting changes before changing the column widths.

## Steps 1 2 3 4

1. Start Excel, click **Tools** on the menu bar, click **Customize**, click the **Options tab** in the Customize dialog box, click **Reset my usage data** to restore the default settings, click **Yes**, then click **Close**

2. Open the worksheet **EX C-1** from your Project Disk, then save it as **Ad Expenses**
   The store advertising worksheet appears in Figure C-1. Numeric data can be displayed in a variety of ways, such as having a leading dollar sign. When formatting, you select the range to be formatted up to the last entry in a column or row by selecting the first cell, pressing and holding [Shift], pressing [End], then pressing [→] for the row, or [↓] for the column.

3. Select the range **E4:E32**, then click the **Currency Style button** 💲 on the Formatting toolbar
   Excel adds dollar signs and two decimal places to the Cost ea. column data. Excel automatically resizes the column to display all the information supplied by the new formatting. Another option for formatting dollar values is to apply the comma format, which does not include the $ sign.

4. Select the range **G4:I32**, then click the **Comma Style button** 🔳 on the Formatting toolbar
   The values in columns G, H, and I display the comma format. You can also format percentages using the Formatting toolbar.

5. Select the range **J4:J32**, click the **Percent Style button** 🔳 on the Formatting toolbar, then click the **Increase Decimal button** 🔳 on the Formatting toolbar to show one decimal place
   The % of Total column is now formatted with a percent sign (%) and one decimal place. Dates can be reformatted to display ranges in a variety of ways.

6. Select the range **B4:B31**, click **Format** on the menu bar, then click **Cells**
   The Format Cells dialog box opens with the Number tab in front and the Date format already selected. See Figure C-2. There are many types of date formats from which to choose.

7. Select the (first) format **14-Mar-98** in the Type list box, then click **OK**
   You decide you don't need the year to appear in the Inv Due column.

8. Select the range **C4:C31**, click **Format** on the menu bar, click **Cells**, click **14-Mar** in the Type list box, then click **OK**
   Compare your worksheet to Figure C-3.

9. Save your work

**FIGURE C-1: Advertising expense worksheet**

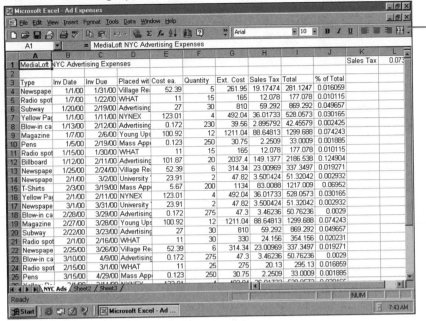

Your toolbars may not match the toolbars in the figures

**FIGURE C-2: Format Cells dialog box**

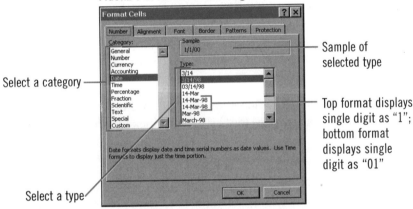

Sample of selected type

Select a category

Top format displays single digit as "1"; bottom format displays single digit as "01"

Select a type

**FIGURE C-3: Worksheet with formatted values**

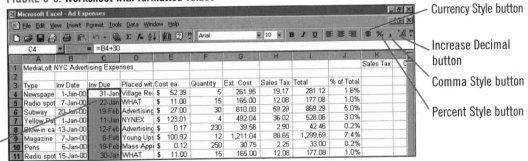

Currency Style button

Increase Decimal button

Comma Style button

Percent Style button

Modified date formats

## Using the Format Painter

A cell's format can be "painted" into other cells using the Format Painter button on the Standard toolbar. This is similar to using drag and drop to copy information, but instead of copying cell contents, you copy only the cell format. Select the cell containing the desired format, then click. The pointer changes to. Use this pointer to select the cell or range you want to contain the painted format.

# Using Fonts and Font Sizes

## Excel 2000

A **font** is the name given to a collection of characters (letters, numerals, symbols, and punctuation marks) with a specific design. The **font size** is the physical size of the text, measured in units called **points**. The default font in Excel is 10 point Arial. You can change the font, the size, or both of any entry or section in a worksheet by using the Format command on the menu bar or by using the Formatting toolbar. Table C-1 shows several fonts in different sizes. Now that the data is formatted, Jim wants to change the font and size of the labels and the worksheet title so that they are better distinguished from the data.

## Steps

**QuickTip**

You can also open the Format Cells dialog box by right-clicking selected cells, then clicking Format Cells.

1. Press **[Ctrl][Home]** to select cell A1

2. Click **Format** on the menu bar, click **Cells**, then click the **Font tab** in the Format Cells dialog box
   See Figure C-5.

3. Scroll down the **Font list** to see an alphabetical listing of the many fonts available on your computer, click **Times New Roman** in the Font list box, click **24** in the Size list box, then click **OK**
   The title font appears in 24 point Times New Roman, and the Formatting toolbar displays the new font and size information. Column headings can be enlarged to make them stand out. You can also change a font and increase the font size using the Formatting toolbar.

4. Select the range **A3:J3**, then click the **Font list arrow** on the Formatting toolbar
   Notice that the fonts on this font list actually look like the font they represent.

5. Click **Times New Roman** in the Font list, click the **Font Size list arrow**, then click **14** in the Font Size list
   Compare your worksheet to Figure C-6. Notice that some of the column headings are now too wide to display fully in the column. Excel does not automatically adjust column widths to accommodate formatting, you have to adjust column widths manually. You'll learn to do this in a later lesson.

6. Save your work

### Using the Formatting toolbar to change fonts and font sizes

The font and font size of the active cell appear on the Formatting toolbar. Click the Font list arrow, as shown in Figure C-4, to see a list of available fonts. Notice that each font name is displayed in the selected font. If you want to change the font, first select the cell, click the Font list arrow, then click the font you want. You can change the size of selected text in the same way, by clicking the Font Size list arrow to display a list of available point sizes.

**FIGURE C-4: Available fonts on the Formatting toolbar**

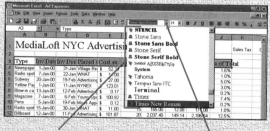

Available fonts installed on your computer (yours may differ)

Font list arrow

FIGURE C-5: Font tab in the Format Cells dialog box

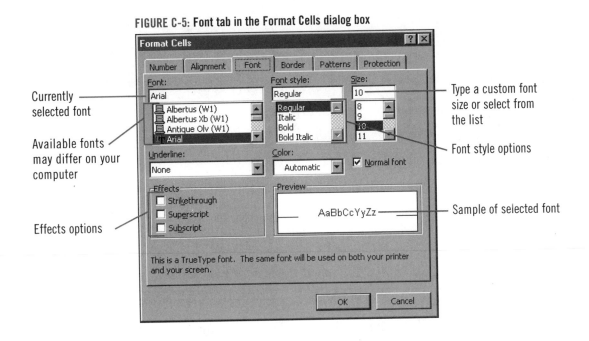

Currently selected font

Available fonts may differ on your computer

Effects options

Type a custom font size or select from the list

Font style options

Sample of selected font

FIGURE C-6: Worksheet with formatted title and labels

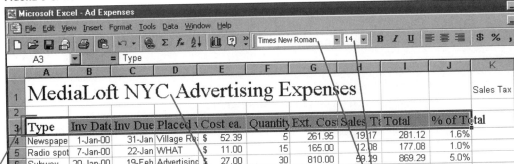

Column headings now 14 point Times New Roman

Title after changing to 24 point Times New Roman

Font and font size of active cell or range

TABLE C-1: Types of fonts

| font | 12 point | 24 point | font | 12 point | 24 point |
|---|---|---|---|---|---|
| Arial | Excel | Excel | Palatino | Excel | Excel |
| Comic Sans MS | Excel | Excel | Times | Excel | Excel |

# Changing Attributes and Alignment of Labels

**Attributes** are styling features such as bold, italics, and underlining that you can apply to affect the way text and numbers look in a worksheet. You can also change the **alignment** of labels and values in cells to be left, right, or center. Attributes and alignment can be applied from the Formatting toolbar, or from the Alignment tab of the Format Cells dialog box. See Table C-2 for a list and description of the available attribute and alignment buttons. ◀——— Now that he has applied the appropriate fonts and font sizes to his worksheet labels, Jim wants to further enhance the worksheet's appearance by adding bold and underline formatting and centering some of the labels.

## Steps

**1.** Press **[Ctrl][Home]** to move to cell A1, then click the **Bold button** 🅱 on the Formatting toolbar
The title Advertising Expenses appears in bold.

**2.** Select the range **A3:J3**, then click the **Underline button** 🆄 on the Formatting toolbar
Excel underlines the text in the column headings in the selected range.

> **QuickTip**
> Overuse of any attribute can be distracting and make a workbook less readable. Be consistent, adding emphasis the same way throughout.

**3.** Click cell **A3**, click the **Italics button** 🅸 on the Formatting toolbar, then click 🅱
The word "Type" appears in boldface italic type. Notice that the Bold, Italics, and Underline buttons are indented. You can apply one or more attributes to text simultaneously.

**4.** Click 🅸
Excel removes italics from cell A3 but the bold and underline formatting attributes remain.

> **QuickTip**
> Use formatting shortcuts on any selected range: [Ctrl][B] to bold, [Ctrl][I] to italicize, and [Ctrl][U] to underline.

**5.** Select the range **B3:J3**, then click 🅱
Bold formatting is added to the rest of the labels in the column headings. You want to center the title over the data columns A through J.

**6.** Select the range **A1:J1**, then click the **Merge and Center button** 🖽 on the Formatting toolbar
Merge creates one cell out of the 10 cells across the row, then Center centers the text in that newly created large cell. The title "MediaLoft NYC Advertising Expenses" is centered across ten columns. The alignment within individual cells can be changed using toolbar buttons.

> **QuickTip**
> To clear all formatting, click Edit on the menu bar, point to Clear, then click Formats.

**7.** Select the range **A3:J3**, then click the **Center button** ▤ on the Formatting toolbar
Compare your screen to Figure C-7. Although they may be difficult to read, notice that all the headings are centered within their cells.

**8.** Save your work

**TABLE C-2: Attribute and Alignment buttons on the Formatting toolbar**

| button | description | button | description |
|--------|-------------|--------|-------------|
| 🅱 | Bolds text | ▤ | Aligns text on the left side of the cell |
| 🅸 | Italicizes text | ▤ | Centers text horizontally within the cell |
| 🆄 | Underlines text | ▤ | Aligns text on the right side of the cell |
| ⊞ | Adds lines or borders | 🖽 | Centers text across columns, and combines two or more selected adjacent cells into one cell |

**FIGURE C-7: Worksheet with formatting attributes applied**

Title centered across columns →

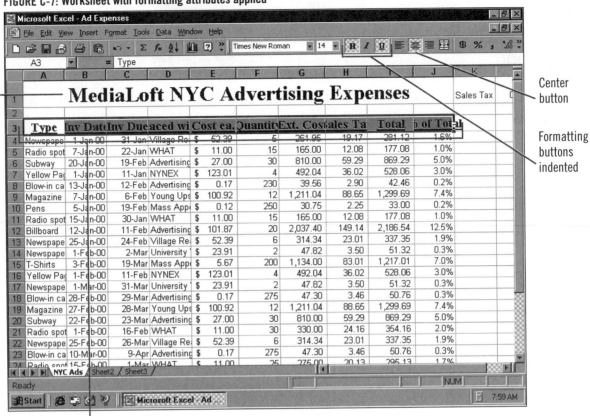

Column headings centered, bold, and underlined

Center button

Formatting buttons indented

## Using AutoFormat

Excel also has 17 predefined worksheet formats to make formatting easier and to give you the option of consistently styling your worksheets. AutoFormats are designed for worksheets with labels in the left column and top rows, and totals in the bottom row or right column. To use AutoFormatting, select the data to be formatted instantly—or place your mouse pointer anywhere within the range to be selected—click Format on the menu bar, click AutoFormat, then select a format from the sample boxes, as shown in Figure C-8.

**FIGURE C-8: AutoFormat dialog box**

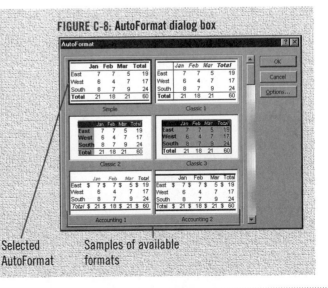

Selected AutoFormat

Samples of available formats

# Excel 2000

# Adjusting Column Widths

As your worksheet formatting continues, you might need to adjust the width of the columns to make your worksheet more usable. The default column width is 8.43 characters wide, a little less than one inch. With Excel, you can adjust the column width for one or more columns using the mouse or the Column command on the Format menu. Table C-3 describes the commands available on the Format Column menu. You can also adjust the height of rows to accommodate larger font sizes. ✐━━ Jim notices that some of the labels in column A have been truncated and don't fit in the cells. He decides to adjust the widths of the columns so that the labels display fully.

## Steps

**1.** Position the pointer on the column line between columns A and B selector buttons

The pointer changes to ↔, as shown in Figure C-9. You position the pointer on the right edge of the column that you are adjusting. Then you can drag the column edge, resizing it using the mouse.

**2.** Click and drag the ↔ pointer to the right until column A is wide enough to accommodate all of the text entries in column A

Yellow Pages is the widest entry. The **AutoFit** feature lets you use the mouse to resize a column so it automatically accommodates the widest entry in a cell.

**3.** Position the pointer on the column line between columns B and C in the column selector until it changes to ↔, then double-click

The width of column B is automatically resized to fit the widest entry, in this case, the column label.

**4.** Use **AutoFit** to resize columns C, D, and J

You can also use the Column Width command on the Format menu to adjust several columns to the same width. Columns can be adjusted by selecting any cell in the column.

**5.** Select the range **F5:I5**

**6.** Click **Format** on the menu bar, point to **Column**, then click **Width**

The Column Width dialog box appears. Move the dialog box, if necessary, by dragging it by its title bar so you can see the contents of the worksheet. The column width measurement is based on the number of characters in the Normal font (in this case, Arial).

**7.** Type **11** in the Column Width text box, then click **OK**

The column widths change to reflect the new settings. See Figure C-10. If "#######" displays after you adjust a column of values, the column is too narrow to display the contents. You need to increase column width until it is wide enough to display the values.

**8.** Save your work

### QuickTip

To reset columns to the default width, select the columns, then use the Column Standard Width command on the Format menu. Click OK in the dialog box to accept the default width.

## CLUES TO USE

### Specifying row height

The Row Height command on the Format menu allows you to customize row height to improve readability. Row height is calculated in points, units of measure also used for fonts—one inch equals 72 points. The row height must exceed the size of the font you are using. Normally, you don't need to adjust row heights manually. If you format something in a row to be a larger point size, Excel will adjust the row to fit the largest point size in the row. You can also adjust row height by placing the ⊥ pointer under the row selector button and dragging to the desired height.

**FIGURE C-9: Preparing to change the column width**

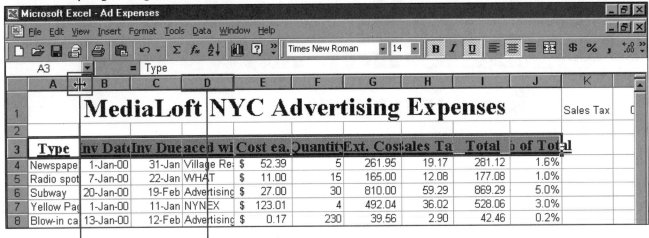

Resize pointer
between columns
A and B

Column D
selector button

**FIGURE C-10: Worksheet with column widths adjusted**

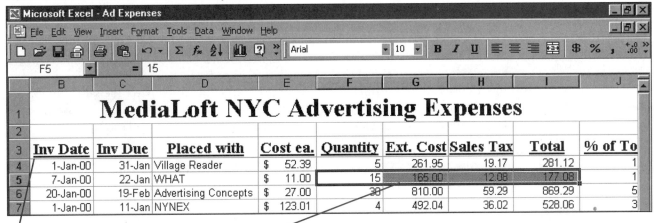

Columns widened
to display text

Columns widened to
same width

**TABLE C-3: Format Column commands**

| command | description |
| --- | --- |
| Width | Sets the width to a specific number of characters |
| AutoFit Selection | Fits the widest entry |
| Hide | Hide(s) column(s) |
| Unhide | Unhide(s) column(s) |
| Standard Width | Resets to default widths |

# Inserting and Deleting Rows and Columns

As you modify a worksheet, you might find it necessary to insert or delete rows and columns to keep your worksheet current. For example, you might need to insert rows to accommodate new inventory products or remove a column of yearly totals that are no longer current. ✏️ Jim has already improved the appearance of his worksheet by formatting the labels and values in the worksheet. Now he decides to improve the overall appearance of the worksheet by inserting a row between the last row of data and the totals. Jim has located a row of inaccurate data that should be deleted, as well as a column that is not necessary.

## Steps 1 2 3 4

**1.** Right-click cell **A32**, then click **Insert**

The Insert dialog box opens. See Figure C-11. You can choose to insert a column or a row, or you can shift the data in the cells in the active column right or in the active row down. An additional row between the last row of data and totals will visually separate the totals.

**2.** Click the **Entire Row option button**, then click **OK**

A blank row is inserted between the totals and the Billboard data for March 2000. Excel inserts rows above the cell pointer and inserts columns to the left of the cell pointer. When you insert a new row, the contents of the worksheet shift down from the newly inserted row. Notice that the formula result in cell E33 has not changed. When you insert a new column, the contents of the worksheet shift to the right from the point of the new column. To insert a single row, you can also click the row selector immediately below where you want the new row, right-click, and then click Insert. To insert multiple rows, select the same number of rows as you want to insert. A row can easily be selected for deletion using its **row selector button**, the gray box containing the row number to the left of the worksheet.

**3.** Click the **row 27 selector button**

Hats from Mass Appeal Inc. will no longer be part of the advertising campaign. All of row 27 is selected, as shown in Figure C-12.

**4.** Click **Edit** in the menu bar, then click **Delete**

Excel deletes row 27, and all rows below this shift up one row.

**5.** Click the **column J selector button**

The percentage information is calculated elsewhere and is no longer needed in this worksheet.

**6.** Click **Edit** in the menu bar, then click **Delete**

Excel deletes column J. The remaining columns to the right shift left one column. You are satisfied with the appearance of the worksheet and decide to save the changes.

**7.** Save your work

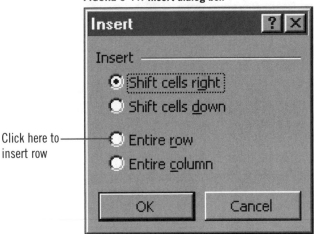

FIGURE C-11: Insert dialog box

Click here to insert row

FIGURE C-12: Worksheet with row 27 selected

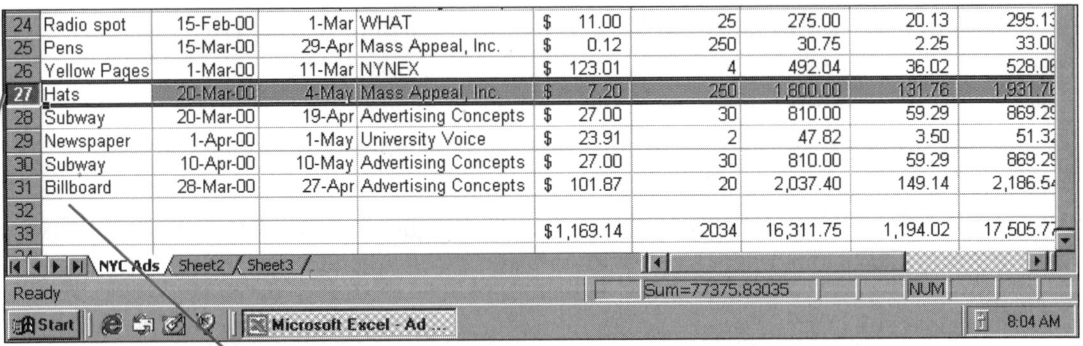

| 24 | Radio spot | 15-Feb-00 | 1-Mar | WHAT | $ | 11.00 | 25 | 275.00 | 20.13 | 295.13 |
| 25 | Pens | 15-Mar-00 | 29-Apr | Mass Appeal, Inc. | $ | 0.12 | 250 | 30.75 | 2.25 | 33.00 |
| 26 | Yellow Pages | 1-Mar-00 | 11-Mar | NYNEX | $ | 123.01 | 4 | 492.04 | 36.02 | 528.06 |
| 27 | Hats | 20-Mar-00 | 4-May | Mass Appeal, Inc. | $ | 7.20 | 250 | 1,800.00 | 131.76 | 1,931.76 |
| 28 | Subway | 20-Mar-00 | 19-Apr | Advertising Concepts | $ | 27.00 | 30 | 810.00 | 59.29 | 869.29 |
| 29 | Newspaper | 1-Apr-00 | 1-May | University Voice | $ | 23.91 | 2 | 47.82 | 3.50 | 51.32 |
| 30 | Subway | 10-Apr-00 | 10-May | Advertising Concepts | $ | 27.00 | 30 | 810.00 | 59.29 | 869.29 |
| 31 | Billboard | 28-Mar-00 | 27-Apr | Advertising Concepts | $ | 101.87 | 20 | 2,037.40 | 149.14 | 2,186.54 |
| 32 | | | | | | | | | | |
| 33 | | | | | $1,169.14 | | 2034 | 16,311.75 | 1,194.02 | 17,505.77 |

NYC Ads / Sheet2 / Sheet3 /

Ready                    Sum=77375.83035          NUM

Start    Microsoft Excel - Ad                    8:04 AM

Row 27 selector button

Inserted row

Excel 2000

## CLUES TO USE

### Using dummy columns and rows

When you add or delete a column or row within a range used in a formula, Excel automatically adjusts the formula to reflect the change. However, when you add a column or row at the end of a range used in a formula, you must modify the formula to reflect the additional column or row. To eliminate having to edit the formula, you can include a dummy column and dummy row which is a blank column or row included at the bottom of—but within—the range you use for that formula, as shown in Figure C-13. Then if you add another column or row to the end of the range, the formula will automatically be modified to include the new data.

FIGURE C-13: Formula with dummy row

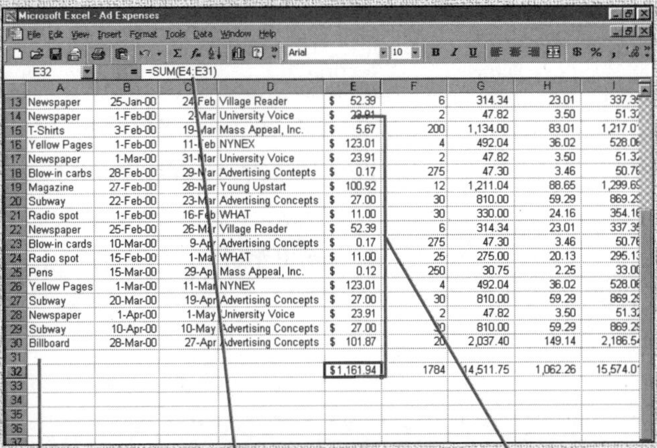

Dummy row          Formula with dummy row          Rows included in formula

# Applying Colors, Patterns, and Borders

You can use colors, patterns, and borders to enhance the overall appearance of a worksheet and to improve its readability. You can add these enhancements using the Patterns tab in the Format Cells dialog box or by using the Borders and Color buttons on the Formatting toolbar. You can apply color or patterns to the background of a cell or range or to cell contents. And, you can apply borders to all the cells in a worksheet or only to selected cells. See Table C-4 for a list of border buttons and their functions. Jim decides to add a pattern, a border, and color to the title of the worksheet. This will give the worksheet a more professional appearance.

## Steps

1. Press **[Ctrl][Home]** to select cell **A1**, then click the **Fill Color list arrow** 🎨▾ on the Formatting toolbar
   The color palette appears.

**QuickTip**

Use color sparingly. Excessive use can divert the reader's attention away from the data in the worksheet.

2. Click **Turquoise** (fourth row, fourth color from the right)
   Cell A1 has a turquoise background, as shown in Figure C-14. Notice that Cell A1 spans columns A-I because of the Merge and Center command used for the title.

3. Click **Format** on the menu bar, then click **Cells**
   The Format Cells dialog box opens.

4. Click the **Patterns tab**, as shown in Figure C-15, if it is not already displayed
   When choosing a background pattern, consider that a high contrast between foreground and background increases the readability of the cell contents.

5. Click the **Pattern list arrow**, click the **Thin Diagonal Crosshatch Pattern** (third row, last pattern on the right), then click **OK**
   A border also enhances a cell's appearance. Unlike underlining, which is a text formatting tool, borders extend the width of the cell.

6. Click the **Borders list arrow** ▦▾ on the Formatting toolbar, then click the **Thick Bottom Border** (second row, second border from the left) on the Borders palette
   It can be difficult to view a border while the cell or range formatted with a border is selected.

7. Click cell **A3**
   The border is a nice enhancement. Font color can distinguish labels in a worksheet.

**QuickTip**

The default color on the Fill Color and Font Color buttons changes to the last color you selected.

8. Select the range **A3:I3**, click the **Font Color list arrow** 🅰▾ on the Formatting toolbar, then click **Blue** (second row from the top, third color from the right) on the palette
   The text changes color, as shown in Figure C-16.

9. Click the **Print Preview button** 🔍 on the Standard toolbar, preview the first page, click **Next** to preview the second page, click **Close** on the Print Preview toolbar, then save your work

### Using color to organize a worksheet

You can use color to give a distinctive look to each part of a worksheet. For example, you might want to apply a light blue to all the rows containing one category of data and a light green to all the rows containing another category of data. Be consistent throughout a group of worksheets, and try to avoid colors that are too bright and distracting.

FIGURE C-14: Background color added to cell

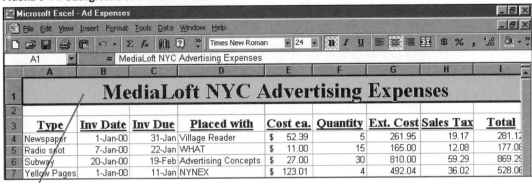

Cell A1 is affected by
fill color

FIGURE C-15: Patterns tab in the Format Cells dialog box

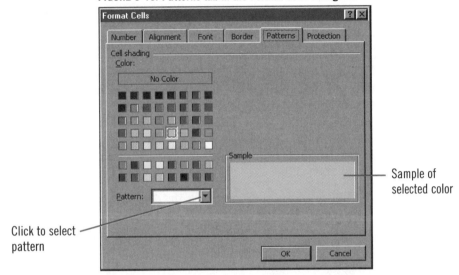

Click to select
pattern

Sample of
selected color

FIGURE C-16: Worksheet with colors, patterns, and border

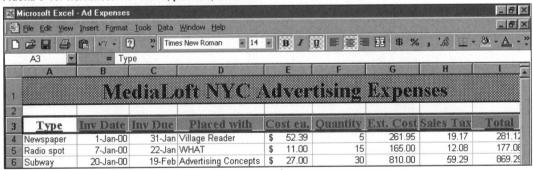

TABLE C-4: Border buttons

| button | function | button | function | button | function |
|---|---|---|---|---|---|
| | Top Border | | Inside Horizontal Border | | Thick Bottom Border |
| | Bottom Border | | Inside Vertical Border | | Top and Bottom Border |
| | Left Border | | Outside Border | | Top and Double Bottom Border |
| | Right Border | | No Border | | Top and Thick Bottom Border |
| | Inside Border | | Bottom Double Border | | Thick Border |

# Using Conditional Formatting

Excel 2000

Formatting attributes make worksheets look professional and help distinguish different data. These same attributes can be applied depending on specific outcomes in cells. Automatically applying formatting attributes based on cell values is called **conditional formatting**. If the data meets your criteria, Excel applies the formats you specify. You might, for example, want advertising costs above a certain number to display in red boldface and lower values to display in blue. ▰▰▰ Jim wants the worksheet to include conditional formatting so that extended advertising costs greater than $175 display in red boldface. He creates the conditional format in the first cell in the extended cost column.

1. **Click cell G4**
   Use the scroll bars if necessary, to make column G visible.

2. **Click Format on the menu bar, then click Conditional Formatting**
   The Conditional Formatting dialog box opens, as shown in Figure C-17. Depending on the logical operator you've selected (such as "greater than" or "not equal to"), the Conditional Formatting dialog box displays different input fields. You can define up to three different conditions that let you determine outcome parameters, and then assign formatting attributes to each one. The condition is defined first. The default setting for the first condition is "Cell Value Is" "between."

**Trouble?**

If the Office Assistant appears, close it by clicking the No, don't provide help now button.

3. **To change the current condition, click the Operator list arrow, then click greater than or equal to**
   The first condition is that the cell value must be greater than or equal to some value. See Table C-5 for a list of options. You can use a constant, formula, cell reference, or date. That value is set in the third box.

4. **Click the Value text box, then type 175**
   Once the value is assigned, the condition's formatting attributes are defined in the Format Cells dialog box.

5. **Click Format, click the Color list arrow, click Red (third row, first column on the left), click Bold in the Font style list box, click OK, then click OK to close the Conditional Formatting dialog box**
   The value, 261.95, in cell G4 is formatted in bold red numbers because it is greater than 175, meeting the condition to apply the format. The conditional format, like any other formatting, can be copied to other cells in a column.

6. **With cell G4 selected, click the Format Painter button ▨ on the Standard toolbar, then drag the ✛▟ Formatting pointer to select the range G5:G30**
   Once the formatting is copied, you reposition the cell pointer to review the results.

7. **Click cell G4**
   Compare your results to Figure C-18. All cells with values greater than or equal to 175 in column G are displayed in bold red text.

8. **Press [Ctrl][Home] to move to cell A1**

9. **Save your work**

FIGURE C-17: Conditional Formatting dialog box

Click to select operator

Click to delete existing condition(s)

Click to add additional condition(s)

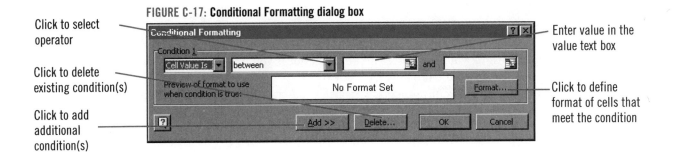

Enter value in the value text box

Click to define format of cells that meet the condition

FIGURE C-18: Worksheet with conditional formatting

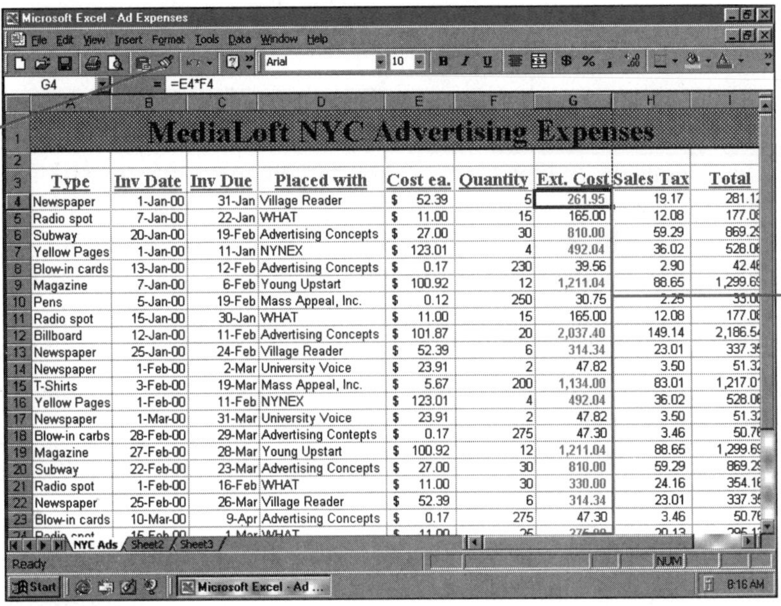

Format Painter button

Results of conditional formatting

TABLE C-5: Conditional Formatting Options

| option | mathematical equivalent | option | mathematical equivalent |
|---|---|---|---|
| Between | $X>Y<Z$ | Greater than | $Z>Y$ |
| Not between | $B \not> C \not< A$ | Less than | $Y<Z$ |
| Equal to | $A=B$ | Greater than or equal to | $A>=B$ |
| Not equal to | $A \neq B$ | Less than or equal to | $Z<=Y$ |

## Deleting conditional formatting

Because it's likely that the conditions you define will change, any of the conditional formats defined can be deleted. Select the cell(s) containing conditional formatting, click Format on the menu bar, click Conditional Formatting, then click the Delete button. The Delete Conditional Format dialog box opens, as shown in Figure C-19. Click the checkboxes for any of the conditions you want to delete, then click OK. The previously assigned formatting is deleted—leaving the cell's contents intact.

FIGURE C-19: Delete Conditional Format dialog box

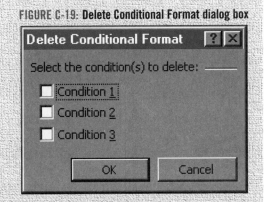

**Excel 2000**

# Checking Spelling

You may think your worksheet is complete, but if you haven't checked for spelling errors, you risk undermining the professional value of your work. A single misspelled word can cast doubt on the validity of your numbers. The spell checker in Excel is also shared by Word, PowerPoint, and Access, so any words you've added to the dictionary using those programs are available in Excel. Jim has completed the formatting for his worksheet and is ready to check its spelling.

## Steps

1. **Click the Spelling button** 📇 **on the Standard toolbar**
   The Spelling dialog box opens, as shown in Figure C-20, with MediaLoft selected as the first misspelled word in the worksheet. The spell checker starts from the active cell and compares words in the worksheet to those in its dictionary. Any word not found in the dictionary causes the spell checker to stop. At that point, you can decide to Ignore, Change, or Add the word to the active dictionary. For any word, (such as MediaLoft or "Inv", the abbreviation of invoice) you have the option to Ignore or Ignore All cases the spell checker cites as incorrect.

2. **Click Ignore All for MediaLoft**
   The spell checker found the word "cards" misspelled and offers "crabs" as one possible alternative. As words are found, you can choose to ignore them, fix the error, or select from a list of alternatives.

3. **Scroll through the Suggestions list, click cards, then click Change**
   The word "Concepts" is also misspelled and the spell checker suggests the correct spelling.

4. **Click Change**
   When no more incorrect words are found, Excel displays the message box shown in Figure C-21.

5. **Click OK**

6. **Press [Ctrl][Home]**

7. **Type your name in cell A2**

8. **Save your work, then preview and print the worksheet**

9. **Click File on the menu bar, then click Exit to close the workbook and exit Excel**

### Modifying the spell checker

Each of us uses words specific to our profession or task. Because the dictionary supplied with Microsoft Office cannot possibly include all the words that each of us needs, it is possible to add words to the dictionary shared by all the components in the suite. To customize the Microsoft Office dictionary used by the spell checker, click Add when a word that you know to be correct (but was not in the dictionary) is found. From then on, that word will no longer be considered misspelled by the spell checker.

**FIGURE C-20: Spelling dialog box**

Misspelled word

Type replacement word here or click a suggestion

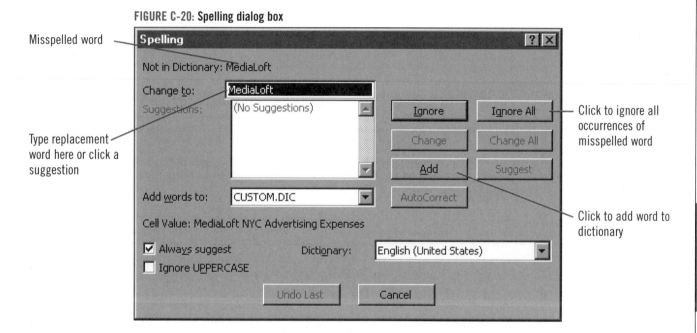

Click to ignore all occurrences of misspelled word

Click to add word to dictionary

**FIGURE C-21: Spelling completed alert box**

# Practice

## ► Concepts Review

Label each element of the Excel worksheet window shown in Figure C-22.

FIGURE C-22

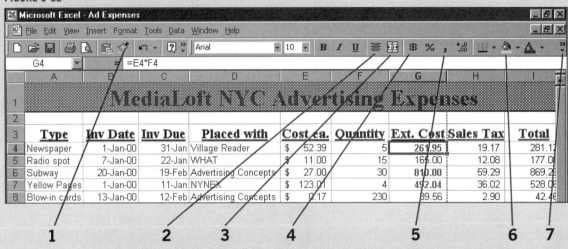

Match command or button with the statement that describes it.

8. Format Cells
9. Edit Delete
10. Format Conditional Formatting
11.
12. $
13. ✓

a. Changes appearance of cell depending on result
b. Erases the contents of a cell
c. Checks the spelling in a worksheet
d. Changes the appearance of selected cells
e. Pastes the contents of the Clipboard in the current cell
f. Changes the format to Currency

Select the best answer from the list of choices.

14. Which button increases the number of decimal places in selected cells?
   a. ⧉
   b. ⧉
   c. ⧉
   d. ⧉

15. Each of the following operators can be used in conditional formatting, *except*
   a. Equal to.
   b. Greater than.
   c. Similar to.
   d. Not between.

16. How many conditional formats can be created in any cell?
   a. 1
   b. 2
   c. 3
   d. 4

**17. Which button center-aligns the contents of a single cell?**
  **a.** ▦                         **c.** ▤
  **b.** ▤                         **d.** ▤

**18. Which of the following is an example of the comma format?**
  **a.** $5,555.55              **c.** 55.55%
  **b.** 5555.55              **d.** 5,555.55

## ▶ Skills Review

### 1. Format values.
  **a.** Start Excel and open a new workbook.
  **b.** Enter the information from Table C-6 in your worksheet. Begin in cell A1, and do not leave any blank rows or columns.
  **c.** Add the bold attribute to the equipment descriptions, as well as the Description and Totals labels.
  **d.** Add the italics attribute to the Price and Sold labels.
  **e.** Apply the Comma format to the Price and Sold data.
  **f.** Insert formulas in the Totals column (multiply the price by the number sold).
  **g.** Apply the Currency format to the Totals data.
  **h.** Save this workbook as "Sports Equipment" on your Project Disk.

**TABLE C-6**

| Best Sports Supreme, Inc. | | | |
| --- | --- | --- | --- |
| Quarterly Sales Sheet | | | |
| Description | Price | Sold | Totals |
| Ski boots | 250 | 1104 | |
| Rollerblades | 175 | 1805 | |
| Baseball bats | 95 | 1098 | |
| Footballs | 35 | 1254 | |

### 2. Use fonts and font sizes.
  **a.** Select the range of cells containing the column titles.
  **b.** Change the font of the column titles to Times New Roman.
  **c.** Increase the font size of the column titles to 14 point.
  **d.** Resize the columns as necessary.
  **e.** Select the range of values in the Price column.
  **f.** Format the range using the Currency Style button.
  **g.** Resize the columns, if necessary.
  **h.** Save your changes.

### 3. Change attributes and alignment of labels.
  **a.** Select the worksheet title Best Sports Supreme, Inc., then click the Bold button to apply boldface to the title.
  **b.** Use the Merge and Center button to center the title over columns A through D.
  **c.** Select the label Quarterly Sales Sheet, then click the Underline button to apply underlining to the label.
  **d.** Select the range of cells containing the column titles, then click the Center button to center the column titles.
  **e.** Save your changes, then preview and print the workbook.

### 4. Adjust column widths.
  **a.** Use the AutoFit feature to resize the Price column.
  **b.** Use the Format menu to resize the Description column to 16 and the Sold column to 9.
  **c.** Save your changes.

### 5. Insert and delete rows and columns.
**a.** Insert a new row between rows 4 and 5.

**b.** Add Best Sports Supreme's newest product—a baseball jersey—in the newly inserted row. Enter "45" for the price and "360" for the number sold.

**c.** Use the fill handle to copy the formula in cell D4 to cell D5.

**d.** Add a new column between the Description and Price columns with the title "Location."

**e.** Delete the "Location" column.

**f.** Save your changes, then preview the workbook.

### 6. Apply colors, patterns, and borders.
**a.** Add a border around the value data.

**b.** Apply a lime background color to the Description column.

**c.** Apply a green background to the column labels in cells B3:D3.

**d.** Change the color of the font in the first row of the data to green.

**e.** Add a pattern fill to the title in Row 1.

**f.** Type your name in an empty cell, then save your work.

**g.** Print the worksheet, then close the workbook.

### 7. Use conditional formatting.
**a.** Open the file EX C-2 from your Project Disk and save it as "Quarterly Report."

**b.** Create conditional formatting that changes values to blue if they are greater than 2500, and changes them to green if less than 700.

**c.** Use the Bold button and Center button to format the column headings and row titles.

**d.** Column A should be wide enough to accommodate the contents of cells A3:A9.

**e.** AutoFit the remaining columns.

**f.** Use Merge and Center in Row 1 to center the title over columns A:E.

**g.** Format the title Reading Room, Inc. using 14 point Times New Roman text. Fill the cell with a color and pattern of your choice.

**h.** Type your name in an empty cell, then apply a green background and make the text color yellow.

**i.** Use the Edit menu to clear the cell formats of the cell with your name, then save your changes.

### 8. Check spelling.
**a.** Check the spelling in the worksheet using the spell checker.

**b.** Correct any spelling errors.

**c.** Save your changes, then preview and print the workbook.

**d.** Save, close the workbook, then exit Excel.

# ► Independent Challenges

**1.** Now that the Beautiful You Salon's accounting records are on Excel, they would like you to work on the inventory. Although more items will be added later, enough have been entered in a worksheet for you to begin your modifications.

To complete this independent challenge:

**a.** Start Excel, open the workbook EX C-3 on your Project Disk, and save it as "BY Inventory."

**b.** Create a formula that calculates the value of the inventory on hand for each item.

**c.** Use an absolute reference to calculate the sale price of each item.

**d.** Use enhancements to make the title, column headings, and row headings more attractive.

**e.** Make sure all columns are wide enough to see the data.

**f.** Add a row under #2 Curlers for "Nail Files," price paid $0.25, sold individually (each), with 59 on hand.

**g.** Before printing, preview the file so you know what the worksheet will look like. Adjust any items as needed, check spelling, and print a copy.

**h.** Use conditional formatting to display which items have 25 or less on hand. Choose colors and formatting.

**i.** Use cell formatting to add borders around the data in the Item column.

**j.** Delete the row with #3 Curlers.

**k.** Type your name in an empty cell, then preview and print the worksheet.

**l.** Save, close the workbook, then exit Excel.

**2.** Continuing your efforts with the Community Action Center, you need to examine the membership in comparison to the community more closely. To make the existing data look more professional and easier to read, you've decided to use attributes and your formatting abilities.

To complete this independent challenge:

**a.** Start Excel, open the workbook EX C-4 on your Project Disk, and save it as "Community Action."

**b.** Remove any blank columns.

**c.** Format the Annual Revenue column using the Currency format.

**d.** Make all columns wide enough to fit their data.

**e.** Use formatting enhancements, such as fonts, font sizes, and text attributes to make the worksheet more attractive.

**f.** Center-align the contents of cells containing column labels.

**g.** Design conditional formatting so that Number of Employee data greater than 50 employees displays in blue.

**h.** Before printing, preview the file so you know what the worksheet will look like. Adjust any items as needed, check spelling, type your name in an empty cell, save your work, and then print a copy.

**i.** Close the workbook and exit Excel.

**3.** Classic Instruments is a Miami-based company that manufactures high-quality pens and markers. As the finance manager, one of your responsibilities is to analyze the monthly reports from your five district sales offices. Your boss, Joanne Bennington, has just asked you to prepare a quarterly sales report for an upcoming meeting. Since several top executives will be attending this meeting, Joanne reminds you that the report must look professional. In particular, she asks you to emphasize the company's surge in profits during the last month and to highlight the fact that the Northeastern district continues to outpace the other districts.

To complete this independent challenge:

**a.** Plan and build a worksheet that shows the company's sales during the last three months. Make sure you include:

- The number of pens sold (units sold) and the associated revenues (total sales) for each of the five district sales offices. The five Classic Instruments sales districts include: Northeastern, Midwestern, Southeastern, Southern, and Western.
- Calculations that show month-by-month totals and a three-month cumulative total.
- Calculations that show each district's share of sales (percent of units sold).
- Formatting enhancements to emphasize the recent month's sales surge and the Northeastern district's sales leadership.

**b.** Prepare a worksheet plan that states your goal, lists the worksheet data you'll need, and identifies the formulas for the different calculations.

**c.** Sketch a sample worksheet on a piece of paper, indicating how the information should be organized and formatted. How will you calculate the totals? What formulas can you copy to save time and keystrokes? Do any of these formulas need to use an absolute reference? How will you show dollar amounts? What information should be shown in bold? Do you need to use more than one font? More than one point size?

**d.** Start Excel, then build the worksheet with your own sales data. Enter the titles and labels first, then enter the numbers and formulas. Save the workbook as "Classic Instruments" on your Project Disk.

**e.** Make enhancements to the worksheet. Adjust the column widths as necessary. Change the row height of row 1 to 30 points. Format labels and values, and change attributes and alignment.

**f.** Add a column that calculates a 15% increase in sales. Use an absolute cell reference in this calculation.

**g.** Type your name in an empty cell.

**h.** Before printing, preview the file so you know what the worksheet will look like. Adjust any items as needed, check spelling, and then print a copy.

**i.** Save your work before closing the file and exiting Excel.

**WEB WORK**

**4.** As the MediaLoft office manager, you've been asked to assemble data on currently available office suites for use in a business environment. You use the World Wide Web to retrieve information about current software and then post the information on the MediaLoft intranet site. You also create an attractive worksheet for distribution to department managers.
To complete this independent challenge:

**a.** Start Excel, then open a new workbook and save it as "Software Comparison" on your Project Disk.

**b.** Connect to the Internet, go to the MediaLoft intranet site at http://www.course.com/illustrated/MediaLoft, then click the link for the Accounting page.

**c.** Print the Office Suite Analysis, disconnect from the Internet, then enter the data in the Software Comparison workbook.

**d.** Create a title for the worksheet in cell A1. Use the Merge and Center command to center the title over the worksheet columns.

**e.** Make sure each column is resized to accommodate its widest contents.

**f.** Format the labels for each suite manufacturer in bold, 12 point, Times New Roman font.

**g.** Format the labels for the type of program (for example, spreadsheets) in italics, 12 point, Times New Roman font.

**h.** Create a background color and a border for the title. Use a pattern to enhance the text.

**i.** Right-align the label for the suite price.

**j.** Use conditional formatting so that suites costing more than $375 display in red.

**k.** Type your name in a visible worksheet cell.

**l.** Save and print your work, then exit Excel.

# ► Visual Workshop

Create the worksheet shown in Figure C-23, using skills you learned in this unit. Open the file EX C-5 on your Project Disk and save it as "Projected March Advertising Invoices." Create a conditional format in the Cost ea. column so that entries greater than 60 are displayed in red. (*Hint:* The only additional font used in this exercise is Times New Roman. It is 22 points in row 1, and 16 points in row 3.)

FIGURE C-23

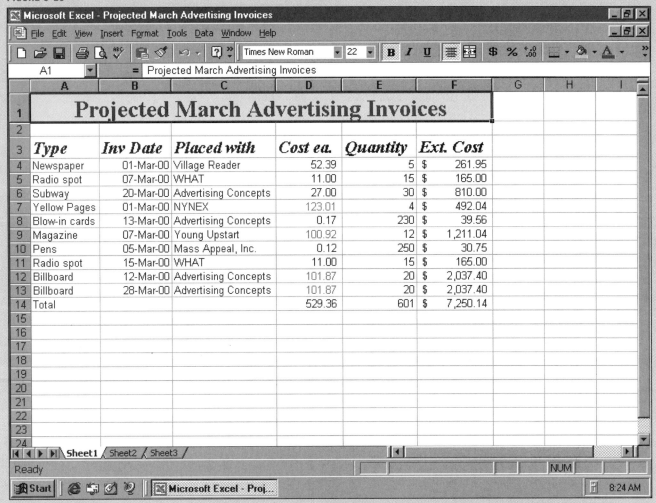

| Type | Inv Date | Placed with | Cost ea. | Quantity | Ext. Cost |
|---|---|---|---|---|---|
| Newspaper | 01-Mar-00 | Village Reader | 52.39 | 5 | $ 261.95 |
| Radio spot | 07-Mar-00 | WHAT | 11.00 | 15 | $ 165.00 |
| Subway | 20-Mar-00 | Advertising Concepts | 27.00 | 30 | $ 810.00 |
| Yellow Pages | 01-Mar-00 | NYNEX | 123.01 | 4 | $ 492.04 |
| Blow-in cards | 13-Mar-00 | Advertising Concepts | 0.17 | 230 | $ 39.56 |
| Magazine | 07-Mar-00 | Young Upstart | 100.92 | 12 | $ 1,211.04 |
| Pens | 05-Mar-00 | Mass Appeal, Inc. | 0.12 | 250 | $ 30.75 |
| Radio spot | 15-Mar-00 | WHAT | 11.00 | 15 | $ 165.00 |
| Billboard | 12-Mar-00 | Advertising Concepts | 101.87 | 20 | $ 2,037.40 |
| Billboard | 28-Mar-00 | Advertising Concepts | 101.87 | 20 | $ 2,037.40 |
| Total | | | 529.36 | 601 | $ 7,250.14 |

# Working
## with Charts

### Objectives

- ▶ **Plan and design a chart**
- [MOUS] ▶ **Create a chart**
- [MOUS] ▶ **Move and resize a chart**
- [MOUS] ▶ **Edit a chart**
- [MOUS] ▶ **Format a chart**
- [MOUS] ▶ **Enhance a chart**
- [MOUS] ▶ **Annotate and draw on a chart**
- [MOUS] ▶ **Preview and print a chart**

Worksheets provide an effective way to organize information, but they are not always the best format for presenting data to others. Information in a selected range or worksheet can easily be converted to the visual format of a chart. Charts graphically communicate the relationships of data in a worksheet. In this unit, you will learn how to create a chart, how to edit a chart and change the chart type, how to add text annotations and arrows to a chart, and how to preview and print a chart. ✐ For the annual meeting Jim Fernandez needs to create a chart showing the six-month sales history at MediaLoft for the stores in the eastern division. He wants to illustrate the trend of growth in this division.

# Planning and Designing a Chart

Before creating a chart, you need to plan the information you want your chart to show and how you want it to look. In early June, the Marketing department launched a regional advertising campaign for the eastern division. The results of the campaign were increased sales during the fall months. Jim wants his chart for the annual meeting to illustrate the growth trend of sales in MediaLoft's eastern division stores and to highlight this dramatic sales increase.

**Jim uses the worksheet shown in Figure D-1 and the following guidelines to plan the chart:**

### Determine the purpose of the chart, and identify the data relationships you want to communicate visually

You want to create a chart that shows sales throughout MediaLoft's eastern division from July through December. In particular, you want to highlight the increase in sales that occurred as a result of the advertising campaign.

### Determine the results you want to see, and decide which chart type is most appropriate to use

Different charts have different strengths and display data in various ways. How you want your data displayed—and how you want that data interpreted—can help you determine the best chart type to use. Table D-1 describes several different types of charts and when each one is best used. Because you want to compare data (sales in multiple locations) over a time period (the months July through December), you decide to use a column chart.

### Identify the worksheet data you want the chart to illustrate

You are using data from the worksheet titled "MediaLoft Eastern Division Stores" as shown in Figure D-1. This worksheet contains the sales data for the four stores in the eastern division from July through December.

### Sketch the chart, then use your sketch to decide where the chart elements should be placed

You sketch your chart as shown in Figure D-2. You put the months on the horizontal axis (the **x-axis**) and the monthly sales figures on the vertical axis (the **y-axis**). The **tick marks** on the y-axis create a scale of measure for each value. Each value in a cell you select for your chart is a **data point**. In any chart, a **data marker** visually represents each data point, which in this case is a column. A collection of related data points is a **data series**. In this chart, there are four data series (Boston, Chicago, Kansas City, and New York), so you include a **legend** to make it easy to identify them.

FIGURE D-1: Worksheet containing sales data

| | A | B | C | D | E | F | G | H | I | J | K |
|---|---|---|---|---|---|---|---|---|---|---|---|
| 1 | | | | MediaLoft Eastern Division Stores | | | | | | | |
| 2 | | | | FY 2000 Sales Following Advertising Campaign | | | | | | | |
| 3 | | | | | | | | | | | |
| 4 | | | | | | | | | | | |
| 5 | | July | August | September | October | November | December | Total | | | |
| 6 | Boston | 12,000 | 12,000 | 15,500 | 20,000 | 21,000 | 20,500 | $103,500 | | | |
| 7 | Chicago | 14,500 | 16,000 | 17,500 | 18,000 | 18,500 | 19,000 | $101,000 | | | |
| 8 | Kansas City | 9,500 | 10,000 | 15,000 | 16,000 | 17,000 | 15,500 | $103,500 | | | |
| 9 | New York | 15,000 | 13,000 | 16,500 | 19,000 | 20,000 | 21,000 | $ 83,000 | | | |
| 10 | Total | $ 51,000 | $ 51,000 | $ 64,500 | $ 73,000 | $ 76,500 | $ 76,000 | $391,000 | | | |
| 11 | | | | | | | | | | | |
| 12 | | | | | | | | | | | |

Microsoft Excel - MediaLoft Sales-Eastern Division

File  Edit  View  Insert  Format  Tools  Data  Window  Help

Arial  10  B  I  U

L24

FIGURE D-2: Sketch of the column chart

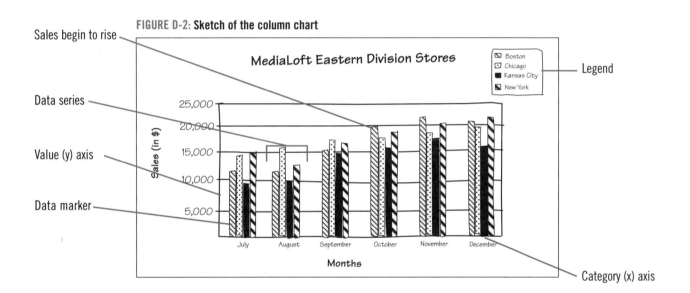

TABLE D-1: Commonly used chart types

| type | button | description |
|---|---|---|
| Area | | Shows how volume changes over time |
| Bar | | Compares distinct objects over time using a horizontal format; sometimes referred to as a horizontal bar chart in other spreadsheet programs |
| Column | | Compares distinct objects over time using a vertical format; the Excel default; sometimes referred to as a bar chart in other spreadsheet programs |
| Line | | Compares trends over even time intervals; similar to an area chart |
| Pie | | Compares sizes of pieces as part of a whole; can have slices pulled away from the pie, or "exploded" |
| XY (scatter) | | Compares trends over uneven time or measurement intervals; used in scientific and engineering disciplines for trend spotting and extrapolation |
| Combination | none | Combines a column and line chart to compare data requiring different scales of measure |

**Excel 2000**

# Creating a Chart

To create a chart in Excel, you first select the range containing the data you want to chart. Once you've selected a range, you can use the Excel Chart Wizard to lead you through the process of creating the chart. Using the worksheet containing the sales data for the eastern division, Jim creates a chart that shows the growth trend that occurred as a result of the advertising campaign.

### Steps

**QuickTip**

To reset toolbars, click Tools on the menu bar, click Customize, click Reset my usage data, click Yes, then click Close.

**1. Start Excel, reset your toolbars to their default settings, open the workbook EX D-1 from your Project Disk, then save it as MediaLoft Sales-Eastern Division**
You want the chart to include the monthly sales figures for each of the eastern division stores, as well as month and store labels. You don't include the Total columns because the monthly figures make up the totals and these figures would skew the chart.

**Trouble?**

Click the More Buttons button ⊠ to locate buttons that are not visible on your toolbars.

**2. Select the range A5:G9, then click the Chart Wizard button 🛄 on the Standard toolbar**
This range includes the cells that will be charted. The Chart Wizard opens. The Chart Wizard - Step 1 of 4 - Chart Type dialog box lets you choose the type of chart you want to create. See Figure D-3. You can see a preview of the chart by clicking and holding the Press and Hold to View Sample button.

**3. Click Next to accept Column, the default chart type**
The Chart Wizard - Step 2 of 4 - Chart Source Data dialog box lets you choose the data being charted and whether the series are in rows or columns. You want to chart the effect of sales for each store over the time period. Currently, the rows are accurately selected as the data series, as specified by the Series in option button located under the Data range. Since you selected the data before clicking the Chart Wizard button, Excel converted the range to absolute values and the correct range =Sheet1!$A$5:$G$9 displays in the Data range text box.

**4. Click Next**
The Chart Wizard - Step 3 of 4 - Chart Options dialog box shows a sample chart using the data you selected. Notice that the store locations (the rows in the selected range) are plotted according to the months (the columns in the selected range), and that the months were added as labels for each data series. Notice also that there is a legend showing each location and its corresponding color on the chart. Here, you can choose to keep the legend, add a chart title, gridlines, data labels, data table, and add axis titles.

**5. Click the Chart title text box, then type MediaLoft Sales - Eastern Division**
After a moment, the title appears in the Sample Chart box. See Figure D-4.

**6. Click Next**
In the Chart Wizard - Step 4 of 4 - Chart Location dialog box, you determine the placement of the chart in the workbook. You can display a chart as an object on the current sheet, on any other existing sheet, or on a newly created chart sheet. A **chart sheet** in a workbook contains only a chart that is linked to the worksheet data. Displaying the chart as an object in the sheet containing the data will help Jim emphasize his point at the annual meeting.

**Trouble?**

If you are using a small monitor, your chart may appear distorted. If so, you'll need to move it to a blank area of the worksheet and then enlarge it before continuing with the lessons in this unit. See your instructor or technical support person for assistance.

**7. Click Finish**
The column chart appears and the Chart toolbar opens, either docked, as shown in Figure D-5, or floating. Your chart might be in a different location and look slightly different. You will adjust the chart's location and size in the next lesson. The **selection handles**, the small squares at the corners and sides of the chart's border, indicate that the chart is selected. Anytime a chart is selected, as it is now, a blue border surrounds the data range, a green border surrounds the row labels, and a purple border surrounds the column labels. If you want to delete a chart, select it, then press [Delete].

**8. Save your work**

**FIGURE D-3: First Chart Wizard dialog box**

Selected chart

Chart types

Chart sub-types for selected chart

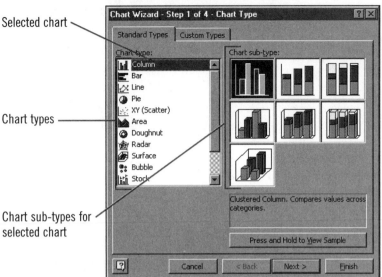

**FIGURE D-4: Third Chart Wizard dialog box**

Type the chart title here

Sample chart

Title added

Legend

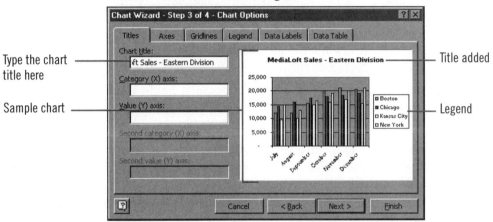

**FIGURE D-5: Worksheet with column chart**

Your toolbars may not match those in the figures

Column labels

Row labels

Data range

Month labels on x-axis

Title

Legend

Selection handles

Chart toolbar

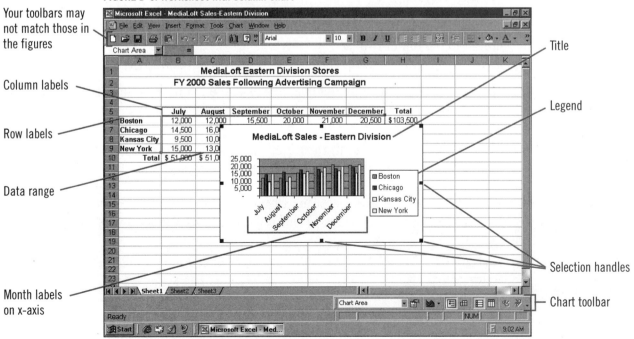

# Moving and Resizing a Chart

Charts are graphics, or drawn **objects**, and are not in a specific cell or range address. You can move a chart anywhere on a worksheet without affecting formulas or data in the worksheet. Resize a chart to improve its appearance by dragging the selection handles. You can even put a chart on another sheet without worrying about cell formulas. Drawn objects such as charts contain other objects that you can move and resize. To move an object, select it, then drag it or cut and copy it to a new location. To resize an object, use the selection handles. When you select a chart object, the name of the selected object appears in the Chart Objects list box on the Chart toolbar, and in the name box. ✏️ Jim wants to increase the size of the chart and position it below the worksheet data. He also wants to change the position of the legend.

**QuickTip**

When a chart is selected, the Chart menu appears on the menu bar.

1. **Make sure the chart is still selected, then position the pointer over the chart**
   The pointer shape ↕ indicates that you can move the chart or use a selection handle to resize it. For a table of commonly used pointers, refer to Table D-2. On occasion, the Chart toolbar obscures your view. You can dock the toolbar to make it easier to see your work.

2. **If the chart toolbar is floating, click the Chart toolbar's title bar, drag it to the right edge of the status bar until it docks, then release the mouse button**
   The toolbar is docked on the bottom of the screen.

3. **Place the ↕ pointer on the chart, press and hold the left mouse button, using ✥ drag the upper left edge of the chart to the top of row 13 and the left edge of the chart to the left border of column A, then release the mouse button**
   A dotted outline of the chart perimeter appears as the chart is being moved. The chart is in the new location. Resizing a chart doesn't affect the data in the chart, only the way the chart looks on the sheet.

4. **Position the pointer on the right-middle selection handle until it changes to ↔, then drag the right edge of the chart to the right edge of column H**
   The chart is widened. See Figure D-6.

5. **Position the pointer over the top middle selection handle until it changes to ↕, then drag it to the top of row 12**

6. **If the labels for the months do not fully display, position the pointer over the bottom middle selection handle until it changes to ↕, then drag down to display the months**
   You can move the legend to improve the chart's appearance. You want to align the top of the legend with the top of the plot area.

7. **Click the legend to select it, then drag the legend using the ↕ to the upper-right corner of the chart until it is aligned with the plot area**
   Selection handles appear around the legend when you click it; "Legend" appears in the Chart Objects list box on the Chart toolbar as well as in the name box, and a dotted outline of the legend perimeter appears as you drag. Changing the original Excel data modifies the legend text.

8. **Click cell A9, type NYC, then click** ☑
   See Figure D-7. The legend is repositioned and the legend entry for the New York City store is changed.

9. **Save your work**

**FIGURE D-6: Worksheet with resized and repositioned chart**

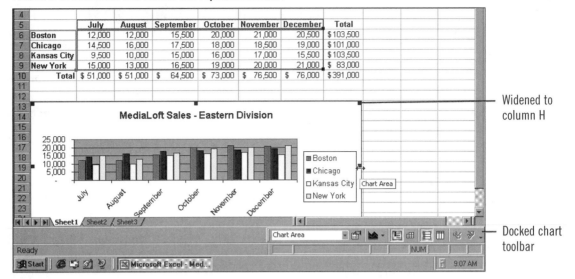

Widened to column H

Docked chart toolbar

**FIGURE D-7: Worksheet with repositioned legend**

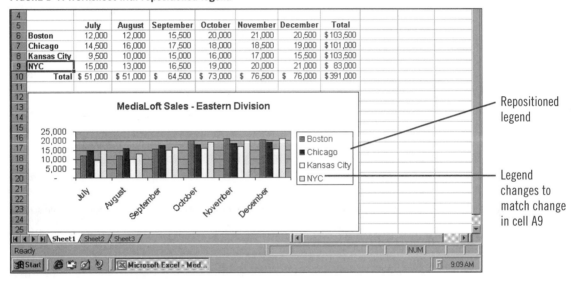

Repositioned legend

Legend changes to match change in cell A9

**TABLE D-2: Commonly used pointers**

| name | pointer | use | name | pointer | use |
|---|---|---|---|---|---|
| Diagonal resizing | ↗ or ↖ | Change chart shape from corners | I-beam | I | Edit chart text |
| Draw | + | Create shapes | Move chart | ✛ | Change chart location |
| Horizontal resizing | ↔ | Change chart shape from left to right | Vertical resizing | ↕ | Changes chart shape from top to bottom |

**CLUES TO USE**

## Identifying chart objects

There are many objects within a chart and Excel makes it easy to identify each of them. Placing your mouse pointer over a chart object causes a ScreenTip for that object to appear, whether the chart is selected or not. If a chart—or any object in it—is selected, the ScreenTips still appear. In addition, the name of the selected chart object appears in the name box and the Chart Object list box on the Chart toolbar.

# Editing a Chart

Once you've created a chart, it's easy to modify it. You can change data values in the worksheet, and the chart will automatically be updated to reflect the new data. You can also easily change chart types using the buttons on the Chart toolbar. Jim looks over his worksheet and realizes he entered the wrong data for the Kansas City store in November and December. After he corrects this data, he wants to see how the same data looks using different chart types.

**Trouble?**

If you cannot see the chart and data together on your monitor, click View on the menu bar, click Zoom, then click 75%.

1. If necessary, scroll the worksheet so that you can see both the chart and row 8, containing the Kansas City sales figures, then place your mouse pointer over the data point to display **Series "Kansas City" Point "December" Value "15,500"**
As you correct the values, the columns for November and December in the chart automatically change.

2. Click cell **F8**, type **18000** to correct the November sales figure, press [→], type **19500** in cell **G8**, then click ☑
The Kansas City columns for November and December reflect the increased sales figures. See Figure D-9. The totals are also updated in column H and row 10.

3. Select the chart by clicking anywhere within the chart border, then click the **Chart Type list arrow** ▲▼ on the Chart toolbar
The chart type buttons appear on the Chart Type palette. Table D-3 describes the chart types available.

4. Click the **Bar Chart button** ▤ on the palette
The column chart changes to a bar chart. See Figure D-10. You look at the bar chart, take some notes, and then decide to convert it back to a column chart. You now want to see if the large increase in sales would be better presented with a three-dimensional column chart.

**QuickTip**

Experiment with different formats for your charts until you get just the right look.

5. Click the **Chart Type list arrow** ▤▼, then click the **3-D Column Chart button** 📊 on the palette
A three-dimensional column chart appears. You notice that the three-dimensional column format is more crowded than the two-dimensional format but gives you a sense of volume.

6. Click the **Chart Type list arrow** 📊▼, then click the **Column Chart button** 📊 on the palette

7. Save your work

### Rotating a chart

In a three-dimensional chart, columns or bars can sometimes be obscured by other data series within the same chart. You can rotate the chart until a better view is obtained. Double-click the chart, click the tip of one of its axes (select the Corners object), then drag the handles until a more pleasing view of the data series appears. See Figure D-8.

Click to rotate chart

**FIGURE D-8: 3-D chart rotated with improved view of data series**

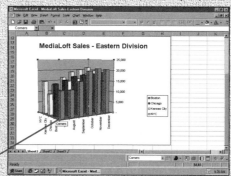

FIGURE D-9: Worksheet with new data entered for Kansas City

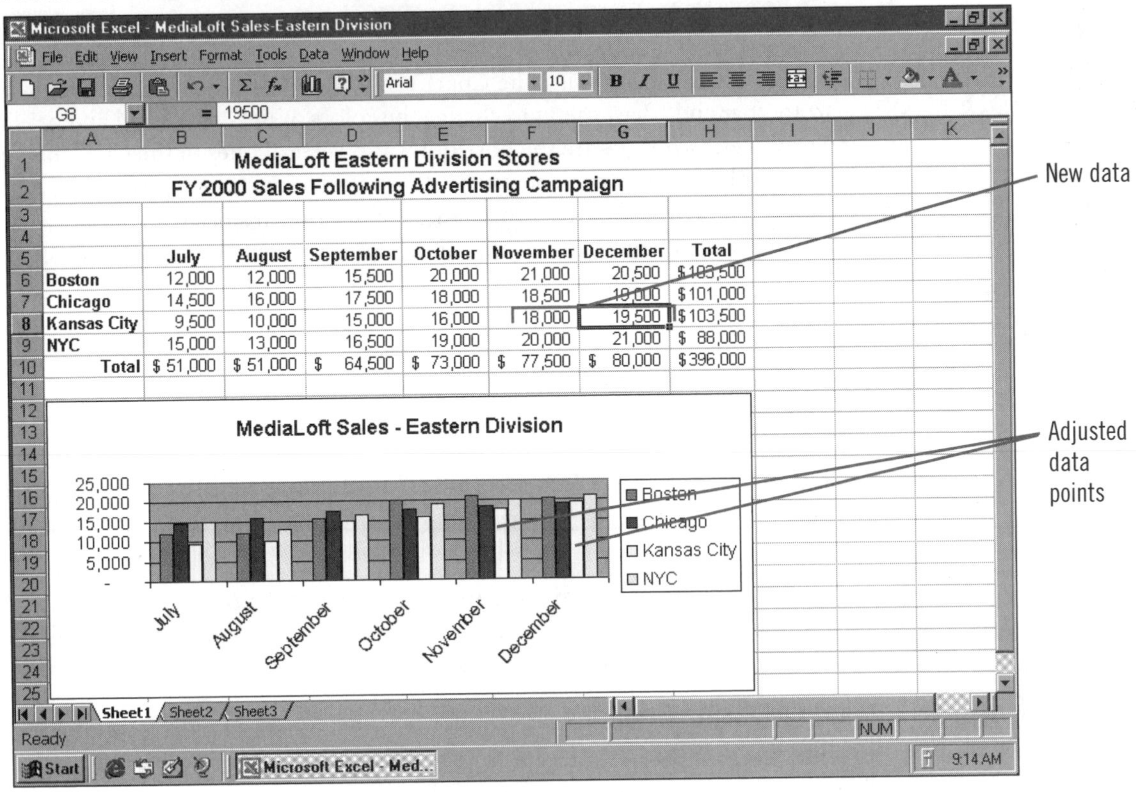

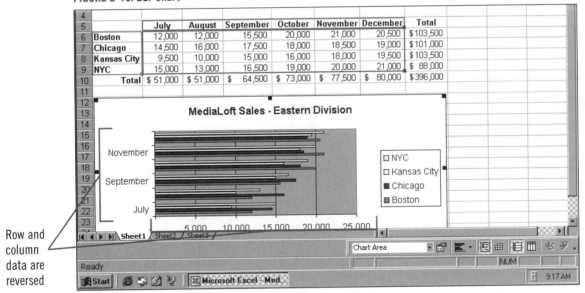

New data

Adjusted
data
points

FIGURE D-10: Bar chart

Row and
column
data are
reversed

TABLE D-3: Commonly used chart type buttons

| click | to display a | click | to display a | click | to display a | click | to display a |
|---|---|---|---|---|---|---|---|
| | area chart | | pie chart | | 3-D area chart | | 3-D pie chart |
| | bar chart | | (xy) scatter chart | | 3-D bar chart | | 3-D surface chart |
| | column chart | | doughnut chart | | 3-D column chart | | 3-D cylinder chart |
| | line chart | | radar chart | | 3-D line chart | | 3-D cone chart |

# Formatting a Chart

After you've created a chart using the Chart Wizard, you can easily modify its appearance. Use the Chart toolbar and Chart menu to change the colors of data series and add or eliminate a legend and gridlines. **Gridlines** are the horizontal and vertical lines in the chart that enable the eye to follow the value on an axis. The button that selects the chart type changes to the last chart type selected. The corresponding Chart toolbar buttons are listed in Table D-4. ➤ Jim wants to make some changes in the appearance of his chart. He wants to see if the chart looks better without gridlines, and he wants to change the color of a data series.

## Steps 1 2 3 4

1. **Make sure the chart is still selected**

   Horizontal gridlines currently appear in the chart.

2. **Click Chart on the menu bar, click Chart Options, click the Gridlines tab in the Chart Options dialog box, then click the Major Gridlines checkbox for the Value (Y) axis to remove the check**

   The gridlines disappear from the sample chart in the dialog box, as shown in Figure D-11. Even though gridlines extend from the tick marks on an axis across the plot area, they are not always necessary to the chart's readability.

   **QuickTip**

   Minor gridlines show the values between the tick marks.

3. **Click the Major Gridlines checkbox for the Value (Y) axis, then click the Minor Gridlines checkbox for the Value (Y) axis**

   Both major and minor gridlines appear in the sample.

4. **Click the Minor Gridlines checkbox for the Value (Y) axis, then click OK**

   The minor gridlines disappear, leaving only the major gridlines on the Value axis. You can change the color of the columns to better distinguish the data series.

5. **With the chart selected, double-click any light blue column in the NYC data series**

   Handles appear on all the columns in the NYC data series, and the Format Data Series dialog box opens, as shown in Figure D-12.

   **QuickTip**

   Add values, labels, and percentages to your chart using the Data Labels tab in the Chart Options dialog box.

6. **Click the Patterns tab, if necessary, click the fuschia box (in the fourth row, first on the left), then click OK**

   All the columns for the series are fuschia, and the legend changes to match the new color. Compare your finished chart to Figure D-13.

7. **Save your work**

**TABLE D-4: Chart enhancement buttons**

| button | use |
|---|---|
| 📋 | Displays formatting dialog box for the selected object on the chart |
| 📊 | Selects chart type (chart type on button changes to last chart type selected) |
| 📑 | Adds/Deletes legend |
| ⊞ | Creates a data table within the chart |
| 📋 | Charts data by row |
| ▥ | Charts data by column |
| 📐 | Angles selected text downward |
| 📐 | Angles selected text upward |

**FIGURE D-11: Chart Options dialog box**

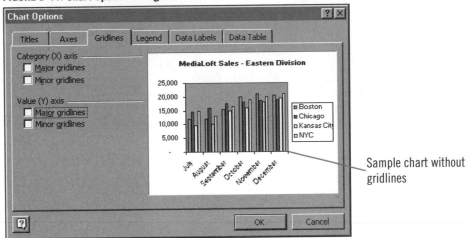

Sample chart without gridlines

**FIGURE D-12: Format Data Series dialog box**

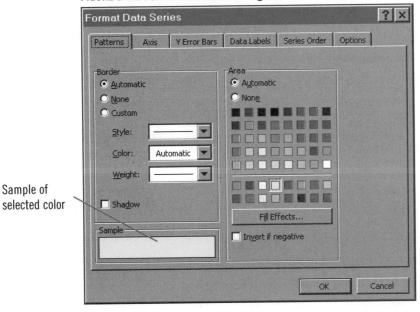

Sample of selected color

**FIGURE D-13: Chart with formatted data series**

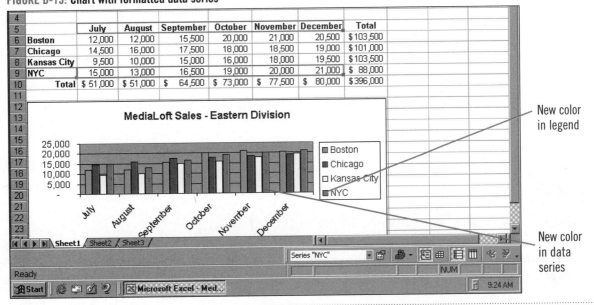

New color in legend

New color in data series

# Enhancing a Chart

There are many ways to enhance a chart to make it easier to read and understand. You can create titles for the x-axis and y-axis, add graphics, or add background color. You can even format the text you use in a chart. Jim wants to improve the appearance of his chart by creating titles for the x-axis and y-axis. He also decides to add a drop shadow to the title.

## Steps

**1.** Make sure the chart is selected, click **Chart** on the menu bar, click **Chart Options**, click the **Titles tab** in the Chart Options dialog box, then type **Months** in the Category (X) axis text box

Descriptive text on the x-axis helps a user understand the chart. The word "Months" appears below the month labels in the sample chart, as shown in Figure D-14.

> **QuickTip**
>
> To edit the text, position the pointer over the selected text box until it changes to I, click, then edit the text.

**2.** Click the **Value (Y) axis text box**, type **Sales (in $)**, then click **OK**

A selected text box containing "Sales (in $)" appears rotated 90 degrees to the left of the y-axis. Once the Chart Options dialog box is closed, you can move the Value or Category axis titles to new positions by clicking on an edge of the object and dragging it.

**3.** Press **[Esc]** to deselect the Value-axis title

Next you decide that a border with a drop shadow will enhance the chart title.

**4.** Click the **chart title MediaLoft Sales – Eastern Division** to select it

You can create a drop shadow using the Format button on the Chart toolbar.

> **QuickTip**
>
> The Format button opens a dialog box with the appropriate formatting options for the selected chart element. The ScreenTip for the button changes depending on the selected object.

**5.** Click the **Format Chart Title button** on the Chart toolbar to open the Format Chart Title dialog box, make sure the **Patterns tab** is selected, then click the **Shadow checkbox**

A border with a drop shadow surrounds the title. You can continue to format the title.

**6.** Click the **Font tab** in the Format Chart Title dialog box, click **Times New Roman** in the Font list, click **Bold Italic** in the Font style list, click **OK,** then press **[Esc]** to deselect the chart title

A border with a drop shadow appears around the chart title, and the chart title text is reformatted.

**7.** Click the **Category Axis Title**, click, click the **Font tab**, select **Times New Roman** in the Font list, then click **OK**

The Category Axis Title appears in the Times New Roman font.

**8.** Click the **Value Axis Title**, click, click the **Font tab**, click **Times New Roman** in the Font list, click **OK**, then press **[Esc]** to deselect the title

The Value Axis Title appears in the Times New Roman font. Compare your chart to Figure D-15.

**9.** Save your work

## Changing text font and alignment in charts

The font and the alignment of axis text can be modified to make it more readable or to better fit within the plot area. With a chart selected, double-click the axis text to be modified. The Format Axis dialog box appears. Click the Font or the Alignment tab, make the desired changes, then click OK.

**FIGURE D-14:** Sample chart with Category (X) axis text

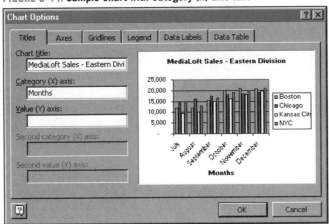

**FIGURE D-15:** Enhanced chart

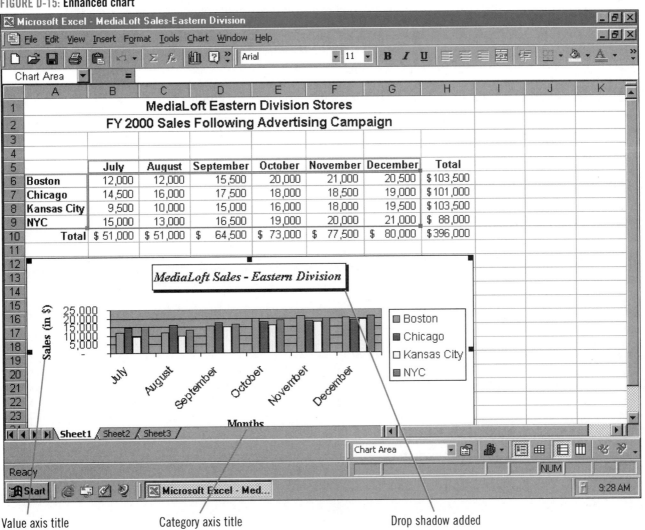

Value axis title

Category axis title

Drop shadow added

# Annotating and Drawing on a Chart

You can add arrows and text annotations to point out critical information in your charts. Text annotations are labels that you add to a chart to further describe the data in it. You can draw lines and arrows that point to the exact locations you want to emphasize. ✐  Jim wants to add a text annotation and an arrow to highlight the October sales increase.

## Steps 1 2 3 4

**1. Make sure the chart is selected**

To call attention to the Boston October sales increase, you can draw an arrow that points to the top of the Boston October data series with the annotation, "Due to ad campaign." With the chart selected, simply typing text in the formula bar creates annotation text.

**2. Type Due to ad campaign, then click the Enter button 🗹**

As you type, the text appears in the formula bar. After you confirm the entry, the text appears in a selected text box within the chart window.

**3. Point to an edge of the text box so the pointer changes to ⬚**

**4. Drag the text box above the chart, as shown in Figure D-16, then release the mouse button**

You can add an arrow to point to a specific area or item in a chart using the Drawing toolbar.

**5. Click the Drawing button 🗹 on the Standard toolbar**

The Drawing toolbar appears.

**6. Click the Arrow button 🗹 on the Drawing toolbar**

The pointer changes to ＋ and the status bar displays "Click and drag to insert an AutoShape." When you draw an arrow, the point farthest from where you start will have the arrowhead.

**7. Position ＋ under the 't' in the word "to" in the text box, press and hold the left mouse button, drag the line to the Boston column in the October sales series, then release the mouse button**

An arrowhead appears, pointing to Boston October sales. The arrowhead is a selected object in the chart and can be resized, formatted, or deleted just like any other object. Compare your finished chart to Figure D-17.

**8. Click 🗹 to close the Drawing toolbar**

**9. Save your work**

### Trouble?

If the pointer changes to ⬚ or ↔, release the mouse button, click outside the text box area to deselect it, then select the text box and repeat Step 3.

### QuickTip

You can insert text and an arrow in the data section of a worksheet by clicking the Text Box button 🗹 on the Drawing toolbar, drawing a text box, typing the text, and then adding the arrow.

**FIGURE D-16: Repositioning text annotation**

Outline of repositioned annotation

Selected floating text box

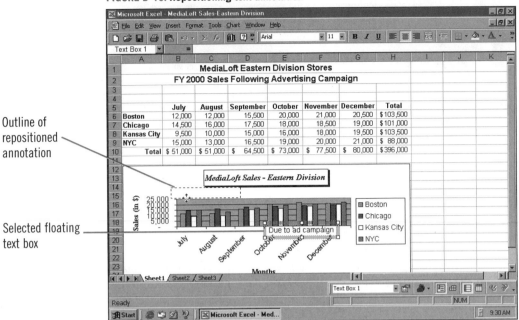

**FIGURE D-17: Completed chart with text annotation and arrow**

Repositioned text annotation

Arrow

Boston October sales

Drawing toolbar

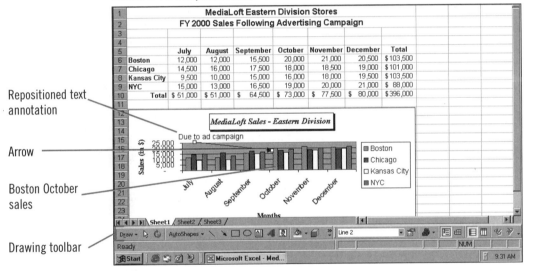

## Exploding a pie slice

Just as an arrow can call attention to a data series, you can emphasize a pie slice by exploding it, or pulling it away from, the pie chart. Once the pie chart is selected, click the pie to select it, click the desired slice to select only the slice, then drag the slice away from the pie, as shown in Figure D-18. After you change the chart type, you may need to adjust arrows within the chart.

**FIGURE D-18: Exploded pie slice**

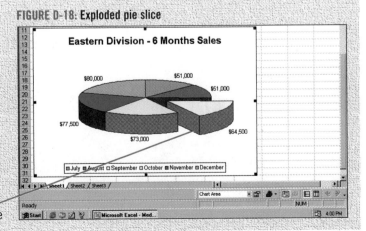

September sales slice pulled from pie

# Previewing and Printing a Chart

After you complete a chart to your satisfaction, you will need to print it. Previewing a chart gives you a chance to see what your chart looks like before you print it. You can print a chart by itself, or as part of the worksheet. ▄▄▄▄▄ Jim wants to print the chart for the annual meeting. He will print the worksheet and the chart together, so that the shareholders can see the actual sales numbers for the eastern division stores.

## Steps 1234

1. **Press [Esc] twice to deselect the arrow and the chart, click cell A35, type your name, press [Enter], then press [Ctrl][Home]**
   If you wanted to print only the chart without the data, you would leave the chart selected. Including your name on a worksheet insures that you'll be able to identify your work when it is printed.

**Trouble?**

Click Margins on the Print Preview toolbar to display Margin lines in the Print Preview window.

2. **Click the Print Preview button 🔍 on the Standard toolbar**
   The Print Preview window opens. You decide that the chart and data would make better use of the page if they were printed in **landscape** orientation—that is, with the text running the long way on the page. Altering the page setup changes the orientation of the page.

3. **Click Setup on the Print Preview toolbar to open the Page Setup dialog box, then click the Page tab**

4. **Click the Landscape option button in the Orientation section as shown in Figure D-19, then click OK**
   Because each page has a left default margin of 0.75", the chart and data will print too far over to the left of the page. You can change this setting using the Margins tab.

5. **Click Setup, click the Margins tab, click the Center on page Horizontally checkbox, then click OK**
   The data and chart are positioned horizontally on the page. See Figure D-20.

6. **Click Print to display the Print dialog box, then click OK**
   The data and chart print and you are returned to the worksheet. If you want, you can choose to preview (and print) only the chart.

7. **Select the chart, then click the Print Preview button 🔍**
   The chart appears in the Print Preview window. If you wanted to, you could print the chart by clicking the Print button on the Print Preview toolbar.

8. **Click Close on the Print Preview toolbar**

9. **Save your work, then close the workbook and exit Excel**

### Using the Page Setup dialog box for a chart

When a chart is selected, a different Page Setup dialog box opens than when neither the chart nor data is selected. The Center on Page options are not always available. To accurately position a chart on the page, you could click the Margins button on the Print Preview toolbar. Margin lines appear on the screen and show you exactly how the margins display on the page. The exact placement appears in the status bar when you press and hold the mouse button on the margin line. You can drag the lines to the exact setting you want.

**FIGURE D-19:** Page tab of the Page Setup dialog box

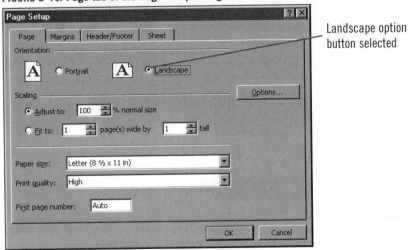

Landscape option button selected

**FIGURE D-20:** Chart and data ready to print

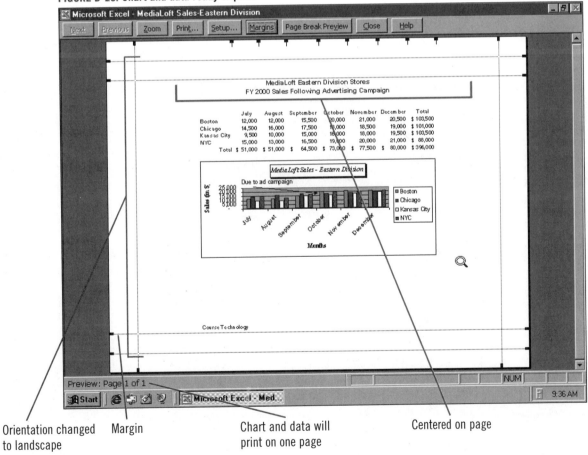

Orientation changed to landscape

Margin

Chart and data will print on one page

Centered on page

# Practice

## ► Concepts Review

Label each element of the Excel chart shown in Figure D-21.

FIGURE D-21

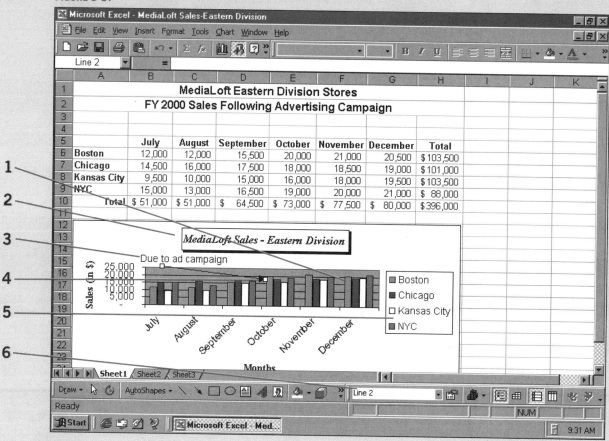

Match each chart type with the statement that describes it.

7. **Column**
8. **Area**
9. **Pie**
10. **Combination**
11. **Line**

a. Shows how volume changes over time
b. Compares data as parts of a whole
c. Displays a column and line chart using different scales of measurement
d. Compares trends over even time intervals
e. Compares data over time—the Excel default

Select the best answer from the list of choices.

**12. The object in a chart that identifies patterns used for each data series is a**
   a. Data point.
   b. Plot.
   c. Legend.
   d. Range.

**13. What is the term for a row or column on a chart?**
   a. Range address
   b. Axis title
   c. Chart orientation
   d. Data series

**14. The orientation of a page whose dimensions are 11" by 8½" is**
   a. Sideways.
   b. Longways.
   c. Portrait.
   d. Landscape.

**15. The Value axis is the**
   a. X-axis.
   b. Z-axis.
   c. D-axis.
   d. Y-axis.

**16. The Category axis is the**
   a. X-axis.
   b. Z-axis.
   c. D-axis.
   d. Y-axis.

**17. Which pointer is used to resize a chart object?**
   a. I
   b. ↙
   c. ✛
   d. +

# ▶ Skills Review

## 1. Create a chart.

**a.** Start Excel, open a new workbook, then save it as "Software Usage" to your Project Disk.

**b.** Enter the information from Table D-5 in your worksheet in range A1:F6. Resize columns and rows.

**c.** Save your work.

**d.** Select the range you want to chart.

**e.** Click the Chart Wizard button.

**f.** Complete the Chart Wizard dialog boxes and build a column chart on the same sheet as the data, having a different color bar for each department. Title the chart "Software Usage by Department."

**g.** Save your work.

TABLE D-5

|  | Excel | Word | PowerPoint | Access | Publisher |
|---|---|---|---|---|---|
| Accounting | 22 | 15 | 2 | 2 | 1 |
| Marketing | 13 | 35 | 35 | 5 | 32 |
| Engineering | 23 | 5 | 3 | 1 | 0 |
| Personnel | 10 | 25 | 10 | 2 | 25 |
| Production | 6 | 5 | 22 | 0 | 22 |

## 2. Move and resize a chart.

**a.** Make sure the chart is still selected.

**b.** Move the chart beneath the data.

**c.** Drag the chart's selection handles so it is as wide as the screen.

**d.** Move the legend below the charted data. (*Hint:* Change the legend's position using the Legend button on the Chart toolbar.)

**e.** Save your work.

## 3. Edit a chart.

**a.** Change the value in cell B3 to "6." Notice the change in the chart.

**b.** Select the chart by clicking it.

**c.** Click the Chart Type list arrow on the Chart toolbar.

**d.** Click the 3-D Column Chart button.

**e.** Rotate the chart to move the data.

**f.** Change the chart back to a column chart.

**g.** Save your work.

## 4. Format a chart.

**a.** Make sure the chart is still selected.

**b.** Use the Chart Options dialog box to turn off the displayed gridlines.

**c.** Change the font used in the Category and Value labels to Times New Roman.

**d.** Turn the major gridlines back on.

**e.** Change the title's font to Times New Roman.

**f.** Save your work.

5. **Enhance a chart.**
   a. Make sure the chart is still selected, click Chart on the menu bar, click Chart Options, then click the Titles tab.
   b. Click the Category (X) axis text box, then type "Software" in the selected text box below the x-axis.
   c. Click the Value (Y) axis text box, type "Users" in the selected text box to the left of the y-axis, then click OK.
   d. Change the legend entry for "Production" to "Art."
   e. Add a drop shadow to the title.
   f. Save your work.

6. **Annotate and draw on a chart.**
   a. Select the chart.
   b. Create the text annotation "Need More Users."
   c. Drag the text annotation under the title.
   d. Click the Arrow button on the Drawing toolbar.
   e. Click below the text annotation, drag the arrow so it points to the area containing the Access columns, then release the mouse button.
   f. Save your work.

7. **Preview and print a chart.**
   a. Deselect the chart and type your name in cell A30.
   b. Preview the chart and data to see how it will look when printed.
   c. Change the paper orientation to landscape.
   d. Center the data and chart horizontally and vertically on the page.
   e. Click Print in the Print Preview window.
   f. Select the chart.
   g. Preview, then print only the chart.
   h. Save your work, close the workbook, then exit Excel.

Excel 2000

# ▶ Independent Challenges

**1.** You are the operations manager for the Springfield Theater Group. Each year the city of Springfield applies to various state and federal agencies for matching funds. The city's marketing department wants you to create charts for a report that will be used to document the number of productions in previous years. You need to create charts that show the number of previously produced plays.

To complete this independent challenge:

a. Sketch a sample worksheet on a piece of paper describing how you will create the charts. Which type of chart is best suited for the information you need to display? What kind of chart enhancements will be necessary? Will a 3-D effect make your chart easier to understand?

b. Start Excel, open the workbook EX D-2 from your Project Disk, then save it as "Theater Group."

c. Create a column chart for the data.

d. Change at least one of the colors used in a data series.

e. Create at least two additional charts for the same data to show how different chart types display the same data.

f. After creating the charts, make the appropriate enhancements. Include chart titles, legends, and value and category titles.

g. Add data labels.

h. Type your name in a cell in the worksheet.

i. Before printing, preview the file so you know what the charts will look like. Adjust any items as needed.

j. Save your work. Print the worksheet (charts and data).

k. Close the workbook and exit Excel.

**2.** One of your responsibilities at the Beautiful You Salon is to re-create the company's records using Excel. Another is to convince the current staff that Excel can make daily operations easier and more efficient. You've decided to create charts using the previous year's operating expenses. These charts will be used at the next monthly meeting.

To complete this independent challenge:

a. Decide which data in the worksheet should be charted. Sketch two sample charts. What type of charts are best suited for the information you need to display? What kind of chart enhancements will be necessary?

b. Start Excel, open the workbook EX D-3 from your Project Disk, and save it as "BY Expense Charts."

c. Create a column chart containing the expense data for all four quarters.

d. Using the same data, create two additional charts using different chart types.

e. Add annotated text and arrows (to the initial chart) highlighting any important data or trends that you can see from the charts.

f. In one chart, change the colors of data series, and in another chart, use black-and-white patterns only.

g. Type your name in a cell in the worksheet.

h. Before printing, preview the file so you know what the charts will look like. Adjust any items as needed.

i. Print the charts. Save your work.

j. Close the workbook and exit Excel.

**3.** The Step Lightly Ad Agency is delighted with the way you've organized their membership roster using Excel. The Board of Directors wants to assess certain advertising expenses and has asked you to prepare charts that can be used in their presentation.

To complete this independent challenge:

**a.** Start Excel, open the workbook EX D-4 from your Project Disk, and save it as "Step Lightly."

**b.** Use the raw data for the sample shown in the range A16:B24 to create charts.

**c.** Decide what types of charts would be best suited for this type of data. Sketch two sample charts. What kind of chart enhancements will be necessary?

**d.** Create at least three different chart types that show the distribution of advertising expenses.

**e.** Add annotated text and arrows highlighting important data, such as the largest expense.

**f.** Change the color of at least one data series.

**g.** Add Category and Value axis titles; add a chart title. Format the titles with a font of your choice. Place a drop shadow around the chart title.

**h.** Type your name in a cell in the worksheet.

**i.** Before printing, preview the file so you know what the charts will look like. Adjust any items as needed. Be sure the chart is placed appropriately on the page.

**j.** Print the charts, save your work, then close the workbook and exit Excel.

**4.** During the second quarter of the year, the New York City MediaLoft store decided to analyze sales by type of book for a three-month period. Sales have been steadily increasing and the manager of the store is planning to renovate the space. Depending on which books sell best for the store location, the manager will reallocate the selling floor space accordingly. To be able to present this information to see which types of books are the best sellers, you will chart the analysis to get a graphical representation of the distributions. You decide to create two types of charts for the same data.

To complete this independent challenge:

**a.** Start Excel, open a new workbook, and save it on your Project Disk as "New York Analysis."

**b.** Connect to the Internet, go to the MediaLoft intranet site at http://www.course.com/illustrated/MediaLoft, then click the link for the Accounting page.

**c.** Copy the New York Analysis data into your worksheet.

**d.** Create a column chart with the data series in rows on the same worksheet as the data. Include a descriptive title and the following text: "Type of Book" in the Category axis, and "Sales" in the Value axis.

**e.** Place the chart on the same sheet as the data.

**f.** Move the chart so that it is below the data and the left side of the chart is in column A.

**g.** Format the legend so that it is placed along the bottom of the chart.

**h.** Change the color of the Science Fiction data series to fuschia.

**i.** Remove the gridlines.

**j.** Using the same data, create a 3-D bar chart (use the Clustered bar with the 3-D visual effect) with the data series in rows on a new sheet.

**k.** Add appropriate title(s) to the worksheet and axes.

**l.** Format the Value axis so the numbers display no decimal places, and a 1000 separator (comma).

**m.** Type your name in a visible cell in the worksheet containing the data.

**n.** Preview the chart and change margins as needed.

**o.** Print the worksheet data and column chart, making setup modifications as necessary.

**p.** Print the 3-D bar chart making any setup modifications as necessary.

**q.** Save the workbook and exit Excel.

# ▶ Visual Workshop

Modify a worksheet using the skills you learned in this unit, using Figure D-22 for reference. Open the file EX D-5 from your Project Disk, and save it as "Quarterly Advertising Budget." Create the chart, then change the data to reflect Figure D-22. Type your name in cell A13, save, preview, and then print your results.

**FIGURE D-22**

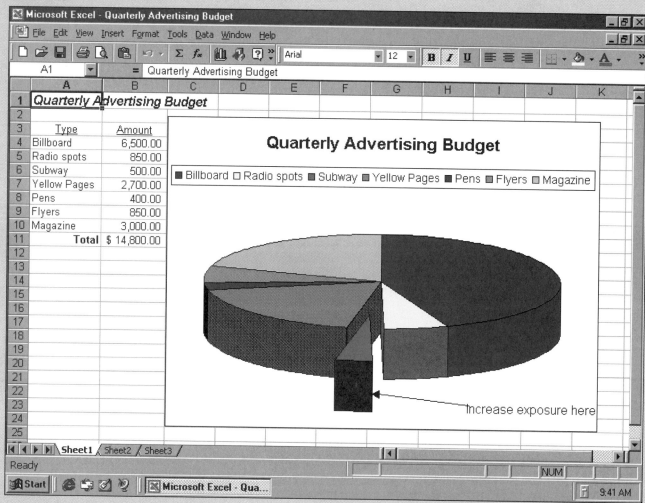

# Working
## with Formulas and Functions

## Objectives

- MOUS ► **Create a formula with several operators**
- MOUS ► **Use names in a formula**
- MOUS ► **Generate multiple totals with AutoSum**
- MOUS ► **Use dates in calculations**
- MOUS ► **Build a conditional formula with the IF function**
- MOUS ► **Use statistical functions**
- MOUS ► **Calculate payments with the PMT function**
- MOUS ► **Display and print formula contents**

Without formulas, Excel would simply be an electronic grid with text and numbers. Used with formulas, Excel becomes a powerful data analysis software tool. As you learn how to analyze data using different types of formulas, including those that call for functions, you will discover more ways to use Excel. In this unit, you will gain a further understanding of Excel formulas and learn how to build several Excel functions.  Top management at MediaLoft has asked Jim Fernandez to analyze various company data. To do this, Jim creates several worksheets that require the use of formulas and functions. Because management is considering raising salaries for store managers, Jim's first task is to create a report that compares the payroll deductions and net pay for store managers before and after a proposed raise.

# Creating a Formula with Several Operators

You can create formulas that contain a combination of cell references (for example, Z100 and B2), operators (for example, * [multiplication] and − [subtraction]), and values (for example, 99 or 1.56). You also can create a single formula that performs several calculations. If you enter a formula with more than one operator, Excel performs the calculations in a particular sequence based on algebraic rules called **precedence**; that is, Excel performs the operation(s) within the parentheses first, then performs the other calculations. See Table E-1. ✍︎ Jim has been given the gross pay and payroll deductions for the first payroll period and needs to complete his analysis. He also has preformatted, with the Comma style, any cells that are to contain values. Jim begins by entering a formula for net pay that subtracts the payroll deductions from gross pay.

## Steps

**QuickTip**

To return personalized tool-bars and menus to their default state, click Tools on the menu bar, click Customize, click the Options tab in the Customize dialog box, click Reset my usage data to restore the default settings, click Yes, click Close, then close the Drawing toolbar if it is displayed.

1. Start Excel if necessary, open the workbook titled **EX E-1**, then save the workbook as **Pay Info for Store Mgrs**
   The first part of the net pay formula will go in cell B11.

2. Click **Edit** on the menu bar, click **Go To**, then type **B11** in the Reference box and click **OK**
   The Go To command is especially useful when you want to select a cell in a large worksheet.

3. Type **=B6−**
   Remember that you can type cell references in either uppercase or lowercase letters. (Excel automatically converts lowercase cell reference letters to uppercase.) If you make a mistake while building a formula, press [Esc] and begin again. You type the equal sign (=) to tell Excel that a formula follows, B6 to reference the cell containing the gross pay, and the minus sign (−) to indicate that the next entry will be subtracted from cell B6.

**Trouble?**

If you receive a message box indicating "Parentheses do not match," make sure you have included both a left and a right parenthesis.

4. Type **(B7+B8+B9+B10)** then click the **Enter button** 📝 on the formula bar
   The net pay for Payroll Period 1 appears in cell B11, as shown in Figure E-1. (*Note:* Your tool-bars may differ from those in the figure.) Because Excel performs the operations within parentheses first, you can control the order of calculations on the worksheet. (In this case, Excel sums the values in cells B7 through B10 first.) After the operations within the parentheses are completed, Excel performs the operations outside the parentheses. (In this case, Excel subtracts the total of range B7:B10 from cell B6.)

5. Copy the formula in cell **B11** into cells **C11:F11**, then return to cell **A1**
   The formula in cell B11 is copied to the range C11:F11 to complete row 11. See Figure E-2.

6. Save the workbook
   Jim is pleased with the formulas that calculate net pay totals.

**TABLE E-1: Example formulas using parentheses and several operators**

| formula | order of precedence | calculated result |
|---|---|---|
| =36+(1+3) | Add 1 to 3; then add the result to 36 | 40 |
| =(10−20)/10−5 | Subtract 20 from 10; divide that by 10; then subtract 5 | −6 |
| =(10*2)*(10+2) | Multiply 10 by 2; add 10 to 2; then multiply the results | 240 |

**FIGURE E-1:** Worksheet showing formula and result

Result in cell B11

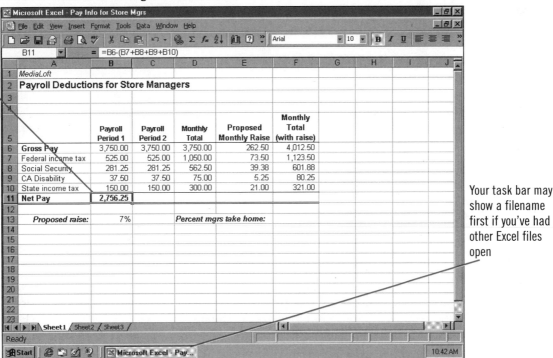

Your task bar may show a filename first if you've had other Excel files open

**FIGURE E-2:** Worksheet with copied formulas

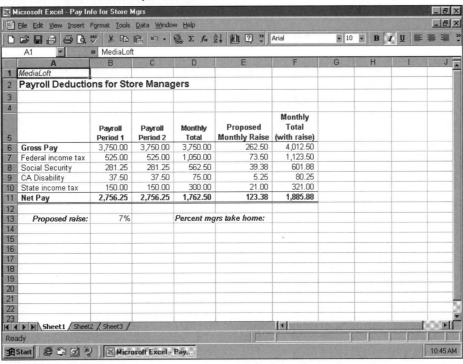

## Using Paste Special to paste formulas and values and to perform calculations

You can use the Paste Special command to quickly enter formulas and values or even to perform quick calculations. Click the cell(s) containing the formula or value you want to copy, click the Copy button 📋 on the Standard toolbar, then right-click the cell where you want the result to appear. In the pop-up menu, choose Paste Special, then choose the feature you want to paste and click OK.

**Excel 2000**

# Using Names in a Formula

You can assign names to cells and ranges. Doing so reduces errors and makes a worksheet easier to follow. You also can use names in formulas. Using names in formulas facilitates formula building and provides a frame of reference for formula logic—the names make formulas easy to recognize and maintain. The formula Revenue − Cost, for example, is much easier to comprehend than the formula A2 − D3. You can produce a list of workbook names and their references at any time. Jim wants to include a formula that calculates the percentage of monthly gross pay the managers would actually take home (net pay) if a 7% raise is granted. He starts by naming the cells he'll use in the calculation.

**Steps 123 4**

**1.** Click cell **F6**, click the **name box** on the formula bar to select the active cell reference, type **Gross_with_Raise**, then press **[Enter]**

The name assigned to cell F6, Gross_with_Raise, appears in the name box. Note that you must type underscores instead of spaces between words. Cell F6 is now named Gross_with_Raise to refer to the monthly gross pay amount that includes the 7% raise. The name box displays as much of the name as fits (Gross_with_…). The net pay cell needs a name.

**QuickTip**

To delete a name, click Insert on the menu bar, point to Name, then click Define. Select the name, click Delete, then click OK.

**2.** Click cell **F11**, click the **name box**, type **Net_with_Raise**, then press **[Enter]**

The new formula will use names instead of cell references.

**3.** Click cell **F13**, type **=Net_with_Raise/Gross_with_Raise**, then click the **Enter button** on the formula bar (make sure you begin the formula with an equal sign)

The formula bar now shows the new formula, and the result, 0.47, appears in the cell. If you add names to a worksheet after all the formulas have been entered, you must click Insert on the menu bar, point to Name, click Apply, click the name or names, then click OK. Cell F13 needs to be formatted in Percent style.

**QuickTip**

If you don't see **%** on your toolbar, click the More Buttons button **?** on the Formatting toolbar.

**4.** Select cell **F13**, click **Format** on the menu bar, click **Style**, click the **Style name list arrow**, click **Percent**, then click **OK**

Notice that the result shown in cell F13, 47%, is rounded to the nearest whole percent as shown in Figure E-3. A **style** is a combination of formatting characteristics, such as bold, italic, and underlined. You can use the Style dialog box instead of the Formatting toolbar to apply styles. You can also use it to remove styles: select the cell that has a style and select Normal in the Style name list. To define your own style, select a cell, format it using the formatting toolbar (such as bold, italic, and 14 point), then open the Style dialog box and type a name for your style. Later, you can apply all those formatting characteristics simply by applying your new style from the dialog box.

**5.** Enter your name into cell **D1**, return to cell A1, then save and print the worksheet

You can use the Label Ranges dialog box (Insert menu, Name submenu, Label command) to designate existing column or row headings as labels. Then instead of using cell references for the column or row in formulas, you can use the labels instead. (This feature is turned off by default. To turn it on, go to Tools/Options/Calculation tab/Accept labels in formulas.)

**6.** Close the workbook

FIGURE E-3: Worksheet formula that includes cell names

Formula with cell names

Name box

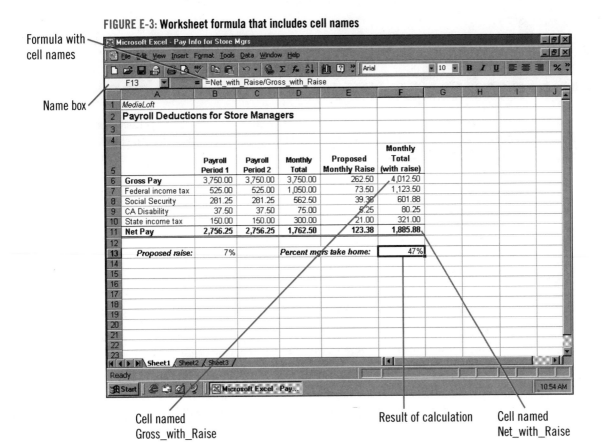

Cell named
Gross_with_Raise

Result of calculation

Cell named
Net_with_Raise

## Producing a list of names

You might want to verify the names you have in a workbook and the cells they reference. To paste a list of names in a workbook, select a blank cell that has several blank cells beside and beneath it. Click Insert on the menu bar, point to Name, then click Paste. In the Paste Name dialog box, click Paste List. Excel produces a list that includes the sheet name and the cell or range the name identifies. See Figure E-4.

FIGURE E-4: Worksheet with pasted list of names

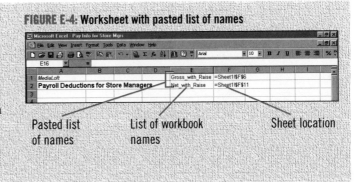

Pasted list of names

List of workbook names

Sheet location

# Generating Multiple Totals with AutoSum

Excel 2000

In most cases, the result of a function is a value derived from a calculation. Functions can also return results such as text, references, or other information about the worksheet. You enter a function, such as AVERAGE, directly into a cell; you can use the Edit Formula button; or you can insert it with the Paste Function. You can use cell references, ranges, names, and formulas as arguments between the parentheses. (Recall that arguments are the information used in calculating the results of a function.) As with other cell entries, you can cut, copy, and paste functions from one area of the worksheet to another and from one workbook to another. The most widely used Excel function, SUM, calculates worksheet totals and can be entered easily using the AutoSum button on the Standard toolbar.

Maria Abbot, MediaLoft's general sales manager, has given Jim a worksheet summarizing store sales. He needs to complete the worksheet totals.

1. **Open the workbook titled EX E-2, type your name into cell D1, then save the workbook as MediaLoft Sales**
   You can use AutoSum to generate two sets of totals at the same time.

2. **Select range B5:E9, press and hold [Ctrl], then select range B11:E15**
   To select nonadjacent cells, you must press and hold [Ctrl] while selecting the additional cells. Compare your selections with Figure E-5. The totals will appear in the last line of each selection.

   **Trouble?**
   If you select the wrong combination of cells, simply click on a single cell and begin again.

3. **Click the AutoSum button Σ on the Standard toolbar**
   When the selected range you want to sum (B5:E9 and B11:E15, in this example) includes a blank cell with data values above it, AutoSum enters the total in the blank cell.

4. **Select range B5:F17, then click Σ**
   Whenever the selected range you want to sum includes a blank cell in the bottom row or right column, AutoSum enters the total in the blank cell. In this case, Excel ignores the data values and totals only the sums. Although Excel generates totals when you click the AutoSum button, it is a good idea to check the results.

5. **Click cell B17**
   The formula bar reads =SUM(B15,B9). See Figure E-6. When generating grand totals, Excel automatically references the cells containing SUM functions with a comma separator between cell references. Excel uses commas to separate multiple arguments in all functions, not just in SUM.

6. **Print the worksheet, then save and close the workbook**

**FIGURE E-5: Selecting nonadjacent ranges using [Ctrl]**

| | A | B | C | D | E | F | G | H |
|---|---|---|---|---|---|---|---|---|
| 1 | *MediaLoft* | | | Jim Fernandez | | | | |
| 2 | **1999 Sales Summary** | | | | | | | |
| 3 | | | | | | | | |
| 4 | ***MediaLoft East*** | Qtr 1 | Qtr 2 | Qtr 3 | Qtr 4 | Total | | |
| 5 | Boston | $ 147,000 | $ 162,000 | $ 157,000 | $ 174,000 | | | |
| 6 | Chicago | 175,000 | 259,000 | 244,000 | 257,000 | | | |
| 7 | Kansas City | 152,000 | 207,000 | 215,000 | 225,000 | | | |
| 8 | New York | 183,000 | 230,000 | 225,000 | 247,000 | | | |
| 9 | Total | | | | | | | |
| 10 | *MediaLoft West* | | | | | | | |
| 11 | Houston | $ 80,000 | $ 117,000 | $ 148,000 | $ 182,000 | | | |
| 12 | San Diego | 63,000 | 95,000 | 152,000 | 186,000 | | | |
| 13 | San Francisco | 103,000 | 145,000 | 182,000 | 220,000 | | | |
| 14 | Seattle | 90,000 | 132,000 | 183,000 | 198,000 | | | |
| 15 | Total | | | | | | | |
| 16 | | | | | | | | |
| 17 | Grand Total | | | | | | | |
| 18 | | | | | | | | |

Ready  Sum= $  5,535,000

Start  Microsoft Excel - Med...  11:09 AM

**FIGURE E-6: Completed worksheet**

B17  = =SUM(B15,B9)

Comma used to separate multiple arguments

| | A | B | C | D | E | F | G | H |
|---|---|---|---|---|---|---|---|---|
| 1 | *MediaLoft* | | | Jim Fernandez | | | | |
| 2 | **1999 Sales Summary** | | | | | | | |
| 3 | | | | | | | | |
| 4 | ***MediaLoft East*** | Qtr 1 | Qtr 2 | Qtr 3 | Qtr 4 | Total | | |
| 5 | Boston | $ 147,000 | $ 162,000 | $ 157,000 | $ 174,000 | $ 640,000 | | |
| 6 | Chicago | 175,000 | 259,000 | 244,000 | 257,000 | 935,000 | | |
| 7 | Kansas City | 152,000 | 207,000 | 215,000 | 225,000 | 799,000 | | |
| 8 | New York | 183,000 | 230,000 | 225,000 | 247,000 | 885,000 | | |
| 9 | Total | $ 657,000 | $ 858,000 | $ 841,000 | $ 903,000 | $ 3,259,000 | | |
| 10 | *MediaLoft West* | | | | | | | |
| 11 | Houston | $ 80,000 | $ 117,000 | $ 148,000 | $ 182,000 | $ 527,000 | | |
| 12 | San Diego | 63,000 | 95,000 | 152,000 | 186,000 | $ 496,000 | | |
| 13 | San Francisco | 103,000 | 145,000 | 182,000 | 220,000 | $ 650,000 | | |
| 14 | Seattle | 90,000 | 132,000 | 183,000 | 198,000 | $ 603,000 | | |
| 15 | Total | $ 336,000 | $ 489,000 | $ 665,000 | $ 786,000 | $ 2,276,000 | | |
| 16 | | | | | | | | |
| 17 | Grand Total | $ 993,000 | $ 1,347,000 | $ 1,506,000 | $ 1,689,000 | $ 5,535,000 | | |
| 18 | | | | | | | | |

Ready

Start  Microsoft Excel - Med...  11:19 AM

**CLUES TO USE**

## Quick calculations with AutoCalculate

To check a total quickly without entering a formula, just select the range you want to sum, and the answer appears in the status bar next to SUM=. You also can perform other quick calculations, such as averaging or finding the minimum value in a selection. To do this, right-click the AutoCalculate area in the status bar and select from the list of options. The option you select remains in effect and in the status bar until you make another selection. See Figure E-7.

**FIGURE E-7: Using AutoCalculate**

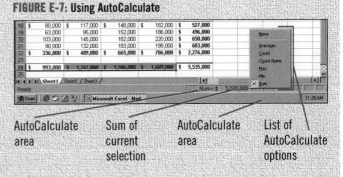

AutoCalculate area   Sum of current selection   AutoCalculate area   List of AutoCalculate options

**WORKING WITH FORMULAS AND FUNCTIONS**  EXCEL E-7 ◄

Excel 2000

Excel 2000

# Using Dates in Calculations

If you enter dates in a worksheet so that Excel recognizes them as dates, you can sort (arrange) the dates and perform date calculations. For example, you can calculate the number of days between your birth date and today, which is the number of days you have been alive. When you enter an Excel date format, Excel considers the entry a date function, converts the date to a serial date number, and stores that number in the cell. A date's converted serial date is the number of days to that date. Excel automatically assigns the serial date of "1" to January 1, 1900 and counts up from there; the serial date of January 1, 2000, for example, is 36,526. Jim's next task is to complete the New York Accounts Payable worksheet. He remembers to enter the worksheet dates in a format that Excel recognizes so that he can use date calculation.

**Steps**

1. Open the workbook titled **EX E-3**, then save the workbook as **New York Payables** to the appropriate folder on your Project Disk
   The calculations will be based on the current date, 4/1/00.

2. Click cell **C4**, type **4/1/00**, then press **[Enter]**
   The date appears in cell C4 just as you typed it. You want to enter a formula that calculates the invoice due date, which is 30 days from the invoice date. The formula adds 30 days to the invoice date.

   **QuickTip**

   You also can perform time calculations in Excel. For example, you can enter an employee's starting time and ending time, then calculate how many hours and minutes he or she worked. You must enter time in a format that Excel recognizes; for example, 1:35 PM (h:mm AM/PM).

3. Click cell **E7**, type **=**, click cell **B7**, type **+30**, then click the **Enter button** 🔲 on the formula bar
   Excel calculates the result by converting the 3/1/00 invoice date to a serial date number, adding 30 to it, then automatically formatting the result as a date. See Figure E-8. You can use the same formula to calculate the due dates of the other invoices.

4. Drag the fill handle to copy the formula in cell E7 into cells **E8:E13**
   Cell referencing causes the copied formula to contain the appropriate cell references. Now you are ready to enter the formula that calculates the age of each invoice. You do this by subtracting the invoice date from the current date. Because each invoice age formula must refer to the current date, you must make cell C4, the current date cell, an absolute reference in the formula.

   **QuickTip**

   If you perform date calculations and the intended numeric result displays as a date, format the cell(s) using a number format.

5. Click cell **F7**, type **=**, click cell **C4**, press **[F4]** to add the absolute reference symbols ($), type **−**, click **B7**, then click 🔲
   The formula bar displays the formula $C$4−B7. The numerical result, 31, appears in cell F7 because there are 31 days between 3/1/00 and 4/1/00. You can use the same formula to calculate the age of the remaining invoices.

6. Drag the fill handle to copy the formula in F7 to the range **F8:F13**, then press **[Ctrl][Home]**
   The age of each invoice appears in column F, as shown in Figure E-9.

7. Save the worksheet

### Using date functions

When you want Excel to perform a calculation using the current date, you can choose date and time options such as NOW, DATE, and TODAY. DATE inserts any date whose month, day, and year you specify as argu-

ments in the formula palette: =DATE(2000,7,6) will produce July 6, 2000, NOW inserts the current date and time, while TODAY inserts today's date only (you don't have to enter arguments for NOW or TODAY).

FIGURE E-8: Worksheet with formula for invoice due date

Formula result automatically calculated as date

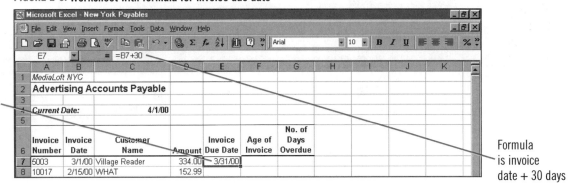

Formula is invoice date + 30 days

FIGURE E-9: Worksheet with copied formulas

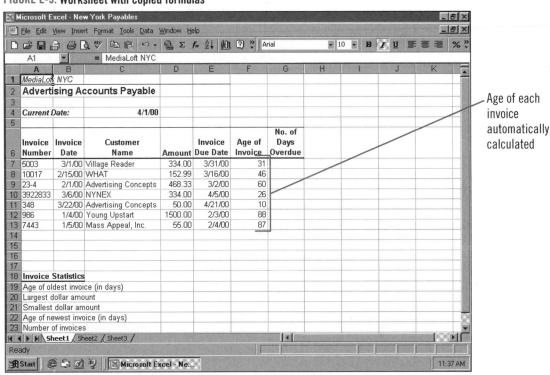

Age of each invoice automatically calculated

## Custom number and date formats

When you use numbers and dates in worksheets or calculations, you can use built-in Excel formats or create your own. The date you entered, 9/1/00, uses the Excel format m/d/yy. You could change it to the format d-mmm, or 1-Sep. The value $3,789 uses the number format $#,### where # represents positive numbers. To apply number formats, click Format on the menu bar, click Cells, then click the Number tab. In the category list, click a category, then specify the exact format in the list or scroll box to the right. To create a custom format, click Custom in the category list, then click a format that resembles the one you want. In the Type box, edit the symbols until they represent the format you want, then click OK. See Figure E-10.

FIGURE E-10: Custom formats on the Number tab in the Format Cells dialog box

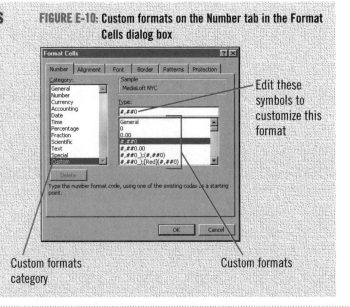

Edit these symbols to customize this format

Custom formats category

Custom formats

## Excel 2000

# Building a Conditional Formula with the IF Function

You can build a conditional formula using an IF function. A **conditional formula** is one that makes calculations based on stated conditions. For example, you can build a formula to calculate bonuses based on a person's performance rating. If a person is rated a 5 (the stated condition) on a scale of 1 to 5, with 5 being the highest rating, he or she receives 10% of his or her salary as a bonus; otherwise, there is no bonus. When the condition is a question that can be answered with a true or false response, Excel calls this stated condition a **logical test**. The IF function has three parts, separated by commas: a condition or logical test, an action to take if the logical test or condition is true, then an action to take if the logical test or condition is false. Another way of expressing this is: IF(test_cond,do_this,else_this). Translated into an Excel IF function, the formula to calculate bonuses would look something like this: IF(Rating=5,Salary*0.10,0). The translation would be: If the rating equals 5, multiply the salary by 0.10 (the decimal equivalent of 10%), then place the result in the selected cell. If the rating does not equal 5, place a 0 in the cell. When entering the logical test portion of an IF statement, you typically use some combination of the comparison operators listed in Table E-2. Jim is almost finished with the worksheet. To complete it, he needs to use an IF function that calculates the number of days each invoice is overdue.

### 1. Click cell G7

The cell pointer is now positioned where the result of the function will appear. You want the formula to calculate the number of days overdue as follows: If the age of the invoice is greater than 30, calculate the days overdue (Age of Invoice − 30), and place the result in cell G7; otherwise, place a 0 (zero) in the cell. The formula will include the IF function and cell references.

### 2. Type =IF(F7>30, (be sure to type the comma)

You have entered the first part of the function, the logical test. Notice that you used the symbol for greater than (>). So far, the formula reads: If Age of Invoice is greater than 30 (in other words, if the invoice is overdue). The next part of the formula tells Excel the action to take if the invoice is over 30 days old.

### 3. Type F7-30, (be sure to type the comma)

This part of the formula, between the first and second commas, is what you want Excel to do if the logical test is true (that is, if the age of the invoice is over 30). Continuing the translation of the formula, this part means: Take the Age of Invoice value and subtract 30. The last part of the formula tells Excel the action to take if the logical test is false (that is, if the age of the invoice is 30 days or less).

### 4. Type 0, then click the Enter button ☑ on the formula bar (you do not have to type the closing parenthesis) to complete the formula

The formula is complete, and the result, 1 (the number of days overdue), appears in cell G7. See Figure E-11.

### 5. Copy the formula in cell G7 into cells G8:G13 and return to cell A1

Compare your results with Figure E-12.

### 6. Save the workbook

FIGURE E-11: **Worksheet with IF function**

Action taken if test is true

Logical test

Commas separate parts of an IF function

Action taken if test is false

Result of function when test is true

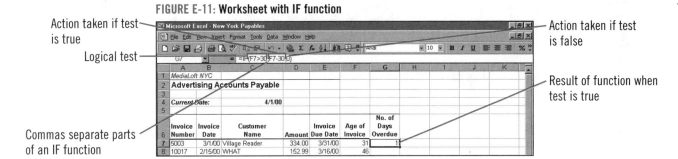

FIGURE E-12: **Completed worksheet**

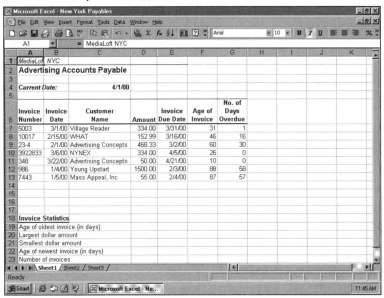

TABLE E-2: **Comparison operators**

| operator | function |
| --- | --- |
| < | Less than |
| > | Greater than |
| = | Equal to |
| <= | Less than or equal to |
| >= | Greater than or equal to |
| <> | Not equal to |

CLUES TO USE

## Inserting and deleting selected cells

As you add formulas to your workbook, you may need to insert or delete cells, not entire rows or columns. When you do this, Excel automatically adjusts cell references to reflect their new locations. To insert cells, click Insert on the menu bar, then click Cells. The Insert dialog box opens, asking if you want to insert a cell and move the selected cell down or to the right of the new one. To delete one or more selected cells, click Edit on the menu bar, click Delete, and, in the Delete dialog box, indicate which way you want to move the adjacent cells. Be careful when using this option that you do not disturb row or column alignment that may be necessary to make sense of the worksheet.

# Excel 2000

# Using Statistical Functions

Excel offers several hundred worksheet functions. A small group of these functions calculates statistics such as averages, minimum values, and maximum values. See Table E-3 for a brief description of these commonly used functions. ◄──── Jim wants to present detailed information about open accounts payable. To do this, he adds some statistical functions to the worksheet. He begins by using the MAX function to calculate the maximum value in a range.

### Trouble?
If you have difficulty clicking cells or ranges when you build formulas, try scrolling to reposition the worksheet area until all participating cells are visible.

**1.** Click cell **D19**, type **=MAX(**, select range **G7:G13**, then press **[Enter]**
Excel automatically adds the right parenthesis after you press [Enter]. The age of the oldest invoice (or maximum value in range G7:G13) is 58 days, as shown in cell D19. Next, Jim builds a formula to calculate the largest dollar amount among the outstanding invoices.

**2.** In cell D20, type **=MAX(**, select range **D7:D13**, then press **[Enter]**
The largest outstanding invoice, for $1500.00, is shown in cell D20. The MIN function finds the smallest dollar amount and the age of the newest invoice.

### Trouble?
If your results do not match those shown here, check your formulas and make sure you did not type a comma following each open parentheses. The formula in cell D20, for example, should be =MAX(D7:D13)

**3.** In cell D21, type **=MIN(**, select range **D7:D13**, then press **[Enter]**; in cell D22, type **=MIN(**, select range **F7:F13**, then press **[Enter]**
The smallest dollar amount owed is $50.00, as shown in cell D21, and the newest invoice is 10 days old. The COUNT function calculates the number of invoices by counting the number of entries in column A.

**4.** In cell D23, type **=**, then click the **Paste Function button** 🔧 on the Standard toolbar to open the Paste Function dialog box

### QuickTip
If you don't see the desired function in the Function name list, scroll to display more function names.

**5.** Under Function category, click **Statistical**, then under Function name, click **COUNT**
After selecting the function name, notice that the description of the COUNT function reads, "Counts the number of cells that contain numbers…" Because the invoice numbers are formatted in General rather than in the Number format, they are considered text entries, not numerical entries, so the COUNT function will not work. There is another function, COUNTA, that counts the number of cells that are not empty and therefore can be used to count the number of invoice number entries.

**6.** Under Function name, click **COUNTA**, then click **OK**
Excel opens the Formula Palette and automatically references the range that is directly above the active cell as the first argument (in this case, range D19:D22, which is not the range you want to count). See Figure E-13. You need to select the correct range of invoice numbers. Because the desired invoice numbers are not visible, you need to collapse the dialog box so that you can select the correct range.

**7.** With the Value1 argument selected in the Formula Palette, click the Value1 **Collapse Dialog Box button** 📑, select range **A7:A13** in the worksheet, click the **Redisplay Dialog Box button** 📄, then click **OK**
Cell D23 confirms that there are seven invoices. Compare your worksheet with Figure E-14.

**8.** Type your name into cell D1, press **[Ctrl][Home]**, then save, print, and close the workbook

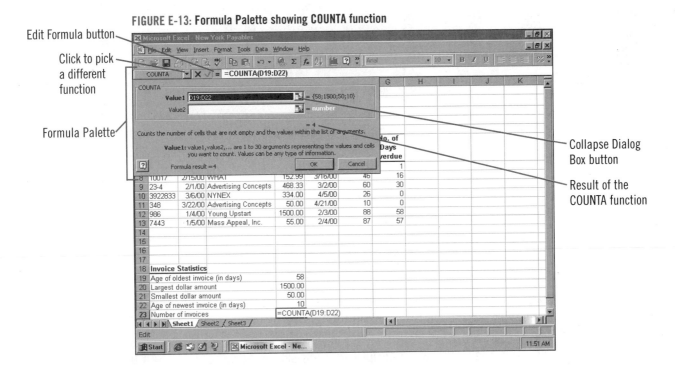

FIGURE E-13: Formula Palette showing COUNTA function

Edit Formula button

Click to pick a different function

Formula Palette

Collapse Dialog Box button

Result of the COUNTA function

FIGURE E-14: Worksheet with invoice statistics

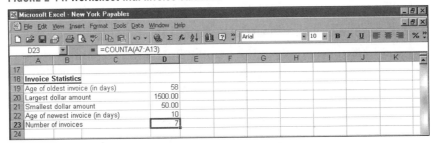

TABLE E-3: Commonly used statistical functions

| function | worksheet action |
|----------|------------------|
| AVERAGE | Calculates an average value |
| COUNT | Counts the number of values |
| COUNTA | Counts the number of nonblank entries |
| MAX | Finds the largest value |
| MIN | Finds the smallest value |
| SUM | Calculates a total |

## Using the Formula Palette to enter and edit formulas

When you use the Paste Function to build a formula, the Formula Palette displays the name and description for the function and each of its arguments, the current result of the function, and the current result of the entire formula. You also can use the Formula Palette to edit functions in formulas. To open the Formula Palette from either a blank cell or one containing a formula, click the Edit Formula button ![=] on the formula bar.

Excel 2000

# Calculating Payments with the PMT Function

PMT is a financial function that calculates the periodic payment amount for money borrowed. For example, if you want to borrow money to buy a car, the PMT function can calculate your monthly payment on the loan. Let's say you want to borrow $15,000 at 9% interest and pay the loan off in five years. The Excel PMT function can tell you that your monthly payment will be $311.38. The parts of the PMT function are: PMT(rate, nper, pv, fv, type). See Figure E-15 for an illustration of a PMT function that calculates the monthly payment in the car loan example. For several months, MediaLoft management has been discussing the expansion of the San Diego store. Jim has obtained quotes from three different lenders on borrowing $25,000 to begin the expansion. He obtained loan quotes from a commercial bank, a venture capitalist, and an investment banker. Now Jim can summarize the information using the Excel PMT function.

1. Open the workbook titled **EX E-4**, then save the workbook as **San Diego Financing**
Jim has already entered all the lender data; you are ready to calculate the commercial loan monthly payment in cell E5.

### QuickTip
It is important to be consistent about the units you use for *rate* and *nper*. If, for example, you express *nper* as the number of *monthly* payments, then you must express the interest rate as a *monthly* rate, not an annual rate.

2. Click cell **E5**, type **=PMT(C5/12,D5,B5)** (make sure you type the commas); then click the **Enter button** on the formula bar
You must divide the annual interest by 12 because you are calculating monthly, not annual, payments. Note that the payment of ($543.56) in cell E5 is a negative amount. (It appears in red on a color monitor.) Excel displays the result of a PMT function as a negative value to reflect the negative cash flow the loan represents to the borrower. Because you want to show the monthly payment value as a positive number, you can convert the loan amount to a positive number by placing a minus sign in front of the cell reference.

3. Edit cell **E5** so it reads **=PMT(C5/12,D5,−B5)**, then click
A positive value of $543.56 now appears in cell E5. See Figure E-16. You can use the same formula to generate the monthly payments for the other loans.

4. With cell **E5** selected, drag the fill handle to select range **E5:E7**
A monthly payment of $818.47 for the venture capitalist loan appears in cell E6. A monthly payment of $1,176.84 for the investment banker loan appears in cell E7. The loans with shorter terms have much higher payments. You will not know the entire financial picture until you calculate the total payments and total interest for each lender.

5. Click cell **F5**, type **=E5*D5**, then press [Tab]; in cell G5, type **=F5−B5**, then click

6. Copy the formulas in cells F5:G5 into the range **FG:G7**, then return to cell A1
You can experiment with different interest rates, loan amounts, or terms for any one of the lenders; the PMT function generates a new set of values automatically. Compare your results with those in Figure E-17.

7. Enter your name into cell **D1**, save the workbook, then print the worksheet

FIGURE E-15: Example of PMT function for car loan

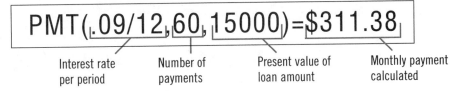

PMT(.09/12, 60, 15000) = $311.38

- Interest rate per period
- Number of payments
- Present value of loan amount
- Monthly payment calculated

FIGURE E-16: PMT function calculating monthly loan payment

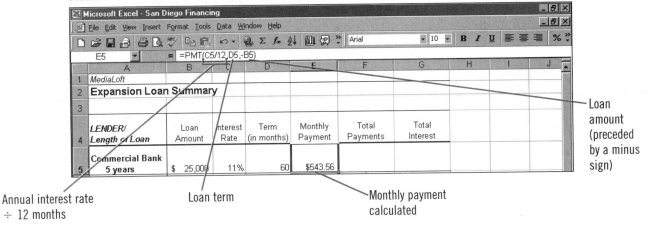

= =PMT(C5/12,D5,-B5)

| LENDER/ Length of Loan | Loan Amount | Interest Rate | Term (in months) | Monthly Payment | Total Payments | Total Interest |
|---|---|---|---|---|---|---|
| Commercial Bank 5 years | $ 25,000 | 11% | 60 | $543.56 | | |

- Loan amount (preceded by a minus sign)
- Annual interest rate ÷ 12 months
- Loan term
- Monthly payment calculated

FIGURE E-17: Completed worksheet

= MediaLoft

| LENDER/ Length of Loan | Loan Amount | Interest Rate | Term (in months) | Monthly Payment | Total Payments | Total Interest |
|---|---|---|---|---|---|---|
| Commercial Bank 5 years | $ 25,000 | 11% | 60 | $543.56 | $ 32,613.63 | $ 7,613.63 |
| Venture Capitalist 3 years | $ 25,000 | 11% | 36 | $818.47 | $ 29,464.85 | $ 4,464.85 |
| Investment Banker 2 years | $ 25,000 | 12% | 24 | $1,176.84 | $ 28,244.08 | $ 3,244.08 |

## CLUES TO USE

### Calculating future value with the FV function

You can use the FV (Future Value) function to determine the amount of money a given monthly investment will amount to, at a given interest rate after a given number of payment periods. The syntax is similar to that of the PMT function: FV(rate,nper,pmt,pv,type). For example, suppose you want to invest $1,000 every month for the next 12 months into an account that pays 12% a year, and you want to know how much you will have at the end of 12 months (that is, its future value). You would enter the function FV(.01,12,−1000), and Excel would return the value $12,682.50 as the future value of your investment. As with the PMT function, the units for the rate and nper must be consistent. If you make monthly payments on a three-year loan at 6% annual interest, you would use the rate 6%/12 and 36 periods (12*3 ). The arguments pv and type are optional; pv is the present value, or the total amount the series of payments is worth now. If you omit it, Excel assumes the pv is 0. The Type argument indicates when the payments are made; 0 is the end of the period and 1 is the beginning of the period.

# Displaying and Printing Formula Contents

Excel usually displays the result of formula calculations in the worksheet area and displays formula contents for the active cell in the formula bar. However, you can instruct Excel to display the formulas directly in the worksheet locations in which they were entered. You can document worksheet formulas by first displaying the formulas, then printing them. These formula printouts are valuable paper-based worksheet documentation. Because formulas are often longer than their corresponding values, landscape orientation is the best choice for printing formulas. Jim is ready to produce a formula printout to submit with the worksheet.

## Steps 1 2 3 4

**1.** Click **Tools** on the menu bar, click **Options**, then click the **View tab**
The View tab of the Options dialog box appears, as shown in Figure E-18.

**2.** Under Window options, click the **Formulas** check box to select it, then click **OK**
The columns widen and retain their original formats.

**3.** Scroll horizontally to bring columns E through G into view
Instead of formula results appearing in the cells, Excel shows the actual formulas. The column widths adjusted automatically to accommodate the formulas.

**4.** Click the **Print Preview button** 🔍 on the Standard toolbar
The status bar reads Preview: Page 1 of 3, indicating that the worksheet will print on three pages. You want to print it on one page and include the row number and column letter headings.

**5.** Click the **Setup button** in the Print Preview window, then click the **Page tab**

**6.** Under Orientation, click the **Landscape option button**; then under Scaling, click the **Fit to option button**
Selecting Landscape instructs Excel to print the worksheet sideways on the page. The Fit to option ensures that the document is printed on a single page.

**7.** Click the **Sheet tab**, under Print click the **Row and column headings check box** to select it, click **OK**, then position the **Zoom pointer** 🔍 over **column A** and click
The worksheet formulas now appear on a single page, in landscape orientation, with row (number) and column (letter) headings. See Figure E-19.

**8.** Click **Print** in the Print Preview window, then click **OK**
After you retrieve the printout, you want to return the worksheet to display formula results. You can do this easily by using a key combination.

**9.** Press **[Ctrl][`]** to redisplay formula results, save and close the workbook, then exit Excel
[Ctrl][`] (grave accent mark) toggles between displaying formula results and displaying formula contents.

### QuickTip
All Page Setup options—such as Landscape orientation, Fit to scaling—apply to the active worksheet and are saved with the workbook.

FIGURE E-18: View tab of the Options dialog box

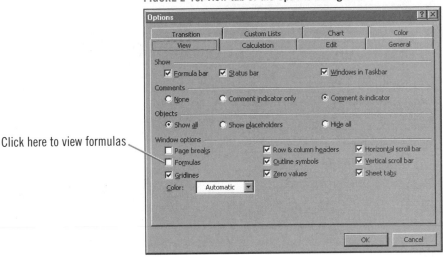

Click here to view formulas

FIGURE E-19: Print Preview window

Column headings

Row headings

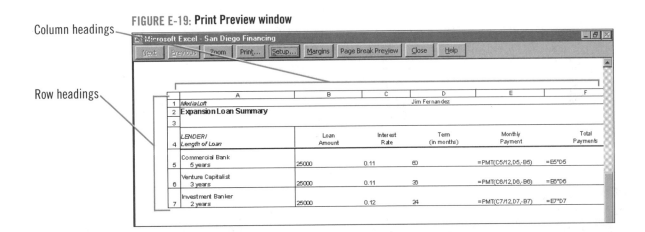

CLUES TO USE

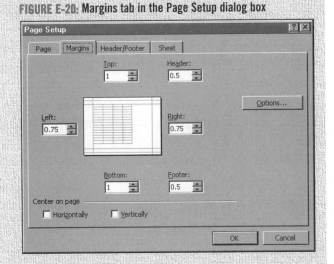

## Setting margins and alignment when printing part of a worksheet

Sometimes you want to print one part of a worksheet. While you may have set margins for printing the whole worksheet, you can set custom margins to print the smaller section. Select the range you want to print, click File on the menu bar, click Print, under Print what click Selection, then click Preview. In the Print Preview window, click Setup, then click the Margins tab. See Figure E-20. Double-click the margin numbers and type new ones. Use the Center on page check boxes to center the range horizontally or vertically. If you plan to print the range again in the future, save the view after you print: Click View on the menu bar, click Custom Views, click Add, then type a view name and click OK.

FIGURE E-20: Margins tab in the Page Setup dialog box

# Practice

## ► Concepts Review

Label each element of the Excel screen shown in Figure E-21.

FIGURE E-21

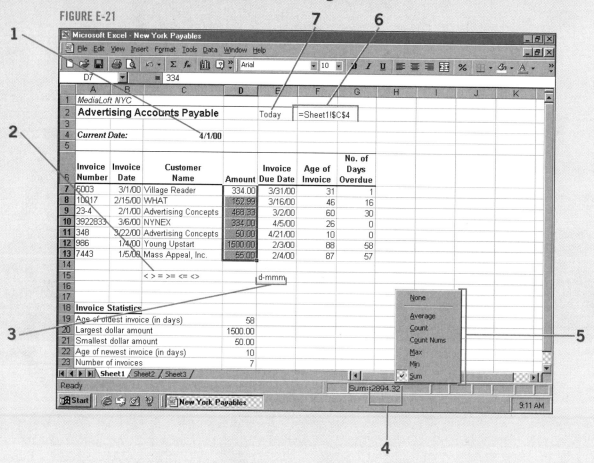

---

## Match each term with the statement that best describes its function.

8. **Parentheses**
9. **COUNTA**
10. **test_cond**
11. **COUNT**
12. **pv**

a. Part of the IF function in which the conditions are stated
b. Function used to count the number of numerical entries
c. Part of the PMT function that represents the loan amount
d. Function used to count the number of nonblank entries
e. Symbols used in formulas to control formula calculation order

Select the best answer from the list of choices.

**13. To generate a positive payment value when using the PMT function, you must**
 a. Enter the function arguments as positive values.
 b. Enter the function arguments as negative values.
 c. Enter the amount being borrowed as a negative value.
 d. Enter the interest rate divisor as a negative value.

**14. When you enter the rate and nper arguments in a PMT function,**
 a. Multiply both units by 12.
 b. Be consistent in the units used.
 c. Divide both values by 12.
 d. Use monthly units instead of annual units.

**15. To express conditions such as less than or equal to, you can use a(n)**
 a. IF function.
 b. Comparison operator.
 c. AutoCalculate formula.
 d. PMT function.

**16. Which of the following statements is false?**
 a. $#,### is an Excel number format.
 b. You can create custom number and date formats in Excel.
 c. You can use only existing number and date formats in Excel.
 d. m/d/yy is an Excel date format.

# ▶ Skills Review

**1. Create a formula with several operators.**
 a. Open workbook EX E-5, enter your name into cell D1, and save the workbook as "Manager Bonuses".
 b. Select cell C15 using the Go To command.
 c. Enter the formula C13+(C14*7).
 d. Use the Paste Special command to paste the values in B4:B10 to G4:G10.

**2. Use names in a formula.**
 a. Name cell C13 "Dept_Bonus".
 b. Name cell C14 "Project_Bonus".
 c. In cell E4, enter the formula Dept_Bonus*D4+Project_Bonus.
 d. Copy the formula in cell E4 into the range E5:E10.
 e. Format range E4:E10 with the Comma Style button.
 f. In cell F4, enter a formula that sums C4 and E4.
 g. Copy the formula in cell F4 into the range F5:F10.
 h. Return to cell A1, then save your work.

**3. Generate multiple totals with AutoSum.**
 a. Select range E4:F11.
 b. Enter the totals using AutoSum.
 c. Format range E11:F11 using the Currency Style button.
 d. Return to cell A1, save your work, then preview and print this worksheet.

4. **Use dates in calculations.**
   a. Make the Merit Pay sheet active.
   b. In cell D6, enter the formula B6+183.
   c. Copy the formula in cell D6 into the range D7:D14.
   d. Use the NOW function to insert the date and time in cell A3, widening the column as necessary.
   e. In cell E18, enter the text "Next Pay Date", and, in cell G18, use the Date function to enter the date 10/1/00.
   f. Save your work.

5. **Build a conditional formula with the IF function.**
   a. In cell F6, enter the formula IF(C6=5,E6*0.05,0).
   b. Copy the formula in cell F6 into the range F7:F14.
   c. Apply the comma format with no decimal places to F6:F14.
   d. Select the range A4:G4 and delete the cells using the Delete command on the Edit menu. Shift the remaining cells up.
   e. Repeat the procedure to delete the cells A15:G15.
   f. Use the Cells command on the Insert menu to insert a cell between Department Statistics and Average Salary, moving the remaining cells down.
   g. Check your formulas to make sure the cell references have been updated.
   h. Save your work.

6. **Use statistical functions.**
   a. In cell C18, enter a function to calculate the average salary in the range E5:E13 with no decimal places.
   b. In cell C19, enter a function to calculate the largest bonus in the range F5:F13.
   c. In cell C20, enter a function to calculate the lowest performance rating in the range C5:C13.
   d. In cell C21, enter a function to calculate the number of entries in range A5:A13.
   e. Enter your name in cell F3, then save, preview, and print this worksheet.

7. **Calculate payments with the PMT function.**
   a. Make the Loan sheet active.
   b. In cell B9, enter the formula PMT(B5/12,B6,−B4).
   c. In cell B10, enter the formula B9*B6.
   d. AutoFit column B, if necessary.
   e. In cell B11, enter the formula B10−B4.
   f. Enter your name in cell C1, then save and print the worksheet.

8. **Display and print formula contents.**
   a. Use the View tab in the Options dialog box to turn formulas on.
   b. Adjust the column widths as necessary.
   c. Save, preview, and print this worksheet in landscape orientation with the row and column headings.
   d. Close the workbook.

# ▶ Independent Challenges

**1.** As manager of Mike's Ice Cream Parlor, you have been asked to create a worksheet that totals the monthly sales of all store products. Your monthly report should include the following:

- Sales totals for the current month for each product
- Sales totals for the last month for each product
- The percent change in sales from last month to this month

To document the report further, you decide to include a printout of the worksheet formulas.

To complete this independent challenge:

**a.** Open the workbook titled EX E-6, type your name into cell D1, then save the workbook as "Mike's Sales" to the appropriate folder on your Project Disk.

**b.** Enter today's date in cell A3. Create and apply a custom format.

**c.** Complete the headings for weeks 2 through 4. Enter totals for each week and current month totals for each product. Calculate the percent change in sales from last month to this month. (*Hint:* The formula in words would be (Current Month-Last Month)/Last Month.)

**d.** After you enter the percent change formula for regular ice cream, copy the formula down the column and format the column with the percentage style.

**e.** Apply a comma format with no decimal places to all numbers and totals.

**f.** Save, preview, then print the worksheet on a single page. If necessary, print in landscape orientation. If you make any page setup changes, save the worksheet again.

**g.** Display and print the worksheet formulas, then print the formulas on one page with row and column headings.

**h.** Close the workbook without saving the changes for displaying formulas.

**2.** You are an auditor with a certified public accounting firm. Fly Away, a manufacturer of skating products, including roller skates and skateboards, has contacted you to audit its financial records. The managers at Fly Away have asked you to assist them in preparing their year-end sales summary. Specifically, they want to add expenses and show the percent of annual expenses that each expense category represents. They also want to show what percent of annual sales each expense category represents. You should include a formula calculating the difference between sales and expenses and another formula calculating expenses divided by sales. The expense categories and their respective dollar amounts are as follows: Building Lease $45,000; Equipment $203,000; Office $23,000; Salary $345,000; Taxes $302,000. Use these expense amounts to prepare the year-end sales and expenses summary for Fly Away.

To complete this independent challenge:

**a.** Open the workbook titled EX E-7, type your name into cell D1, then save the workbook as "Fly Away Sales".

**b.** Name the cell containing the formula for total annual expenses "Annual_Expenses". Use the name Annual_Expenses in the first formula calculating percent of annual expenses. Copy this formula as appropriate and apply the percentage style. Make sure to include a formula that sums all the values for percent of annual expenses, which should equal 1 or 100%.

**c.** Enter a formula calculating what percent of annual sales each expense category represents. Use the name Annual_Sales in the formula and format it appropriately. Enter formulas calculating annual sales minus annual expenses and expenses divided by sales using only the names Annual_Sales and Annual_Expenses. Add formulas for totals as appropriate.

**d.** Format the cells using the Currency, Percent, or Comma style. Widen the columns as necessary to display cell contents.

**e.** Save, preview, then print the worksheet on a single page. If necessary, use landscape orientation. Save any page setup changes you make.

**f.** Display and print worksheet formulas on a single page with row and column headings.

**g.** Close the workbook without saving the changes for displaying formulas.

**3.** As the owner of Custom Fit, a general contracting firm specializing in home-storage projects, you are facing yet another business challenge at your firm. Because jobs are taking longer than expected, you decide to take out a loan to purchase some new power tools. According to your estimates, you need a $5,000 loan to purchase the tools. You check three loan sources: the Small Business Administration (SBA), your local bank, and a consortium of investors. Each source offers you a loan on its own terms. The local bank offers you the loan at 9.5% interest over four years. The SBA will loan you the money at 9% interest, but you have to pay it off in three years. The consortium offers you an 8% loan, but they require you to pay it back in two years. To analyze all three loan options, you decide to build a tool loan summary worksheet. Using the loan terms provided, build a worksheet summarizing your options.

To complete this independent challenge:

**a.** Open a new workbook, type your name in cell A1, then save it as "Custom Fit Loan Options".

**b.** Enter today's date in cell A3.

**c.** Enter labels and worksheet data. You need headings for the loan source, loan amount, interest rate, term or number of payments, monthly payment, total payments, and total interest. Fill in the data provided for the three loan sources.

**d.** Enter formulas as appropriate: a PMT formula for the monthly payment; a formula calculating the total payments based on the monthly payment and term values; and a formula for total interest based on the total payments and the loan amount.

**e.** Format the worksheet as desired.

**f.** Save, preview, then print the worksheet on a single page using landscape orientation. Create a printout of worksheet formulas showing row and column headings. Do not save the worksheet with these settings.

**4.** The MediaLoft accounting department has asked you to analyze overall MediaLoft CD sales and look at ways to improve them. The figures you will need are on the MediaLoft intranet site. This site gives employees access to companywide information. Accounting is considering taking out a $25,000 loan to buy new CD display cases for some of its stores.

To complete this independent challenge:

**a.** Start Excel, then open the File EX E-8, save it as CD Analysis on your Project Disk, and make sure the CD Sales tab is active.

**b.** Connect to the Internet, go to the MediaLoft intranet site at http://www.course.com/Illustrated/MediaLoft. Click the Accounting link, then click the CD Sales Analysis link. Print the CD Sales Analysis, disconnect from the Internet, and then, starting in cell A2, enter this data on the CD Sales sheet in the CD Analysis workbook, except for the Totals row. Enter formulas to calculate the totals in row 11 and label the row. Enter formulas to calculate the category totals in column F and label the column totals.

**c.** In row 13, enter a label in column A that reads "Goals", and enter the following sales goals for each quarter:

| Q1 | Q2 | Q3 | Q4 |
|---|---|---|---|
| 317,000 | 327,000 | 372,000 | 400,000 |

**d.** Enter a formula that totals the goals figures in cell F13.

**e.** In row 15, enter a label called "Real to Goal", and enter formulas for each loan that calculate the difference between goal and actual sales for each quarter and for the year's total.

**f.** In row 17, enter another label called "Status". For each quarter, use the IF function that displays the text "Over Goal" if the Real to Goal total is a positive number (in other words, >0). Otherwise, have it print "Under Goal". Format the cells, AutoFit the columns as necessary, and save the worksheet.

**g.** Go to the CD Loan worksheet and use the PMT function to calculate the monthly payment for each loan, making sure it displays as a positive number.

**h.** Enter a formula in column F that calculates the total interest for each loan. It should multiply the monthly payment by the term of the loan, and then subtract the original loan amount from the result.

i. For each loan, the respective banks have given MediaLoft a certain number of days to respond, after which their loan offers will no longer be valid. In the Inform by column, enter a formula for each loan that adds the number of days in column G to today's date, displaying the date by which MediaLoft must respond. (*Hint:* Use the TODAY function to enter today's date in the formula.)

j. In cells B8:B10, use Excel functions to enter the shortest term, the lowest rate, and the average interest rate, then display and print the formulas for the CD Loan sheet.

k. Print the CD Sales and CD Loan worksheets, then save and close the workbook.

# ▶ Visual Workshop

Create the worksheet shown in Figure E-22. (Hint: Enter the items in range C9:C11 as labels by typing an apostrophe before each formula.) Type your name in row 1, and save the workbook as "Car Payment Calculator" to the appropriate folder on your Project Disk. Preview, then print, the worksheet.

FIGURE E-22

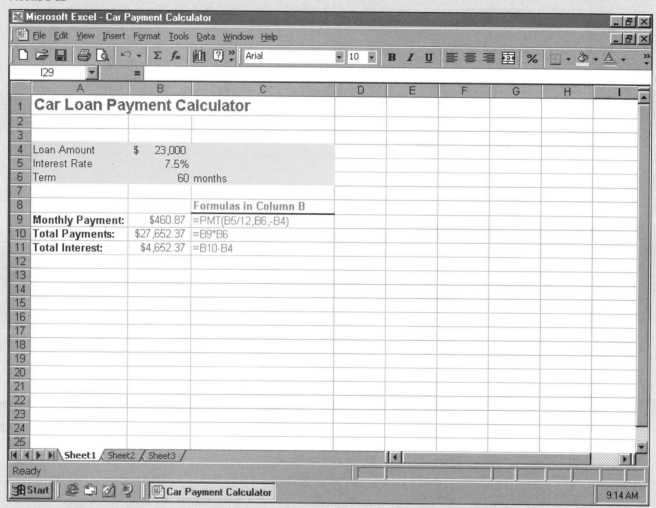

Excel 2000

Unit F

# Managing

## Workbooks and Preparing Them for the Web

### Objectives

- [MOUS] ▶ **Freeze columns and rows**
- [MOUS] ▶ **Insert and delete worksheets**
- [MOUS] ▶ **Consolidate data with 3-D references**
- [MOUS] ▶ **Hide and protect worksheet areas**
- ▶ **Save custom views of a worksheet**
- [MOUS] ▶ **Control page breaks and page numbering**
- [MOUS] ▶ **Create a hyperlink between Excel files**
- [MOUS] ▶ **Save an Excel file as an HTML document**

In this unit you will learn several Excel features to help you manage and print workbook data. You will also learn how to prepare workbooks for publication on the World Wide Web. ✎ MediaLoft's accounting department asks Jim Fernandez to design a timecard summary worksheet to track salary costs for hourly workers. He designs a worksheet using some employees from the MediaLoft Houston store. When the worksheet is complete, the accounting department will add the rest of the employees and place it on the MediaLoft intranet site for review by store managers. Jim will save the worksheet in HTML format for viewing on the site.

**Excel 2000**

# Freezing Columns and Rows

As rows and columns fill up with data, you might need to scroll through the worksheet to add, delete, modify, and view information. Looking at information without row or column labels can be confusing. In Excel, you can temporarily freeze columns and rows, which enables you to view separate areas of your worksheets at the same time. **Panes** are the columns and rows that **freeze**, or remain in place, while you scroll through your worksheet. The freeze feature is especially useful when you're dealing with large worksheets. Sometimes, though, even freezing is not sufficient. In those cases, you can create as many as four areas, or panes, on the screen at one time and move freely within each of them.  Jim needs to verify the total hours worked, hourly pay rate, and total pay for salespeople Paul Cristifano and Virginia Young. Because the worksheet is becoming more difficult to read as its size increases, Jim needs to freeze the column and row labels.

**Steps**

**QuickTip**

To return personalized toolbars and menus to their default state, click Tools on the menu bar, click Customize, click Reset my usage data on the Options tab, click Yes, then click Close.

**1.** Start Excel if necessary, open the workbook titled **EX F-1**, save it as **Timecard Summary**, scroll through the Monday worksheet to view the data and click cell **D6**
You move to cell D6 because you want to freeze columns A, B, and C. By doing so, you will be able to see each employee's last name, first name, and timecard number on the screen when you scroll to the right. Because you want to scroll down the worksheet and still be able to read the column headings, you also freeze the labels in rows 1 through 5. Excel freezes the columns to the left and the rows above the cell pointer.

**2.** Click **Window** on the menu bar, then click **Freeze Panes**
A thin line appears along the column border to the left of the active cell, and another line appears along the row above the active cell indicating that columns A through C and rows 1 through 5 are frozen.

**QuickTip**

To easily change worksheet data without manual scrolling, click Edit on the menu bar, click Replace, then enter text you want to find and text you want to replace it with. Use the Find Next, Replace, and Replace All buttons to find and replace occurrences of the found text with the replacement text.

**3.** Scroll to the right until columns **A** through **C** and **L** through **O** are visible
Because columns A, B, and C are frozen, they remain on the screen; columns D through K are temporarily hidden from view. Notice that the information you are looking for in row 13 (last name, total hours, hourly pay rate, and total pay for Paul Cristifano) is readily available. You jot down Paul's data but still need to verify Virginia Young's information.

**4.** Scroll down until **row 26** is visible
Notice that in addition to columns A through C, rows 1 through 5 remain on the screen as well. See Figure F-1. Jim jots down the information for Virginia Young. Even though a pane is frozen, you can click in the frozen area of the worksheet and edit the contents of the cells there, if necessary.

**QuickTip**

When you open an existing workbook, the cell pointer is in the cell it was in when you last saved the workbook. Press [Ctrl][Home] to return to cell A1 prior to saving and closing a workbook.

**5.** Press **[Ctrl][Home]**
Because the panes are frozen, the cell pointer moves to cell D6, not A1.

**6.** Click **Window** on the menu bar, then click **Unfreeze Panes**
The panes are unfrozen.

**7.** Return to cell A1, then save the workbook

**FIGURE F-1: Scrolled worksheet with frozen rows and columns**

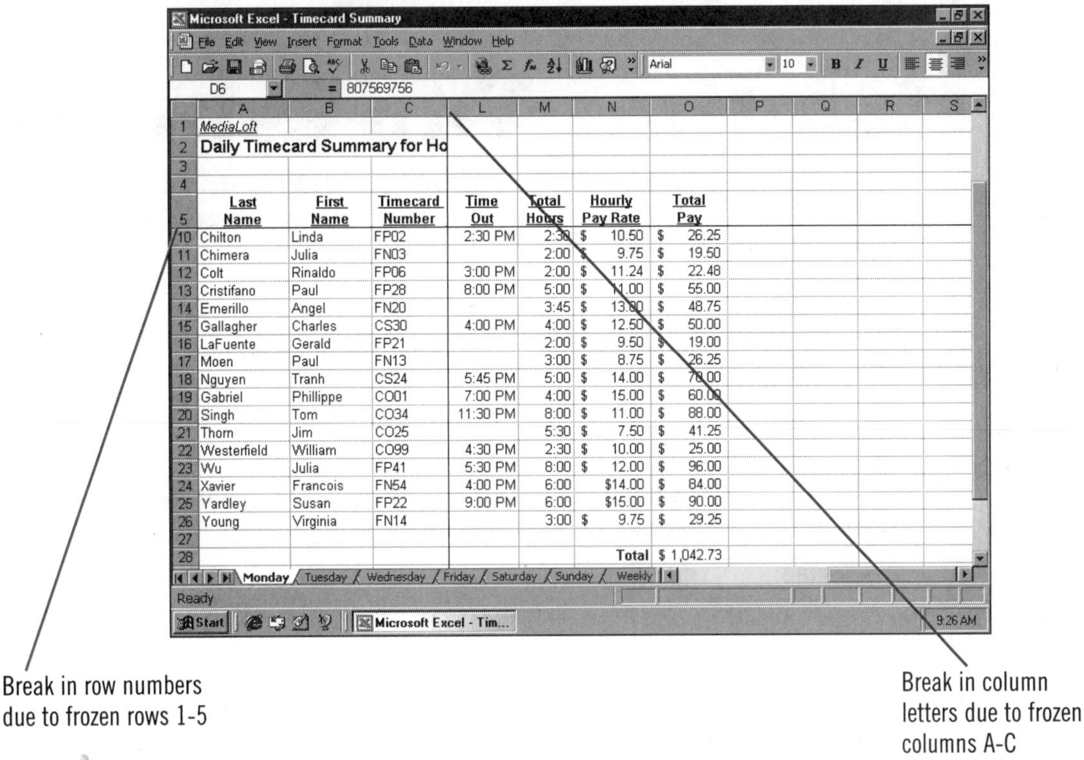
Break in row numbers due to frozen rows 1-5
Break in column letters due to frozen columns A-C

Excel 2000

## Clues to Use: Splitting the worksheet into multiple panes

Excel provides a way to split the worksheet area into vertical and/or horizontal panes, so that you can click inside any one pane and scroll to locate desired information in that pane while the other panes remain in place. See Figure F-2. To split a worksheet area into multiple panes, drag the split box (the small box at the top of the vertical scroll bar or at the right end of the horizontal scroll bar) in the direction you want the split to appear. To remove the split, move the mouse over the split until the pointer changes to a double pointed arrow ÷, then double-click.

**FIGURE F-2: Worksheet split into two horizontal panes**

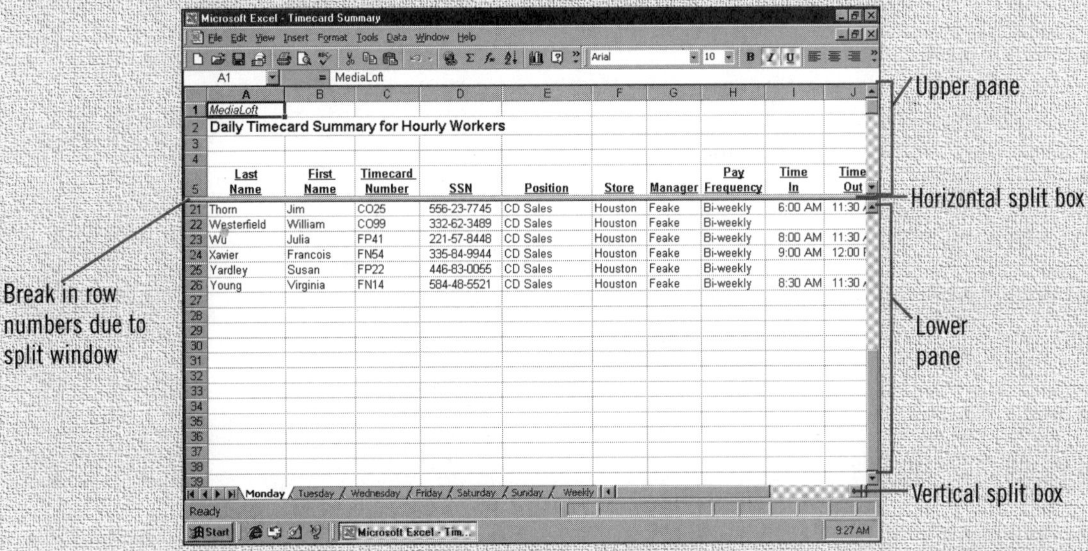
Upper pane
Horizontal split box
Break in row numbers due to split window
Lower pane
Vertical split box

# Inserting and Deleting Worksheets

You can insert and delete worksheets in a workbook as needed. For example, because new workbooks open with only three sheets available (Sheet1, Sheet2, and Sheet3), you need to insert at least one more sheet if you want to have four quarterly worksheets in an annual financial budget workbook. You can do this by using commands on the menu bar or pop-up menu. Jim was in a hurry when he added the sheet tabs to the Timecard Summary workbook. He needs to insert a sheet for Thursday and delete the sheet for Sunday because these Houston workers do not work on Sundays.

1. **Click the Friday sheet tab, click Insert on the menu bar, then click Worksheet**
   Excel automatically inserts a new sheet tab labeled Sheet1 to the left of the Friday sheet.

2. **Rename the Sheet1 tab Thursday**
   Now the tabs read Monday, Tuesday, Wednesday, Thursday, Friday, and Saturday. The tab for the Weekly Summary is not visible, but you still need to delete the Sunday worksheet.

3. **Click the Sunday sheet tab, move the pointer over the Sunday tab, then click the right mouse button**
   A pop-up menu appears. See Figure F-3. The pop-up menu allows you to insert, delete, rename, move, or copy sheets, select all the sheets, or view any Visual Basic programming code in a workbook.

4. **Click Delete on the pop-up menu**
   A message box warns that the selected sheet will be deleted permanently. You must acknowledge the message before proceeding.

5. **Click OK**
   The Sunday sheet is deleted. Next, to check your work, you view a menu of worksheets in the workbook.

6. **Move the mouse pointer over any tab scrolling button, then right-click**
   When you right-click a tab scrolling button, Excel automatically opens a menu of the worksheets in the active workbook. Compare your list with Figure F-4.

7. **Click Monday, return to cell A1, then save the workbook**

**FIGURE F-3: Worksheet pop-up menu**

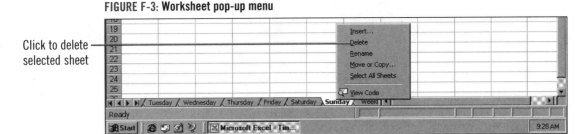

Click to delete selected sheet

**FIGURE F-4: Workbook with menu of worksheets**

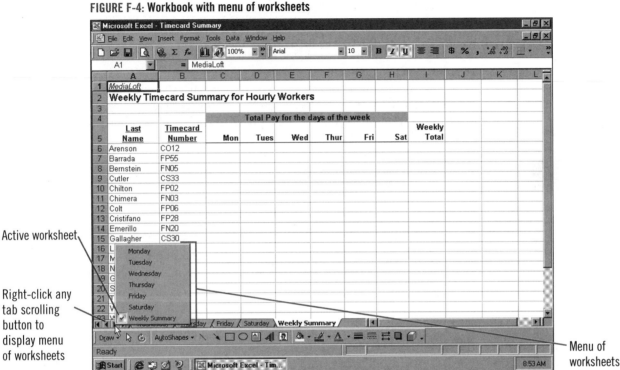

Active worksheet

Right-click any tab scrolling button to display menu of worksheets

Menu of worksheets

## CLUES TO USE

## Specifying headers and footers

As you prepare a workbook for others to view, it is helpful to give them as much data as possible about the worksheet—how many pages, who created it on what date, and the like. You can do this easily in a **header** or **footer**, information that prints at the top or bottom of each printed page. Headers and footers are visible on screen only in Print Preview. To add a header, for example, click View on the menu bar, click Header and Footer, click Custom Header, and you see a dialog box similar to that in Figure F-5. Both the header and the footer are divided into three sections, and you can enter information in any or all of them. Type information such as your name and click the icons to enter the page number ⊞, total pages ⊞, date ⊞, time ⊘, filename ⊡, or sheet name ⊡ to enter codes that represent these items. Click OK, view the preview on the Header and Footer tab, then click OK again.

**FIGURE F-5: Header dialog box**

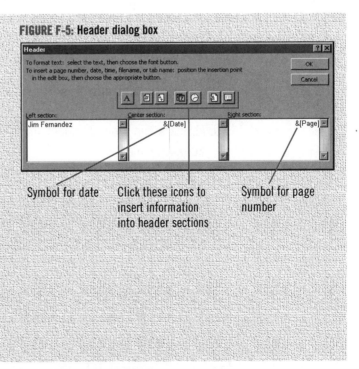

Symbol for date

Click these icons to insert information into header sections

Symbol for page number

# Consolidating Data with 3-D References

When you want to summarize similar data that exists in different sheets or workbooks, you can combine and display it in one sheet. For example, you might have departmental sales figures on four different store sheets that you want to add together, or **consolidate**, on one summary sheet that shows total departmental sales for all stores. The best way to consolidate data is to use cell references to the various sheets on a consolidation, or summary, sheet. Because they reference other sheets that are usually behind the summary sheet, such references effectively create another dimension in the workbook and are called **3-D references**. You can reference data in other sheets and in other workbooks. Referencing cells is a better method than retyping calculated results because the data values on which calculated totals depend might change. If you reference the values instead, any changes to the original values are automatically reflected in the consolidation sheet. ✎ Although Jim does not have timecard data for the remaining days of the week, he wants to test the Weekly Summary sheet that will consolidate the timesheet data. He does this by creating a reference from the total pay data in the Monday sheet to the Weekly Summary sheet. First, he freezes panes to improve the view of the worksheets prior to initiating the reference between them.

1. On the Monday sheet, click cell **D6**, click **Window** on the menu bar, click **Freeze Panes**, then scroll horizontally to bring columns L through O into view

2. Right-click a **tab scrolling button**, then click **Weekly Summary**
   Because the Weekly Summary sheet (which is the consolidation sheet) will contain the reference, the cell pointer must reside there when you initiate the reference. To make a simple **reference** within the same sheet or between sheets, position the cell pointer in the cell to contain the reference, type = (equal sign), position the cell pointer in the cell to be referenced, and then enter the information.

### Trouble?

If you have difficulty referencing cells between sheets, press [Esc] and begin again.

3. While in the Weekly Summary sheet, click cell **C6**, type **=**, activate the Monday sheet, click cell **O6**, then click the **Enter button** 🔲 on the formula bar
   The formula bar reads =Monday!O6. See Figure F-6. *Monday* references the Monday sheet. The ! (exclamation point) is an **external reference indicator** meaning that the cell referenced is outside the active sheet; O6 is the actual cell reference in the external sheet. The result, $33.00, appears in cell C6 of the Weekly Summary sheet, showing the reference to the value displayed in cell O6 of the Monday sheet.

4. While in the Weekly Summary sheet, copy cell **C6** into cells **C7:C26**
   Excel copies the contents of cell C6 with its relative reference down the column. You can test a reference by changing one cell that it is based on and seeing if the reference changes.

5. Activate the Monday sheet, edit cell **L6** to read **6:30 PM**, then activate the Weekly Summary sheet
   Cell C6 now shows $41.25. Changing Beryl Arenson's "time out" from 5:30 to 6:30 increased her pay from $33.00 to $41.25. This makes sense because Beryl's hours went from four to five, and her hourly salary is $8.25. The reference to Monday's total pay was automatically updated in the Weekly Summary sheet. See Figure F-7.

6. Preview, then print the Weekly Summary sheet
   To preview and print an entire workbook, click File on the menu bar, click Print, click to select the Entire Workbook option button, then click Preview. In the Preview window, you can page through the entire workbook. When you click Print, the entire workbook will print.

7. Activate the Monday sheet, then unfreeze the panes

8. Save the workbook

**FIGURE F-6:** Worksheet showing referenced cell

Sheet referenced

Cell referenced

Formula referencing cell

External reference indicator

Referenced value

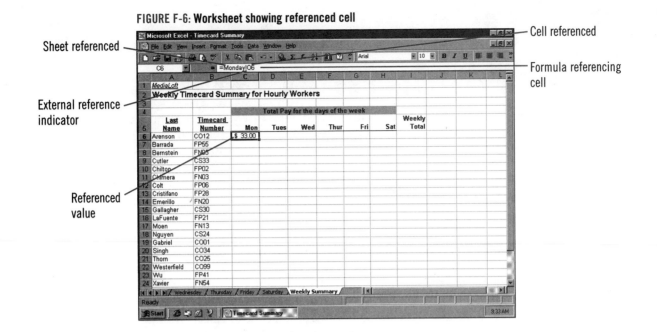

**FIGURE F-7:** Weekly Summary worksheet with updated reference

Updated value

Copied values also reference the Monday sheet

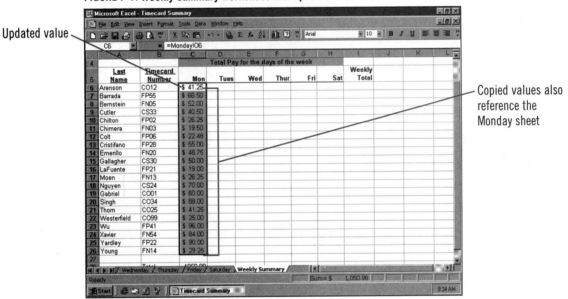

## Consolidating data from different workbooks using linking

Just as you can reference data between cells in a worksheet and between sheets, you can reference data between workbooks dynamically so that changes made in referenced cells in one workbook are reflected in the consolidation sheet in the other workbook. This dynamic referencing is called **linking**. To link a single cell between workbooks, open both workbooks, select the cell to receive the linked data, press = (equal sign), select the cell in the other workbook containing the data to be linked, then press

[Enter]. Excel automatically inserts the name of the referenced workbook in the cell reference. To perform calculations, enter formulas on the consolidation sheet using cells in the supporting sheets. If you are linking more than one cell, you can copy the linked data to the Clipboard, select in the other workbook the upper-left cell to receive the link, click Edit on the menu bar, click Paste Special, then click Paste Link.

**MANAGING WORKBOOKS AND PREPARING THEM FOR THE WEB** EXCEL F-7 ◄

**Excel 2000**

# Hiding and Protecting Worksheet Areas

Worksheets can contain sensitive information that you don't want others to view or alter. To protect such information, Excel gives you two basic options. You can **hide** the formulas in selected cells (or rows, columns, or entire sheets), and you can **lock** selected cells, in which case other people will be able to view the data (values, numbers, labels, formulas, etc.) in those cells but not to alter it in any way. See Table F-1 for a list of options you can use to protect a worksheet. You set the lock and hide options in the Format Cells dialog box. You lock and unlock cells by clicking the Locked check box in the Format Cells dialog box Protection tab, and hide and "unhide" cell formulas by clicking the Hidden check box. The lock and hide options will not function unless an Excel protection feature, which you access via the Tools menu, is also activated. A common worksheet protection strategy is to unlock cells in which data will be changed, sometimes referred to as the **data entry area**, and to lock cells in which the data should not be changed. Then, when you protect the worksheet, the unlocked areas can still be changed. ▸ Because Jim will assign someone to enter the sensitive timecard information into the worksheet, he plans to hide and lock selected areas of the worksheet.

**Steps**

1. Make sure the Monday sheet is active, select range **I6:L27**, click **Format** on the menu bar, click **Cells**, then click the **Protection tab**

   You include row 27, even though it does not contain data, in the event that new data is added to the row later. Notice that the Locked box in the Protection tab is already checked, as shown in Figure F-8. The Locked check box is selected by default, meaning that all the cells in a new workbook start out locked. (Note, however, that cell locking is not applied unless the protection feature is also activated. The protection feature is inactive by default.)

2. Click the **Locked check box** to deselect it, then click **OK**

   Excel stores time as a fraction of a 24-hour day. In the formula for total pay, hours must be multiplied by 24. This concept might be confusing to the data entry person, so you hide the formulas.

3. Select range **O6:O26**, click **Format** on the menu bar, click **Cells**, click the **Protection tab**, click the **Hidden check box** to select it, then click **OK**

   The screen data remains the same (unhidden and unlocked) until you set the protection in the next step.

**QuickTip**

To turn off worksheet protection, click Tools on the menu bar, point to Protection, then click Unprotect Sheet. If prompted for a password, type the password, then click OK. To remove passwords, open the workbook or worksheet using the password, then go to the window where you entered the password, highlight the password, and press [Delete]. Remember that passwords are case sensitive.

4. Click **Tools** on the menu bar, point to **Protection**, then click **Protect Sheet**

   The Protect Sheet dialog box opens. You choose not to use a password.

5. Click **OK**

   You are ready to test the new worksheet protection.

6. Click cell **O6**

   Notice that the formula bar is empty because of the hidden formula setting.

7. In cell **O6**, type **T** to confirm that locked cells cannot be changed, then click **OK**

   When you attempt to change a locked cell, a message box reminds you of the protected cell's read-only status. See Figure F-9.

8. Click cell **I6**, type **9**, and notice that Excel allows you to begin the entry, press **[Esc]** to cancel the entry, then save the workbook

   Because you unlocked the cells in columns I through L before you protected the worksheet, you can make changes to these cells. Jim is satisfied that the Time In and Time Out data can be changed as necessary.

FIGURE F-8: Protection tab in Format Cells dialog box

Click to remove checkmark

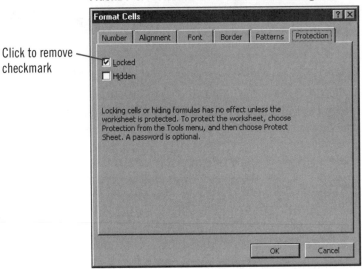

FIGURE F-9: Reminder of protected cell's read-only status

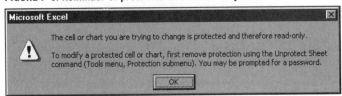

TABLE F-1: Options for hiding and protecting worksheet elements

| task | menu commands |
|------|---------------|
| Hide/Unhide a column | Format, Column, Hide or Unhide |
| Hide/Unhide a formula | Format, Cells, Protection tab, select/deselect Hidden check box |
| Hide/Unhide a row | Format, Row, Hide or Unhide |
| Hide/Unhide a sheet | Format, Sheet, Hide or Unhide |
| Protect workbook | Tools, Protection, Protect Workbook, assign optional password |
| Protect worksheet | Tools, Protection, Protect Sheet, assign optional password |
| Unlock/Relock cells | Format, Cells, Protection tab, deselect/select Locked check box |

*Note:* Some of the hide and protect options do not take effect until protection is enabled.

### Changing workbook properties

You can also password-protect an entire workbook from being opened or modified by changing its file properties. Click File, click Save As, click Tools, then click General Options. Specify the password(s) for opening or modifying the workbook. You can also use this dialog box to offer users an option to open the workbook in read-only format. To make an entire workbook read-only so that users can open but not change it, click Start on the Taskbar, point to Programs, then click Windows Explorer. Locate and click the filename, click File on the menu bar, click Properties, click the General tab, then, under Attributes, select the Read-only check box.

**Excel 2000**

# Saving Custom Views of a Worksheet

A **view** is a set of display and/or print settings that you can name and save, then access at a later time. By using the Excel Custom Views feature, you can create several different views of a worksheet without having to create separate sheets. For example, if you often switch between portrait and landscape orientations when printing different parts of a worksheet, you can create two views with the appropriate print settings for each view. You set the display and/or print settings first, then name the view. Because Jim will generate several reports from his data, he saves the current print and display settings as a custom view. To better view the data to be printed, he decides to use the Zoom box to display the entire worksheet on one screen. The Zoom box has a default setting of 100% magnification and appears on the Standard toolbar.

**Trouble?**

If the Zoom box does not appear on your Standard toolbar, click the More Buttons button 🔃 to view it.

**QuickTip**

To delete views from the active worksheet, select the view in the Views list box, then click Delete.

**Trouble?**

If you receive the message, "Some view settings could not be applied," repeat Step 5 to ensure worksheet protection is turned off.

**QuickTip**

With Report Manager add-in on the View menu, you can group worksheets and their views to be printed in sequence as one large report. If Report Manager is not on your View menu, click Tools/Add-Ins to add it.

1. **With the Monday sheet active, select range A1:028, click the Zoom box list arrow on the Standard toolbar, click Selection, then press [Ctrl][Home] to return to cell A1**
   Excel automatically adjusts the display magnification so that the data selected fits on one screen. See Figure F-10. After selecting the **Zoom box**, you also can pick a magnification percentage from the list or type the desired percentage.

2. **Click View on the menu bar, then click Custom Views**
   The Custom Views dialog box opens. Any previously defined views for the active worksheet appear in the Views box. In this case, Jim had created a custom view named Generic containing default print and display settings. See Figure F-11.

3. **Click Add**
   The Add View dialog box opens, as shown in Figure F-12. Here, you enter a name for the view and decide whether to include print settings and hidden rows, columns, and filter settings. You want to include the selected options.

4. **In the Name box, type Complete Daily Worksheet, then click OK**
   After creating a custom view of the worksheet, you return to the worksheet area. You are ready to test the two custom views. In case the views require a change to the worksheet, it's a good idea to turn off worksheet protection.

5. **Click Tools on the menu bar, point to Protection, then click Unprotect Sheet**

6. **Click View on the menu bar, then click Custom Views**
   The Custom Views dialog box opens, listing both the Complete Daily Worksheet and Generic views.

7. **Click Generic in the Views list box, click Show, preview the worksheet, then close the Preview**
   The Generic custom view returns the worksheet to the Excel default print and display settings. Now you are ready to test the new custom view.

8. **Click View on the menu bar, click Custom Views, click Complete Daily Worksheet in the Views list box, click Show**
   The entire worksheet fits on the screen.

9. **Return to the Generic view, then save your work**
   Jim is satisfied with the custom view of the worksheet he created.

**FIGURE F-10:** Selected data fit to one screen

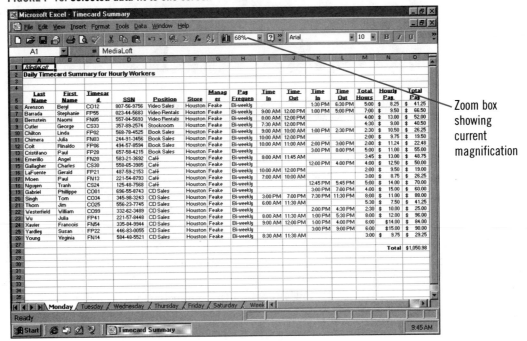

Zoom box showing current magnification

**FIGURE F-11:** Custom Views dialog box

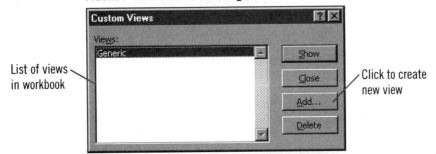

List of views in workbook

Click to create new view

**FIGURE F-12:** Add View dialog box

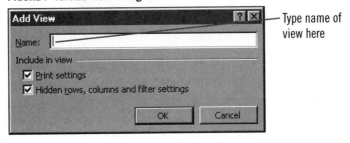

Type name of view here

## Using a workspace

If you work with several workbooks at a time in a particular arrangement, you can create a **workspace** containing information about their location and window sizes. Then, instead of opening each workbook individually, you can just open the workspace, which will automatically display the workbooks in the sizes and locations saved in the workspace. To create a workspace, open the workbooks and locate and size them as you would like them to appear. Click File on the menu bar, click Save Workspace, then type a name for the workspace file. Then open the workspace file and open the workbooks in their saved locations and sizes. Remember, however, that the workspace file does not contain the workbooks themselves, so you still have to back up the original workbook files. To start the workspace automatically when you turn on your computer, place the workspace file only in your XLStart folder.

# Controlling Page Breaks and Page Numbering

The vertical and horizontal dashed lines in worksheets indicate page breaks. Excel automatically inserts a page break when your worksheet data doesn't fit on one page. These page breaks are **dynamic**, which means they adjust automatically when you insert or delete rows and columns and when you change column widths or row heights. Everything to the left of the first vertical dashed line and above the first horizontal dashed line is printed on the first page. You can override the automatic breaks by choosing the Page Break command on the Insert menu. Table F-2 describes the different types of page breaks you can use. Jim wants another report displaying no more than half the hourly workers on each page. To accomplish this, he must insert a manual page break.

**1.** Click cell **A16**, click **Insert** on the menu bar, then click **Page Break**

A dashed line appears between rows 15 and 16, indicating a horizontal page break. See Figure F-13. After you set page breaks, it's a good idea to preview each page.

**2.** Preview the worksheet, then click **Zoom**

Notice that the status bar reads "Page 1 of 4" and that the data for the employees up through Charles Gallagher appears on the first page. Jim decides to place the date in the footer.

> **QuickTip**
>
> To insert the page number in a header or footer section yourself, click 🔲 in the Header or Footer dialog box.

**3.** While in the Print Preview window, click **Setup**, click the **Header/Footer tab**, click **Custom Footer**, click the **Right section box**, click the **Date button** 🔲

**4.** Click the **Left section box**, type your name, then click **OK**

Your name, the page number, and the date appear in the Footer preview area.

> **QuickTip**
>
> To remove a manual page break, select any cell directly below or to the right of the page break, click Insert on the menu bar, then click Remove Page Break.

**5.** In the Page Setup dialog box, click **OK**, and, still in Print Preview, check to make sure all the pages show your name and the page numbers, click **Print**, then click **OK**

**6.** Click **View** on the menu bar, click **Custom Views**, click **Add**, type **Half N Half**, then click **OK**

Your new custom view has the page breaks and all current print settings.

**7.** Make sure cell H16 is selected, then click **Insert** on the menu bar and click **Remove Page Break**

**8.** Save the workbook

TABLE F-2: **Page break options**

| type of page break | where to position cell pointer |
| --- | --- |
| Both horizontal and vertical page breaks | Select the cell below and to the right of the gridline where you want the breaks to occur |
| Only a horizontal page break | Select the cell in column A that is directly below the gridline where you want the page to break |
| Only a vertical page break | Select a cell in row 1 that is to the right of the gridline where you want the page to break |

FIGURE F-13: Worksheet with horizontal page break

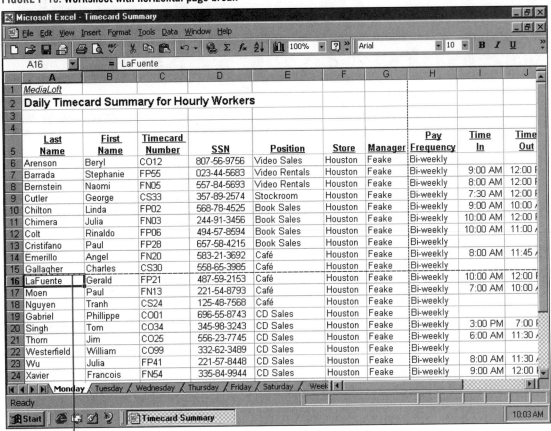

Dashed line indicates horizontal
break after row 15

## Using Page Break Preview

By clicking View on the menu bar, then clicking Page Break Preview, or clicking Page Break Preview in the Print Preview window, you can view and change page breaks manually. (If you see a dialog box asking if you want help, just click OK to close it.) Simply drag the page break lines to the desired location. See Figure F-14. To exit Page Break Preview, click View on the menu bar, then click Normal.

FIGURE F-14: Page Break Preview window

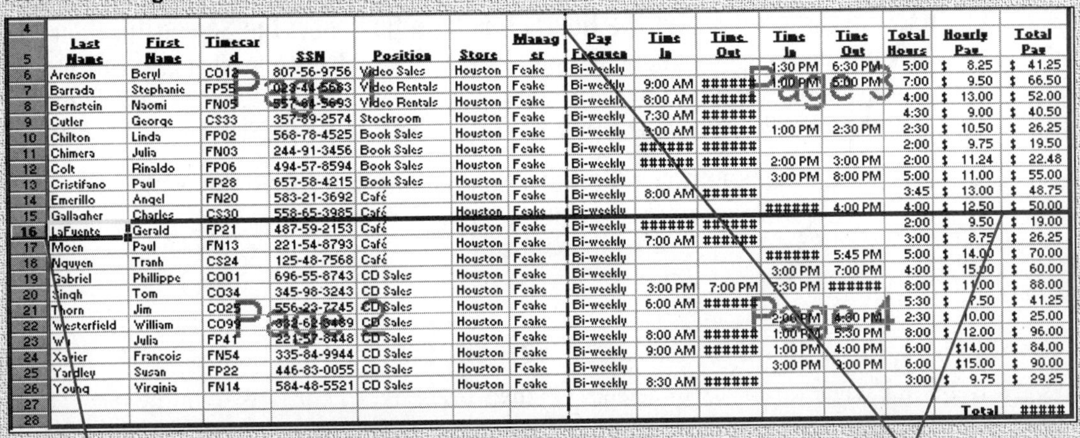

Cell pointer in cell A16

Drag page break lines
to change page breaks

# Creating a Hyperlink between Excel Files

As you manage the content and appearance of your workbooks, you may want the workbook user to have access to information in another workbook. It might be nonessential information or data that is too detailed to place in the workbook itself. In these cases, you can create a **hyperlink**, an object (a filename, a word, a phrase, or a graphic) in a worksheet that, when you click it, will jump to another worksheet, called the **target**. The target can be a document created in another software program or a site on the World Wide Web. For example, in a worksheet that lists customer invoices, at each customer's name, you might create a hyperlink to an Excel file containing payment terms for each customer. You can also use hyperlinks to navigate to other locations in a large worksheet. Jim wants managers who view the Timecard Summary worksheet to be able to view the pay categories for MediaLoft store employees. He creates a hyperlink at the Hourly Pay Rate column heading. Users will click the hyperlink to view the Pay Rate worksheet.

1. Display the Monday worksheet

2. Click **Edit**, click **Go To**, type **N5** (the cell containing **the text Hourly Pay Rate**), then click **OK**

3. Click the **Insert Hyperlink button** 🔗 on the Standard toolbar, then click **Existing File or Web Page**, if necessary
   The Insert Hyperlink dialog box opens. See Figure F-15. The icons under Link to: on the left side of the dialog box let you specify the type of location you want the link to jump to: an existing file or Web page, a place in the same document, a new document, or an e-mail address. Since Jim wants users to display a document he has created, the first icon, Existing File or Web Page, is correct and is already selected.

4. Click **File** under Browse for, then in the Link to File dialog box, navigate to your Project Disk and double-click **Pay Rate Classifications**
   The Insert Hyperlink dialog box reappears with the filename you selected in the Type the file or Web page name text box. This document appears when users click this hyperlink. You can also specify the ScreenTip that users will see when they hold the pointer over the hyperlink.

5. Click **ScreenTip**, type **Click here to see MediaLoft pay rate classifications**, click **OK**, then click **OK** again
   Cell N5 now contains underlined blue text, indicating that it is a hyperlink. After you create a hyperlink, you should check it to make sure it jumps to the correct destination.

6. Move the pointer over the **Hourly Pay Rate text**, view the ScreenTip, then click once
   Notice that when you move the pointer over the text, the pointer changes to 👆, indicating that it is a hyperlink, and the ScreenTip appears. After you click, the Pay Rate Classifications worksheet appears. See Figure F-16. The Web toolbar appears beneath the Standard and Formatting toolbars.

7. Click the **Back button** ⬅ on the Web toolbar, then save the workbook

### Using hyperlinks to navigate large worksheets

Hyperlinks are useful in navigating large worksheets or workbooks. You can create a hyperlink from any cell to another cell in the same worksheet, a cell in another worksheet, or a defined name anywhere in the workbook. Under Link to in the Insert Hyperlink dialog box, click Place in This Document. Then type the cell reference and indicate the sheet, or select the named location in the scroll box.

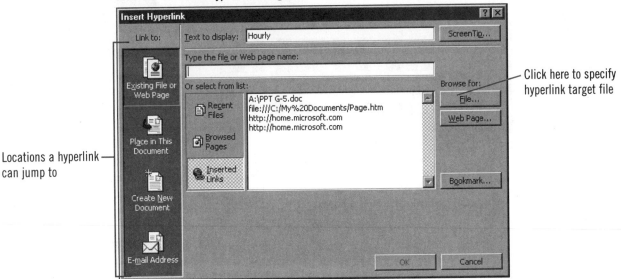

FIGURE F-15: Insert Hyperlink dialog box

Locations a hyperlink can jump to

Click here to specify hyperlink target file

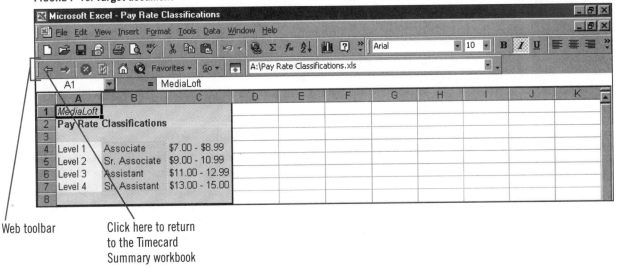

FIGURE F-16: Target document

Web toolbar

Click here to return to the Timecard Summary workbook

## Inserting a picture

As you prepare your workbooks for viewing by others on an intranet or on the Internet, you may want to enhance their appearance by adding pictures. You can easily add your own picture, such as a company logo or a scanned picture, or a picture from the Microsoft Clip Gallery. To insert a Clip Gallery picture on a worksheet, click Insert on the menu bar, point to

Picture, then click Clip Art. Click a category, click the image you want to insert, then click the Insert Clip icon. Close the Insert Clip Art window. The picture is an **object** that you can move, resize, or delete. To move a picture, click and then drag it. To resize it, click it once to select it, then drag one of its corners. To delete it, click to select it, then press [Delete].

# Saving an Excel file as an HTML Document

One way to share Excel data is to publish, or **post**, it online over a network so that others can access it using their Web browsers. The network can be an **intranet**, which is an internal network site used by a particular group of people who work together, or the World Wide Web. The **World Wide Web** is a structure of documents, or pages, connected electronically over a large computer network called the **Internet**, which is made up of smaller networks and computers. If you save and post an entire workbook, users can click worksheet tabs to view each sheet. If you save a single worksheet, you can make the Web page interactive, meaning that users can enter, format, and calculate worksheet data. To post an Excel document to an intranet or the World Wide Web, you must first save it in **HTML (Hypertext Markup Language)**, which is the format that a Web browser can read. Jim saves the entire Timecard Summary workbook in HTML format so it can be posted on the MediaLoft intranet for managers' use.

## Steps 1234

1. **Click File on the menu bar, then click Save as Web Page**
   The Save As dialog box opens. See Figure F-17. By default, the Entire Workbook option button is selected, which is what Jim wants. However, he wants the title bar of the Web page to be more descriptive than the filename.

2. **Click Change Title**
   The Set Page Title dialog box opens.

3. **Type MediaLoft Houston Timecard Summary, then click OK**
   The Page title area displays the new title. The Save as type list box indicates that the workbook will be saved as a Web page, which is in HTML format.

   **QuickTip**

   If you want, you can create a folder in the Save As dialog box. Click the Create new folder button 📁 and in the Save As dialog box, type the name of the new folder and click OK. The new folder automatically opens and appears in the Save in list. When you click Save, the HTML files will be saved in your new folder.

4. **Change the filename to Timecard Summary - Web, then click the Save in list arrow and locate your Project Disk**

5. **Click Save**
   A dialog box appears, indicating that the custom views you saved earlier will not be part of the HTML file.

6. **Click Yes**
   Excel saves the Web page version as an HTML file in the folder location you specified in the Save As dialog box, and in the same place creates a folder in which it places associated files, such as a file for each worksheet. To make the workbook available to others, you would post all these files on a network server. When the save process is complete, the original XLS file closes and the HTML file opens on your screen.

7. **Click File on the menu bar, click Web Page Preview, then maximize the browser window**
   The workbook opens in your default Web browser, which could be Internet Explorer or Netscape, showing you what it would look like if you opened it on an intranet or on the Internet. See Figure F-18. The Monday worksheet appears as it would if it were on a Web site or intranet, with tabs at the bottom of the screen for each daily sheet. If you wanted to use this document online, you would also need to save the target document (Pay Rate Classifications) in HTML format and post it to the Web site.

8. **Click the Weekly Summary tab**
   The Weekly Summary worksheet appears just as it would in Excel.

9. **Close the Web browser window, then close the Timecard Summary - Web workbook and the Pay Rate Classifications workbook, then exit Excel**

FIGURE F-17: Save As dialog box

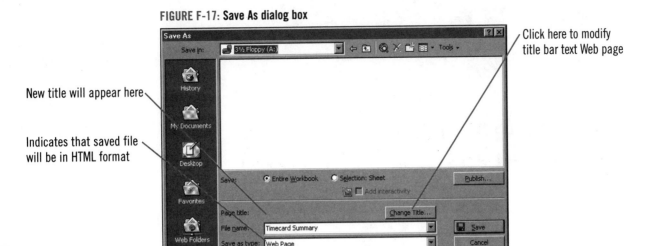

New title will appear here ➤

Indicates that saved file will be in HTML format ➤

Click here to modify title bar text Web page

FIGURE F-18: Workbook in Web page preview

Your browser may be Internet Explorer

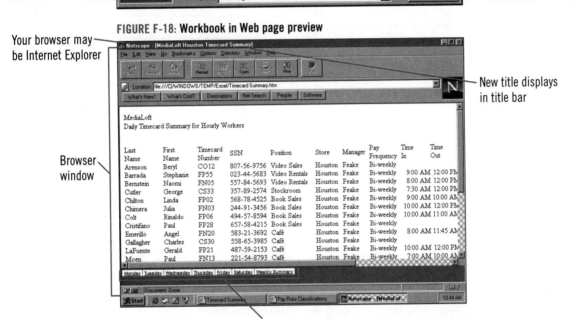

New title displays in title bar

Browser window

Worksheet tabs allow users to view other sheets in browser

## Send a workbook via e-mail

You can send an entire workbook or a worksheet to any e-mail recipient from within Excel. To send a workbook as an attachment to an e-mail message, click File, point to Send to, then click Mail Recipient (as attachment). Fill in the To and Cc information and click Send. See Figure F-19. (If Internet Explorer is not your default Web browser, you may need to respond to additional dialog boxes.) You can also route a workbook to one or more recipients on a routing list that you create. Click File, point to Send to, then click Routing Recipient. Click Create New Contact and enter contact information, then fill in the Routing slip. Depending on your e-mail program, you may have to follow a different procedure. See your instructor or lab resource person for help.

FIGURE F-19: E-mailing an Excel file as an attachment

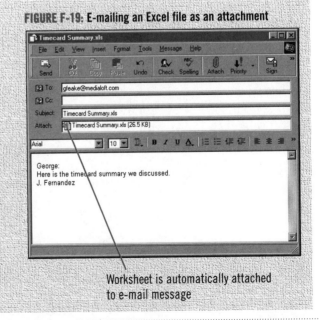

Worksheet is automatically attached to e-mail message

Excel 2000

# Practice

## ▶ Concepts Review

Label each element of the Excel screen shown in Figure F-20.

FIGURE F-20

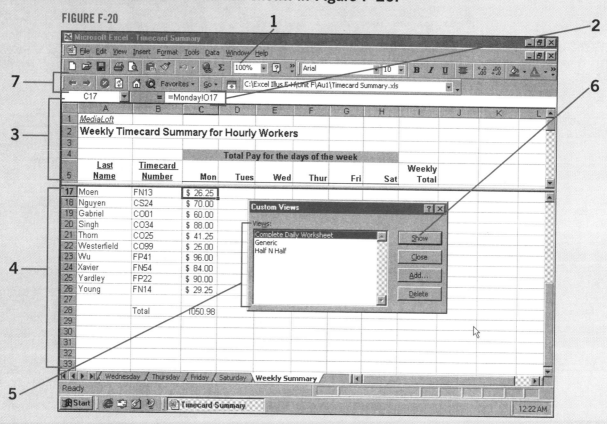

Match each of the terms with the statement that describes its function.

a. Dashed line
b. Hyperlink
c. 3-D reference
d. ☐
e. ⊞

8. Inserts a code to print the total number of pages
9. Uses values from different workbooks
10. Indicates a page break
11. Inserts a code to print the sheet name in a header or footer
12. An object you click to display a target

Select the best answer from the list of choices.

13. You can save frequently used display and print settings by using the _____ feature.
    a. HTML
    b. View menu
    c. Custom Views
    d. Save command

14. You freeze areas of the worksheet to
    a. Freeze data and unlock formulas.
    b. Lock column and row headings in place while you scroll through the worksheet.
    c. Freeze all data in place so that you can see it.
    d. Lock open windows in place.

15. To protect a worksheet, you must first unlock those cells that _____, and then issue the Protect Sheet command.
    a. never change
    b. the user will be allowed to change
    c. have hidden formulas
    d. are locked

# ▶ Skills Review

1. **Freeze columns and rows.**
    a. Open the workbook titled EX F-2, then save it as "Quarterly Household Budget".
    b. Freeze columns A and B and rows 1 through 3 for improved viewing. (*Hint:* Click cell C4 prior to issuing the Freeze Panes command.)
    c. Scroll until columns A and B and F through H are visible.
    d. Press [Ctrl][Home] to return to cell C4.
    e. Unfreeze the panes.

2. **Insert and delete worksheets.**
    a. With the 2001 sheet active, use the sheet pop-up menu to insert a new Sheet1 to its left.
    b. Delete Sheet1.
    c. Add a custom footer to the 2001 sheet with your name on the left side and the page number on the right side.
    d. Add a custom header with the worksheet name on the left side.
    e. Preview and print the worksheet.

3. **Consolidate data with 3-D references.**
    a. In cell C22, enter a reference to cell G7.
    b. In cell C23, enter a reference to cell G18.
    c. Activate the 2002 worksheet.
    d. In cell C4, enter a reference to cell C4 on the 2001 worksheet.
    e. In the 2002 worksheet, copy the contents of cell C4 into cells C5:C6.
    f. Preview the 2002 worksheet, view the Page Break Preview, and drag the page break so all the data fits on one page.
    g. Print the 2002 worksheet and save your work.

4. **Hide and protect worksheet areas.**
   a. On the 2001 sheet, unlock the expense data in the range C10:F17.
   b. Protect the sheet without using a password.
   c. To make sure the other cells are locked, attempt to make an entry in cell D4.
   d. Confirm the message box warning.
   e. Change the first-quarter mortgage expense to $3,400.
   f. Unprotect the worksheet.
   g. Save the workbook.

5. **Save custom views of a worksheet.**
   a. Set the zoom on the 2001 worksheet so all the data fits on your screen.
   b. Make this a new view called "Entire 2001 Budget".
   c. Use the Custom Views dialog box to return to Generic view.
   d. Save the workbook.

6. **Control page breaks and page numbering.**
   a. Insert a page break above cell A9.
   b. Save the view as "Halves".
   c. Preview and print the worksheet, then preview and print the entire workbook.
   d. Save the workbook.

7. **Create a hyperlink between Excel files.**
   a. On the 2001 worksheet, make cell A9 a hyperlink to the file Expense Details, with a ScreenTip that reads "Click here to see expense assumptions".
   b. Test the link, then print the Expense Details worksheet.
   c. Return to the Household Budget worksheet using the Web toolbar.
   d. On the 2002 worksheet, enter the text "Based on 2001 budget" in cell A2.
   e. Make the text in cell A2 a hyperlink to cell A1 in the 2001 worksheet. (*Hint:* Use the Place in this document button.)
   f. Test the hyperlink.
   g. Add any clip art picture to your worksheet, then move and resize it so it doesn't obscure any worksheet information.

8. **Save an Excel file as an HTML document.**
   a. Save the entire budget workbook as a Web page with a title bar that reads "Our Budget" and the file named Quarterly Household Budget - Web.
   b. Preview the Web page in your browser.
   c. Test the worksheet tabs in the browser to make sure they work.
   d. Return to Excel, then close the HTML document.
   e. Close the Expense Details worksheet, then exit Excel.

# ▶ Independent Challenges

**1.** You own PC Assist, a software training company. You have added several new entries to the August check register and are ready to enter September's check activity. Because the sheet for August will include much of the same information you need for September, you decide to copy it. Then you will edit the new sheet to fit your needs for September check activity. You will use sheet referencing to enter the beginning balance and beginning check number. Using your own data, you will complete five checks for the September register.

To complete this independent challenge:

a. Open the workbook entitled EX F-3, then save it as "Update to Check Register".
b. Delete Sheet 2 and Sheet 3, then create a worksheet for September by copying the August sheet.
c. With the September sheet active, delete the data in range A6:E24.

**d.** To update the balance at the beginning of the month, use sheet referencing from the last balance entry in the August sheet.

**e.** Generate the first check number. (*Hint:* Use a formula that references the last check number in August and adds one.)

**f.** Enter data for five checks.

**g.** Add a footer to the September sheet that includes your name left-aligned on the printout and the system date right-aligned on the printout. Add a header that displays the sheet name centered on the printout.

**h.** Save the workbook.

**i.** Preview the entire workbook, then close the Preview window.

**j.** Preview the September worksheet, then print it in landscape orientation on a single page.

**k.** Save and close the workbook, then exit Excel.

**2.** You are a new employee for a computer software manufacturer. You are responsible for tracking the sales of different product lines and determining which computer operating system generates the most software sales each month. Although sales figures vary from month to month, the format in which data is entered does not. Use Table F-3 as a guide to create a worksheet tracking sales across personal computer (PC) platforms by month. Use a separate sheet for each month and create data for three months. Use your own data for the number of software packages sold in the Windows and Macintosh columns for each product. Create a summary sheet with all the sales summary information.

To complete this independent challenge:

**a.** Create a new workbook, then save it as "Software Sales Summary".

**b.** Enter row and column labels, your own data, and formulas for the totals.

**c.** Create a summary sheet that totals the information in all three sheets. Customize the header to include your name and the date. Set the footer to (none). In Page Setup, center the page both horizontally and vertically.

**d.** Save the workbook, then preview and print the four worksheets.

TABLE F-3

|  | Windows | Macintosh | Total |
| --- | --- | --- | --- |
| **Games Software** | | | |
| Space Wars 99 | | | |
| Safari | | | |
| Flight School | | | |
| Total | | | |
| **Business Software** | | | |
| Word Processing | | | |
| Spreadsheet | | | |
| Presentation | | | |
| Graphics | | | |
| Page Layout | | | |
| Total | | | |
| **Utilities Products** | | | |
| Antivirus | | | |
| File recovery | | | |
| Total | | | |

**3.** You are a college student with two roommates. Each month you receive your long-distance telephone bill. Because no one wants to figure out who owes what, you split the bill three ways. You are sure that one of your roommates makes two-thirds of the long-distance calls. To make the situation more equitable, you decide to create a spreadsheet to track the long-distance phone calls each month. Create a workbook with a separate sheet for each roommate. Track the following information for each month's long-distance calls: date of call, time of call (AM or PM), call minutes, location called, state called, area code, phone number, and call charge. Total the charges for each roommate. Create a summary sheet of all three roommates' charges for the month.

To complete this independent challenge:

**a.** Create a new workbook, then save it as "Monthly Long Distance" to the appropriate folder on your Project Disk.

**b.** Enter column headings and row labels to track each call.

**c.** Use your own data, entering at least three long-distance calls for each roommate.

**d.** Create totals for minutes and charges on each roommate's sheet.

**e.** Create a summary sheet that shows each name and uses cell references to display the total minutes and total charges for each person.

**f.** On the summary sheet, create a hyperlink from each person's name to cell A1 of their respective worksheet.

**g.** Create a workbook with the same type of information for the two people in the apartment next door. Save it as "Next Door".

**h.** Use linking to create a 3-D reference that displays that information on your summary sheet so your roommates can compare their expenses with the neighbors'.

**i.** Change the workbook properties to Read only.

**j.** Save the Monthly Long Distance workbook in HTML format and preview it in your Web browser.

**4.** Maria Abbott, general sales manager at MediaLoft, has asked you to create a projection of MediaLoft advertising expenditures for 1999–2002 that she can put on the company intranet. She wants managers to review this information for an advertising discussion at the next managers meeting. The categories and 1999 figures are already on the site.

**a.** Connect to the Internet, go to the MediaLoft intranet site at http://www.course.com/illustrated/MediaLoft, click the Marketing link, then locate and print the Ad Campaign Summary. Close your browser and disconnect from the Internet.

**b.** Start Excel and create a workbook titled "Ad Campaign Projection". Name Sheet1 "1999", enter the categories and numbers from your printout, and use a formula to calculate the total.

**c.** Add an appropriate worksheet name in cell A1.

**d.** Create figures for the years 2000–2002 and put them in the columns to the right of the 1999 figures, then use font and fill colors to make the worksheet attractive.

**e.** Format all numbers in an appropriate format.

**f.** Use formulas to create totals for each year and for each ad type. Format the totals so they stand out from the other figures and use cell borders as appropriate.

**g.** Create a custom view of the worksheet and save the view using a descriptive name.

**h.** Delete the unused sheets.

**i.** Add your name to the footer, then save and print the worksheet.

**j.** Save your workbook as a Web page, using the filename Ad Campaign Projection - Web, adding descriptive text to the title bar.

**k.** Preview the resulting file in your Web Browser, and test the chart tab.

**l.** Close your browser and Excel.

Excel 2000

# ▶ Visual Workshop

Create the worksheet shown in Figure F-21. Save the workbook as "Martinez Agency". Preview, then print, the worksheet. (*Hint:* Notice the hyperlink target on the sheet name at the bottom of the figure.)

FIGURE F-21

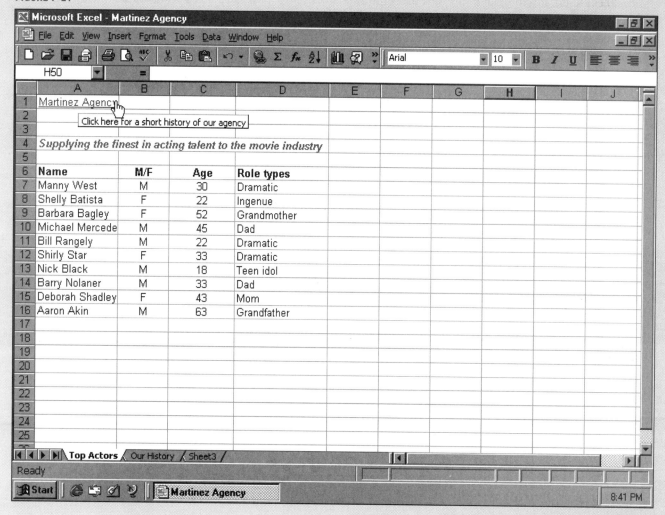

# Automating
## Worksheet Tasks

### Objectives

► **Plan a macro**

MOUS ► **Record a macro**

MOUS ► **Run a macro**

MOUS ► **Edit a macro**

► **Use shortcut keys with macros**

► **Use the Personal Macro Workbook**

► **Add a macro as a menu item**

► **Create a toolbar for macros**

A **macro** is a set of instructions that performs tasks in the order you specify. You create macros to automate frequently performed Excel tasks that require a series of steps. For example, if you usually type your name and date in a worksheet footer, Excel can record the keystrokes in a macro that types the text and inserts the current date automatically. In this unit, you will plan and design a simple macro, then record and run it. Then you will edit the macro. You will also create a macro to run when you use shortcut keys, store a macro in the Personal Macro Workbook, add a macro option to the Tools menu, and create a new toolbar for macros. Jim is creating a macro for the accounting department. The macro will automatically insert text that will identify the worksheet as originating in the accounting department.

# Planning a Macro

You create macros for tasks that you perform on a regular basis. For example, you can create a macro to enter and format text or to save and print a worksheet. To create a macro, you record the series of actions or write the instructions in a special format. Because the sequence of actions is important, you need to plan the macro carefully before you record it. You use commands on the Tools menu to record, run, and modify macros. ⬤▬▬ Jim creates a macro for the accounting department that inserts the text "Accounting Department" in the upper-left corner of any worksheet. He plans the macro using the following guidelines:

## Steps 1 2 3 4

**1. Assign the macro a descriptive name, and write out the steps the macro will perform**
This planning helps eliminate careless errors. Jim decides to name the macro "DeptStamp".
He writes a description of the macro, as shown in Figure G-1. See Table G-1 for a list of macros Jim might create to automate other tasks.

**2. Decide how you will perform the actions you want to record**
You can use the mouse, the keyboard, or a combination of the two. Jim decides to use both the mouse and keyboard.

**3. Practice the steps you want Excel to record and write them down**
Jim wrote down the sequence of actions as he performed them, and he is now ready to record and test the macro.

**4. Decide where to locate the description of the macro and the macro itself**
Macros can be stored in an unused area of the active workbook, in a new workbook, or in the Personal Macro Workbook. Jim stores the macro in a new workbook.

## Macro to create stamp with the department name

| | |
|---|---|
| Name: | DeptStamp |
| Description: | Adds a stamp to the top left of worksheet identifying it as an accounting department worksheet |
| Steps: | 1. Position the cell pointer in cell A1 |
| | 2. Type Accounting Department, then click the Enter button |
| | 3. Click Format on the menu bar, click Cells |
| | 4. Click Font tab, under Font style click Bold, under Underline click Single, and under Color click Red, then click OK |

TABLE G-1: Possible macros and their descriptive names

| description of macro | descriptive name |
|---|---|
| Enter a frequently used proper name, such as Jim Fernandez | JimFernandez |
| Enter a frequently used company name, such as MediaLoft | CompanyName |
| Print the active worksheet on a single page, in landscape orientation | FitToLand |
| Turn off the header and footer in the active worksheet | HeadFootOff |
| Show a frequently used custom view, such as a generic view of the worksheet, setting the print and display settings back to the Excel defaults | GenericView |

### Macros and viruses

When you open an Excel Workbook that has macros, you will see a message asking you if you want to enable or disable macros. This is because macros can contain viruses, destructive software programs that can damage your computer files. If you know your workbook came from a trusted source, click Enable macros. If you are not sure of the workbook's source, click Disable macros. If you disable the macros in a workbook, you will not be able to use them in the workbook. For more information, see the Excel Help topic About Viruses and workbook macros.

# Recording a Macro

The easiest way to create a macro is to record it using the Excel Macro Recorder. You simply turn the Macro Recorder on, enter the keystrokes, select the commands you want the macro to perform, then stop the recorder. As you record the macro, each action is translated into programming code that you can later view and modify. ◀━━ Jim wants to create a macro that enters a department stamp in cell A1 of the active worksheet. He creates this macro by recording his actions.

# Steps

**QuickTip**

To return personalized tool-bars and menus to a default state, click Tools on the menu bar, click Customize, click Reset my usage data on the Options tab, click Yes, then click Close.

**QuickTip**

If information in a text box is selected, you can simply type new information to replace it. This saves you from having to delete the existing entry before typing the new entry.

**Trouble?**

If your results differ from Figure G-4, clear the con-tents of cell A1, then slowly and carefully repeat Steps 2 through 9. When prompted to replace the existing macro at the end of step 5, click Yes.

1. Start Excel if necessary, click the **New button** ▫ on the Standard toolbar, then save the blank workbook as **My Excel Macros**
   Now you are ready to start recording the macro.

2. Click **Tools** on the menu bar, point to **Macro**, then click **Record New Macro**
   The Record Macro dialog box opens. See Figure G-2. Notice the default name Macro1 is selected. You can either assign this name or type a new name. The first character of a macro name must be a letter; the remaining characters can be letters, numbers, or underscores; (spaces are not allowed in macro names; use underscores in place of spaces). This dialog box also allows you to assign a shortcut key for running the macro and to instruct Excel where to store the macro.

3. Type **DeptStamp** in the Macro name box

4. If the Store macro in list arrow box does not read "This Workbook", click the **list arrow** and select **This Workbook**

5. If the Description text box does not contain your name, select the existing name, type your own name, then click **OK**
   The dialog box closes. Excel displays the small Stop Recording toolbar containing the Stop Recording button ▪, and the word "Recording" appears on the status bar. Take your time performing the steps below. Excel records every keystroke, menu option, and mouse action that you make.

6. Press **[Ctrl][Home]**
   The cell pointer moves to cell A1. When you begin an Excel session, macros record absolute cell references. By beginning the recording in cell A1, you ensure that the macro includes the instruction to select cell A1 as the first step.

7. Type **Accounting Department** in cell A1, then click the **Enter button** ☑ on the formula bar

8. Click **Format** on the menu bar, then click **Cells**

9. Click the **Font tab**, in the Font style list box click **Bold**, click the **Underline list arrow** and click **Single**, then click the **Color list arrow** and click **red** (third row, first color on left)
   See Figure G-3.

10. Click **OK**, click the **Stop Recording button** ▪ on the Stop Recording toolbar, click **cell D1** to deselect cell A1, then save the workbook
    Compare your results with Figure G-4.

FIGURE G-2: Record Macro dialog box

Type macro name here

Your setting may differ

Reflects your name and system date

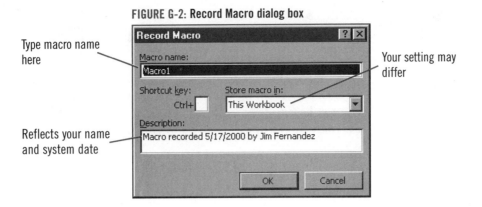

FIGURE G-3: Font tab of the Format Cells dialog box

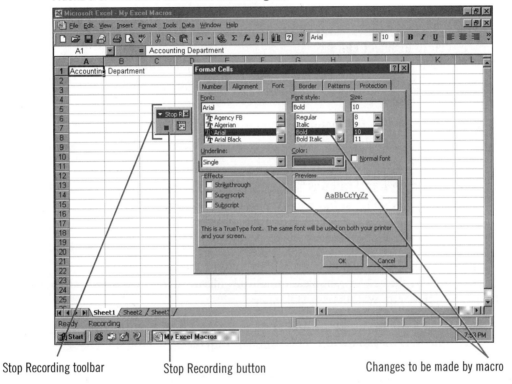

Stop Recording toolbar

Stop Recording button

Changes to be made by macro

FIGURE G-4: Personalized department stamp

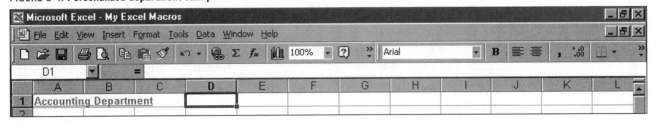

## CLUES TO USE

## Using templates to create a workbook

You can create a workbook using an Excel **template**, a special-purpose workbook with formatting and formulas, such as an invoice or income statement. Click File on the menu bar, click New, click the Spreadsheet Solutions or Business planner templates tab, then double-click any template. Excel opens a workbook using that template design.

# Running a Macro

Once you record a macro, you should test it to make sure that the actions performed are correct. To test a macro, you **run**, or execute, it. One way to run a macro is to select the macro in the Macros dialog box, then click Run. ✐ Jim clears the contents of cell A1 and then tests the DeptStamp macro. After he runs the macro from the My Excel Macros workbook, he decides to test the macro once more from a newly opened workbook.

## Steps

**1.** Click **cell A1**, click **Edit** on the menu bar, point to **Clear**, click **All**, then click any other cell to deselect cell A1

When you delete only the contents of a cell, any formatting still remains in the cell. By using the Clear All option on the Edit menu, you can be sure that the cell is free of contents and formatting.

**2.** Click **Tools** on the menu bar, point to **Macro**, then click **Macros**

The Macro dialog box, shown in Figure G-5, lists all the macros contained in the open workbooks.

**3.** Make sure **DeptStamp** is selected, click **Run**, then deselect cell A1

Watch your screen as the macro quickly plays back the steps you recorded in the previous lesson. When the macro is finished, your screen should look like Figure G-6. As long as the workbook containing the macro remains open, you can run the macro from any open workbook.

**4.** Click the **New button** ▢ on the Standard toolbar

Because the new workbook automatically fills the screen, it is difficult to be sure that the My Excel Macros workbook is still open.

**5.** Click **Window** on the menu bar

A list of open workbooks appears underneath the menu options. The active workbook name (in this case, Book2) appears with a check mark to its left. The My Excel Macros workbook appears on the menu, so you know it's open. See Figure G-7.

**6.** Deselect cell A1 if necessary, click **Tools** on the menu bar, point to **Macro**, click **Macros**, make sure **'My Excel Macros.xls'!DeptStamp** is selected, click **Run**, then deselect cell A1

Cell A1 should look like Figure G-6. Notice that when multiple workbooks are open, the macro name includes the workbook name between single quotation marks, followed by an exclamation point, indicating that the macro is outside the active workbook. Since you use this workbook only to test the macro, you don't need to save it.

**7.** Close Book2 without saving changes

The My Excel Macros workbook reappears.

FIGURE G-5: Macro dialog box

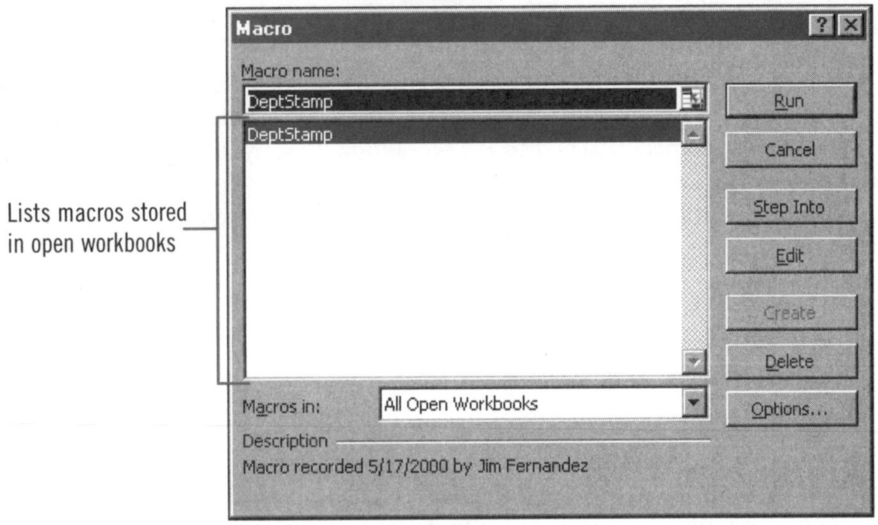

Lists macros stored
in open workbooks

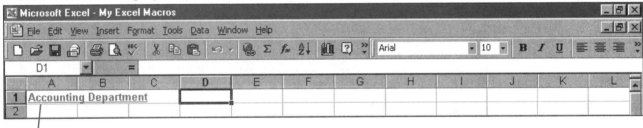

FIGURE G-6: Result of running DeptStamp macro

DeptStamp macro
inserts formatted
text in cell A1

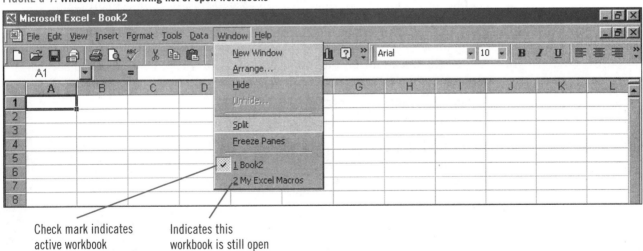

FIGURE G-7: Window menu showing list of open workbooks

Check mark indicates
active workbook

Indicates this
workbook is still open

# Editing a Macro

When you use the Macro Recorder to create a macro, the instructions are recorded automatically in Visual Basic for Applications programming language. Each macro is stored as a **module**, or program code container, attached to the workbook. Once you record a macro, you might need to change it. If you have a lot of changes to make, it might be best to re-record the macro. If you need to make only minor adjustments, you can edit the macro code, or program instructions, directly using the Visual Basic Editor. ✐ Jim wants to modify his macro to change the point size of the department stamp to 12.

## Steps

### QuickTip

Another way to start the Visual Basic Editor is to click Tools on the menu bar, point to Macro, then click Visual Basic Editor, or press [Alt][F11].

**1.** Make sure the My Excel Macros workbook is open, click **Tools** on the menu bar, point to **Macro**, click **Macros**, make sure **DeptStamp** is selected, then click **Edit**

The Visual Basic Editor starts showing the DeptStamp macro steps in a numbered module window (in this case, Module1).

**2.** Maximize the window titled **My Excel Macros.xls – [Module1 (Code)]**, then examine the steps in the macro

See Figure G-8. The name of the macro and the date it was recorded appear at the top of the module window. Notice that Excel translates your keystrokes and commands into words, known as macro code. For example, the line .FontStyle = "Bold" was generated when you clicked Bold in the Format Cells dialog box. When you make changes in a dialog box during macro recording, Excel automatically stores all the dialog box settings in the macro code. You also see lines of code that you didn't generate directly while recording the DeptStamp macro; for example, .Name = "Arial".

**3.** In the line .Size = 10, double-click **10** to select it, then type **12**

Because Module1 is attached to the workbook and not stored as a separate file, any changes to the module are saved automatically when the workbook is saved.

**4.** In the Visual Basic Editor, click **File** on the menu bar, click **Print**, then click **OK** to print the module

Review the printout of Module1.

**5.** Click **File** on the menu bar, then click **Close and Return to Microsoft Excel**

You want to rerun the DeptStamp macro to view the point size edit you made using the Visual Basic Editor.

**6.** Click cell **A1**, click **Edit** on the menu bar, point to **Clear**, click **All**, deselect cell A1, click **Tools** on the menu bar, point to **Macro**, click **Macros**, make sure **DeptStamp** is selected, click **Run**, then deselect cell A1

Compare your results with Figure G-9.

**7.** Save the workbook

**FIGURE G-8: Visual Basic Editor showing Module1**

Name of the macro

Project Explorer with open module selected

Properties window showing properties for selected objects

Macro programming code

Comments appear in green preceded by an apostrophe

Code window

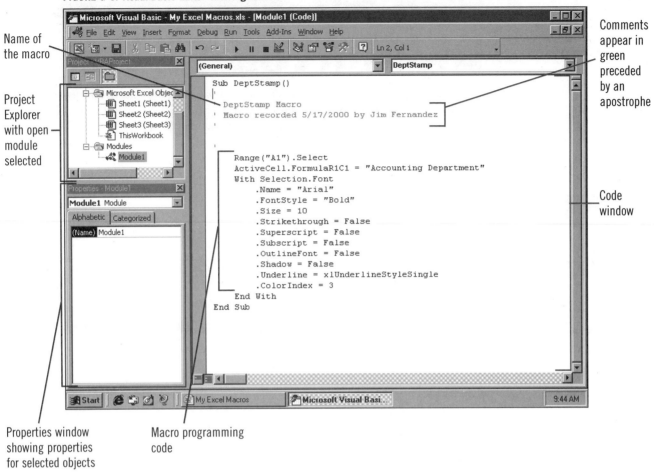

**FIGURE G-9: Result of running edited DeptStamp macro**

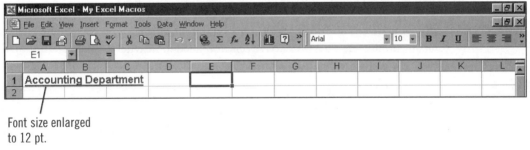

Font size enlarged to 12 pt.

 CLUES TO USE

## Adding comments to code

With practice, you will be able to interpret the lines of code within your macro. Others who use your macro, however, might want to know the function of a particular line. You can explain the code by adding comments to the macro. Comments are explanatory text added to the lines of code. When you enter a comment, you must type an apostrophe (') before the comment text. Otherwise, Excel thinks you have entered a command. On a color monitor, comments appear in green after you press [Enter]. See Figure G-8. You also can insert blank lines in the macro code to make the code more readable. To do this, type an apostrophe, then press [Enter].

Excel 2000

# Using Shortcut Keys with Macros

In addition to running a macro from the Macro dialog box, you can run a macro by assigning a shortcut key combination. Using shortcut keys to run macros reduces the number of keystrokes required to begin macro playback. You assign shortcut key combinations in the Record Macro dialog box. ✐ Jim also wants to create a macro called CompanyName to enter the company name into a worksheet. He assigns a shortcut key combination to run the macro.

## Steps 1 2 3 4

1. **Click cell B2**

   You will record the macro in cell B2. You want to be able to enter the company name anywhere in a worksheet. Therefore, you will not begin the macro with an instruction to position the cell pointer, as you did in the DeptStamp macro.

2. **Click Tools on the menu bar, point to Macro, then click Record New Macro**

   The Record Macro dialog box opens. Notice the option Shortcut key: Ctrl+ followed by a blank box. You can type a letter (A-Z) in the Shortcut key box to assign the key combination of [Ctrl] plus that letter to run the macro. You use the key combination [Ctrl][Shift] plus a letter to avoid overriding any of the Excel's assigned [Ctrl] [letter] shortcut keys, such as [Ctrl][C] for Copy.

3. **With the default macro name selected, type CompanyName, click the Shortcut key text box, press and hold [Shift], type C, then, if necessary, replace the name in the Description box with your name**

   Compare your screen with Figure G-10. You are ready to record the CompanyName macro.

4. **Click OK to close the dialog box**

   By default, Excel records absolute cell references in macros. Beginning the macro in cell B2 causes the macro code to begin with a statement to select cell B2. Because you want to be able to run this macro in any active cell, you need to instruct Excel to record relative cell references while recording the macro.

5. **Click the Relative Reference button [icon] on the Stop Recording toolbar**

   The Relative Reference button is now indented to indicate that it is selected. See Figure G-11. This button is a toggle and retains the relative reference setting until you click it again to turn it off.

> **QuickTip**
>
> When you begin an Excel session, the Relative Reference button is toggled off, indicating that Excel is recording absolute cell references in macros. Once selected, and until it is toggled off again, the Relative Reference setting remains in effect during the current Excel session.

6. **Type MediaLoft in cell B2, click the Enter button [icon] on the formula bar, press [Ctrl][I] to italicize the text, click the Stop Recording button [icon] on the Stop Recording toolbar, then deselect cell B2**

   MediaLoft appears in italics in cell B2. You are ready to run the macro in cell A5 using the shortcut key combination.

7. **Click cell A5, press and hold [Ctrl][Shift], type C, then deselect the cell**

   The result appears in cell A5. See Figure G-12. Because the macro played back in the selected cell (A5) instead of the cell where it was recorded (B2), Jim is convinced that the macro recorded relative cell references.

8. **Save the workbook**

**FIGURE G-10: Record Macro dialog box with shortcut key assigned**

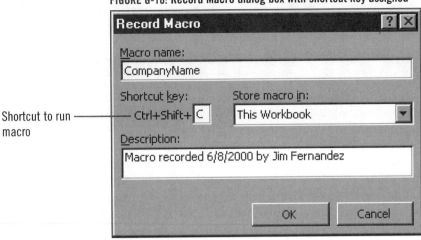

Shortcut to run macro ——

**FIGURE G-11: Stop Recording toolbar with Relative Reference button selected**

Relative Reference button

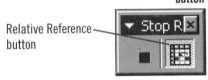

**FIGURE G-12: Result of running the CompanyName macro**

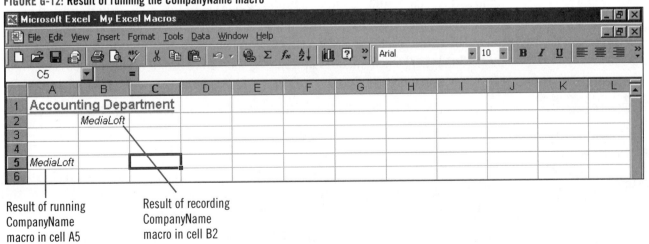

Result of running CompanyName macro in cell A5

Result of recording CompanyName macro in cell B2

# Using the Personal Macro Workbook

You can store commonly used macros in a **Personal Macro Workbook**. The Personal Macro Workbook is always available, unless you specify otherwise, and gives you access to all the macros it contains, regardless of which workbooks are open. The Personal Macro Workbook file is created automatically the first time you choose to store a macro in it. Additional macros are added to the Personal Macro Workbook when you store them there. Jim often adds a footer to his worksheets identifying his department, the workbook name, the worksheet name, the page number, and the current date. He saves time by creating a macro that automatically inserts this footer. Because he wants this macro to be available whenever he uses Excel, Jim decides to store this macro in the Personal Macro Workbook.

## Steps 1234

**1.** From any cell in the active worksheet, click **Tools** on the menu bar, point to **Macro**, then click **Record New Macro**

The Record Macro dialog box opens.

**Trouble?**

If you are prompted to replace an existing macro named FooterStamp, click Yes.

**2.** Type **FooterStamp** in the Macro name box, click the **Shortcut key box**, press and hold **[Shift]**, type **F**, then click the **Store macro in list arrow**

You have named the macro FooterStamp and assigned it the shortcut combination [Ctrl][Shift][F]. Notice that This Workbook is selected by default, indicating that Excel automatically stores macros in the active workbook. See Figure G-13. You also can choose to store the macro in a new workbook or in the Personal Macro Workbook.

**QuickTip**

If you see a message saying that the Personal Macro Workbook needs to be opened, open it, and then begin again from step 1. Once created, the Personal Macro Workbook file is usually stored in the Windows/Application Data/ Microsoft/Excel/XLSTART folder under the name "Personal".

**3.** Click **Personal Macro Workbook**, replace the existing name in the Description text box with your own name, if necessary, then click **OK**

The recorder is on, and you are ready to record the macro keystrokes. (If there is already a macro assigned to this shortcut, display the Personal Macro workbook and delete the FooterStamp macro. Then return to the My Excel Macro workbook and begin again from step 1.)

**4.** Click **File** on the menu bar, click **Page Setup**, click the **Header/Footer tab** (make sure to do this even if it is already active), click **Custom Footer**, in the Left section box, type **Accounting**, click the **Center section box**, click the **File Name button** 🔳, press **[Spacebar]**, type **/**, press **[Spacebar]**, click the **Tab Name button** 🔳 to insert the sheet name, click the **Right section box**, type your name followed by a comma, press **[Spacebar]**, click the **Date button** 🔳, click **OK** to return to the Header/Footer tab

The footer stamp is set up, as shown in Figure G-14.

**QuickTip**

You can copy or move macros stored in other workbooks to the Personal Macro Workbook using the Visual Basic Editor.

**5.** Click **OK** to return to the worksheet, then click the **Stop Recording button** 🔳 on the Stop Recording toolbar

You want to ensure that the macro will set the footer stamp in any active worksheet.

**6.** Activate Sheet2, in cell A1 type **Testing the FooterStamp macro**, press **[Enter]**, press and hold **[Ctrl][Shift]**, then type **F**

The FooterStamp macro plays back the sequence of commands.

**7.** Preview the worksheet to verify that the new footer was inserted

**8.** Print, then save the worksheet

Jim is satisfied that the FooterStamp macro works in any active worksheet. Next, Jim adds the macro as a menu item on the Tools menu.

**FIGURE G-13: Record Macro dialog box showing Store macro in options**

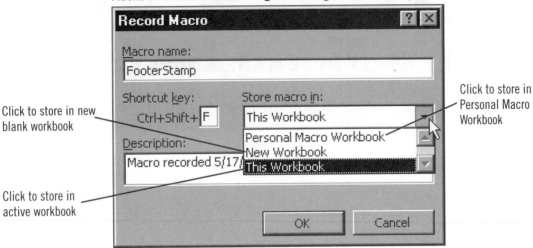

Click to store in new blank workbook

Click to store in active workbook

Click to store in Personal Macro Workbook

**FIGURE G-14: Header/Footer tab showing custom footer settings**

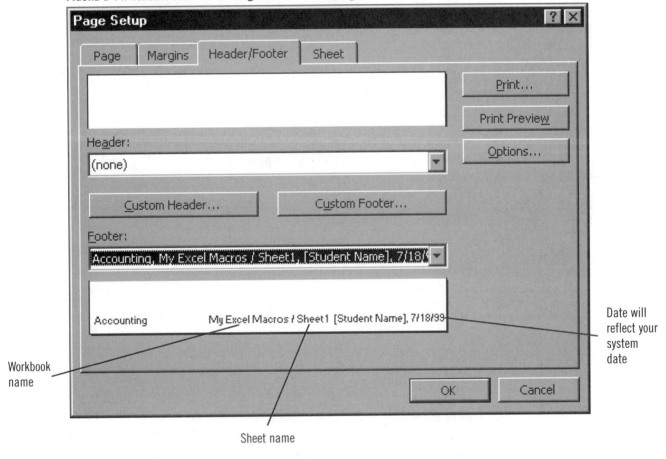

Workbook name

Sheet name

Date will reflect your system date

## CLUES TO USE

### Working with the Personal Macro Workbook

Once created, the Personal Macro Workbook automatically opens each time you start Excel. By default, the Personal Macro Workbook is hidden as a precautionary measure so you don't accidentally add anything to it. When the Personal Macro Workbook is hidden, you can add macros to it but you cannot delete macros from it.

# Adding a Macro as a Menu Item

In addition to storing macros in the Personal Macro Workbook so that they are always available, you can add macros as items on the Excel Worksheet menu bar. The **Worksheet menu bar** is a special toolbar at the top of the Excel screen that you can customize. ◢▬▬▬ To increase the availability of the FooterStamp macro, Jim decides to add it as an item on the Tools menu. First, he adds a custom menu item to the Tools menu, then he assigns the macro to that menu item.

## Steps

1. Click **Tools** on the menu bar, click **Customize**, click the **Commands tab**, then under Categories, click **Macros**
   See Figure G-15.

2. Click **Custom Menu Item** under Commands, drag the selection to **Tools** on the menu bar (the menu opens), then point just under the last menu option, but do not release the mouse button
   Compare your screen to Figure G-16.

3. Release the mouse button
   Now, Custom Menu item is the last item on the Tools menu.

4. With the Tools menu still open, right-click **Custom Menu Item**, select the text in the Name box (&Custom Menu Item), type **Footer Stamp**, then click **Assign Macro**
   Unlike a macro name, the name of a custom menu item can have spaces between words, as do all standard menu items. The Assign Macro dialog box opens.

5. Click **PERSONAL.XLS!FooterStamp** under Macro name, click **OK**, then click **Close**

6. Click the **Sheet3 tab**, in cell A1 type **Testing macro menu item**, press **[Enter]**, then click **Tools** on the menu bar
   The Tools menu appears with the new menu option at the bottom. See Figure G-17.

7. Click **Footer Stamp**, preview the worksheet to verify that the footer was inserted, then close the Print Preview window
   The Print Preview window appears with the footer stamp. Since others using your machine might be confused by the macro on the menu, it's a good idea to remove it.

8. Click **Tools** on the menu bar, click **Customize**, click the **Toolbars tab**, click **Worksheet Menu Bar** to select it, click **Reset**, click **OK** to confirm, click **Close**, then click **Tools** on the menu bar to make sure that the custom item has been deleted
   Because you did not make any changes to your workbook, you don't need to save it. Next, Jim creates a toolbar for macros and adds macros to it.

**FIGURE G-15: Commands tab of the Customize dialog box**

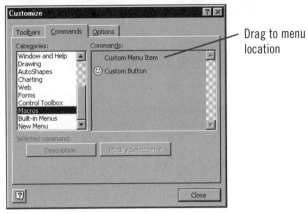

Drag to menu location

**FIGURE G-16: Tools menu showing placement of Custom Menu Item**

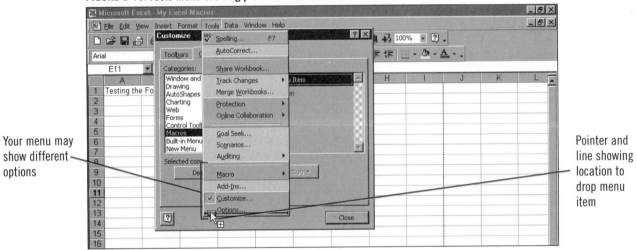

Your menu may show different options

Pointer and line showing location to drop menu item

**FIGURE G-17: Tools menu with new Footer Stamp item**

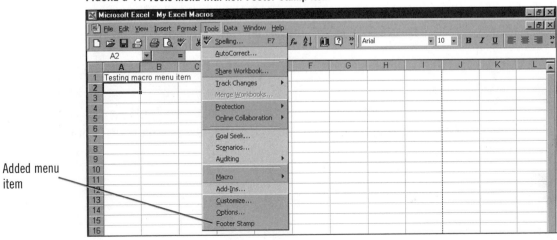

Added menu item

# Creating a Toolbar for Macros

Toolbars contain buttons that allow you to access commonly used commands. You can create your own custom toolbars to organize commands so that you can find and use them quickly. Once you create a toolbar, you then add buttons to access Excel commands such as macros. ➤ Jim has decided to create a custom toolbar called Macros that will contain buttons to run two of his macros.

## Steps

1. With Sheet3 active, click **Tools** on the menu bar, click **Customize**, click the **Toolbars tab**, if necessary, then click **New**
   The New Toolbar dialog box opens, as shown in Figure G-18. Under Toolbar name, a default name of Custom1 is selected.

2. Type **Macros**, then click **OK**
   Excel adds the new toolbar named Macros to the bottom of the list and a small, empty toolbar named Macros opens. See Figure G-19. Notice that you cannot see the entire toolbar name. A toolbar starts small and automatically expands to fit the buttons you assign to it.

3. Click the **Commands tab** in the Customize dialog box, click **Macros** under Categories, then drag the 🙂 **Custom Button** over the new Macros toolbar and release the mouse button
   The Macros toolbar now contains one button. You want the toolbar to contain two macros, so you need to add one more button.

4. Drag the 🙂 **Custom Button** over the Macros toolbar again
   With the two buttons in place, you customize the buttons and assign macros to them.

5. Right-click the left 🙂 on the Macros toolbar, select **&Custom Button** in the Name box, type **Department Stamp**, click **Assign Macro**, click **DeptStamp**, then click **OK**
   With the first toolbar button customized, you are ready to customize the second button.

6. With the Customize dialog box open, right-click the right 🙂 on the Macros toolbar, edit the name to read **Company Name**, click **Change Button Image**, click 🐎 (bottom row, third from the left), right-click 🐎, click **Assign Macro**, click **CompanyName** to select it, click **OK**, then close the Customize dialog box
   The Macros toolbar appears with the two customized macro buttons.

7. Move the mouse pointer over 🙂 on the Macros toolbar to display the macro name (Department Stamp), then click to run the macro; click **cell B2**, move the mouse pointer over 🐎 on the Macros toolbar to display the macro name (Company Name), click 🐎, then deselect the cell
   Compare your screen with Figure G-20. The DeptStamp macro automatically replaces the contents of cell A1.

8. Click **Tools** on the menu bar, click **Customize**, click the **Toolbars tab**, if necessary, under Toolbars click **Macros** to select it, click **Delete**, click **OK** to confirm the deletion, then click **Close**

9. Save, then close the workbooks

FIGURE G-18: New Toolbar dialog box

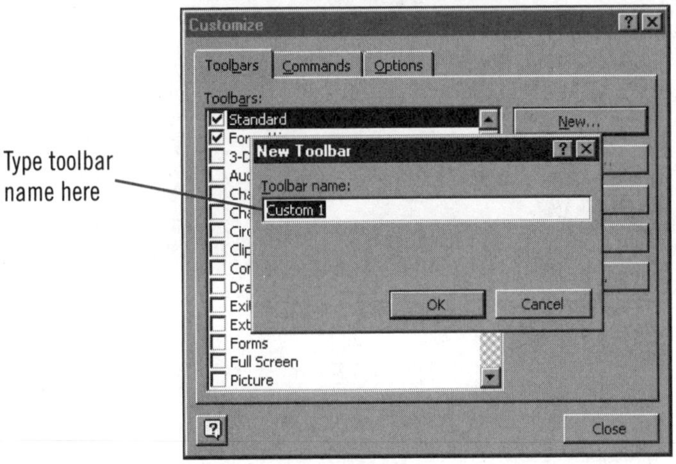

Type toolbar
name here

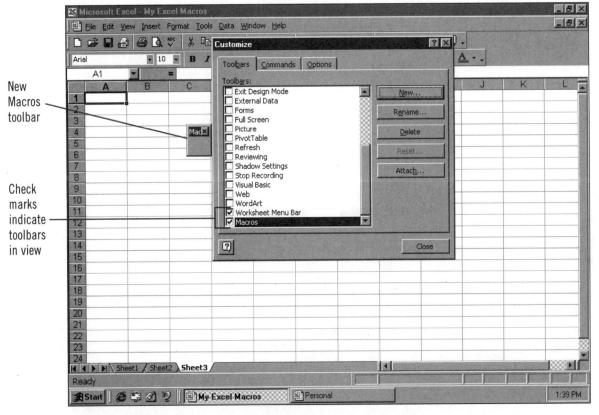

FIGURE G-19: Customize dialog box with new Macros toolbar

New
Macros
toolbar

Check
marks
indicate
toolbars
in view

FIGURE G-20: Worksheet showing Macros toolbar with two customized buttons

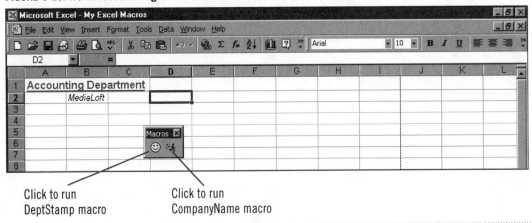

Click to run
DeptStamp macro

Click to run
CompanyName macro

# Practice

## ► Concepts Review

Label each element of the Excel screen shown in Figure G-21.

**FIGURE G-21**

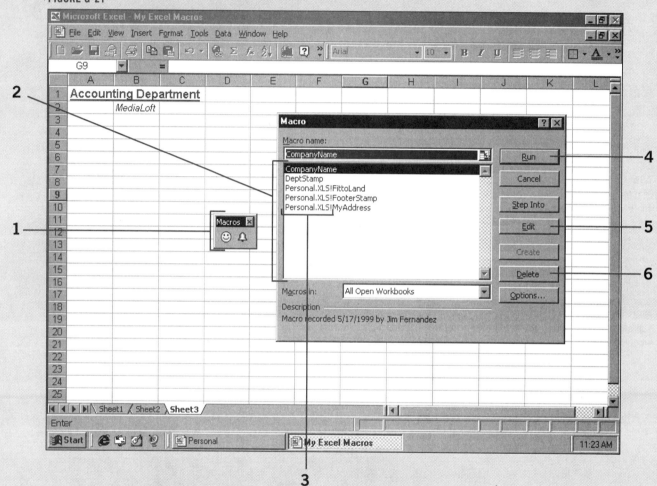

**Select the best answer from the list of choices.**

7. **Which of the following is the best candidate for a macro?**
   a. One-button or one-keystroke commands
   b. Often-used sequences of commands or actions
   c. Seldom-used commands or tasks
   d. Nonsequential tasks

8. **When you are recording a macro, you can execute commands by using**
   a. Only the keyboard.
   b. Only the mouse.
   c. Any combination of the keyboard and the mouse.
   d. Only menu commands.

9. **A macro is stored in**
   a. The body of a worksheet used for data.
   b. An unused area to the far right or well below the worksheet contents.
   c. A module attached to a workbook.
   d. A Custom Menu Item.

10. **Which of the following is *not* true about editing a macro?**
    a. You edit macros using the Visual Basic Editor.
    b. A macro cannot be edited and must be recorded again.
    c. You can type changes directly in the existing macro code.
    d. You can make more than one editing change in a macro.

11. **Why is it important to plan a macro?**
    a. Macros won't be stored if they contain errors.
    b. Planning helps prevent careless errors from being introduced into the macro.
    c. It is very difficult to correct errors you make in a macro.
    d. Planning ensures that your macro will not contain errors.

12. **Macros are recorded with relative references**
    a. Only if the Relative Reference button is selected.
    b. In all cases.
    c. Only if relative references are chosen while recording the macro.
    d. Only if the Absolute Reference button is not selected.

13. **You can run macros**
    a. From the Macro dialog box.
    b. From shortcut key combinations.
    c. As items on menus.
    d. Using all of the above.

## ▶ Skills Review

### 1. Record a macro.

**a.** Create a new workbook, then save it as "Macros". You will record a macro titled "MyAddress" that enters and formats your name, address, and telephone number in a worksheet.

**b.** Store the macro in the current workbook.

**c.** Record the macro, entering your name in cell A1, your street address in cell A2, your city, state, and ZIP code in cell A3, and your telephone number in cell A4.

**d.** Format the information as 14-point Arial bold.

**e.** Add a border and make the text the color of your choice.

**f.** Save the workbook.

### 2. Run a macro.

**a.** Clear cell entries in the range affected by the macro.

**b.** Run the MyAddress macro in cell A1.

**c.** Clear the cell entries generated by running the MyAddress macro.

**d.** Save the workbook.

### 3. Edit a macro.

**a.** Open the MyAddress macro in the Visual Basic Editor.

**b.** Locate the line of code that defines the font size, then change the size to 18 point.

**c.** Edit the selected range to A1:E4, which increases it by three columns to accommodate the changed label size. (*Hint*: It is the second Range line in the macro.)

**d.** Add a comment line that describes this macro.

**e.** Save and print the module, then return to Excel.

**f.** Test the macro in Sheet1.

**g.** Save the workbook.

### 4. Use shortcut keys with macros.

**a.** You will record a macro in the current workbook called "MyName" that records your full name in cell G1.

**b.** Assign your macro the shortcut key combination [Ctrl][Shift][N] and store it in the current workbook.

**c.** After you record the macro, clear cell G1.

**d.** Use the shortcut key combination to run the MyName macro.

**e.** Save the workbook.

### 5. Use the Personal Macro Workbook.

**a.** You will record a new macro called "FitToLand" that sets print orientation to landscape, scaled to fit on a page.

**b.** Store the macro in the Personal Macro Workbook. If you are prompted to replace the existing FitToLand macro, click Yes.

**c.** After you record the macro, activate Sheet2, and enter some test data in row 1 that exceeds one page width.

**d.** In the Page Setup dialog box, return the orientation to portrait and adjust the capital A to 100 percent of normal size.

**e.** Run the macro.

**f.** Preview Sheet2 and verify that it's in landscape view and fits on one page.

**6. Add a macro as a menu item.**
   **a.** On the Commands tab in the Customize dialog box, specify that you want to create a Custom Menu Item.
   **b.** Place the Custom Menu Item at the bottom of the Tools menu.
   **c.** Rename the Custom Menu Item "Fit to Landscape".
   **d.** Assign the macro PERSONAL.XLS!FitToLand to the command.
   **e.** Go to Sheet3 and change the orientation to portrait, then enter some test data in column A.
   **f.** Run the Fit to Landscape macro from the Tools menu.
   **g.** Preview the worksheet and verify that it is in landscape view.
   **h.** Using the Tools, Customize menu options, select the Worksheet Menu bar, and reset.
   **i.** Verify that the command has been removed from the Tools menu.
   **j.** Save the workbook.

**7. Create a toolbar for macros.**
   **a.** With the Macros workbook still open, you will create a new custom toolbar titled "My Info".
   **b.** If necessary, drag the new toolbar onto the worksheet.
   **c.** Display the Macros command category, then drag the Custom Button to the My Info toolbar.
   **d.** Again, drag the Custom Button to the My Info toolbar.
   **e.** Rename the first button "My Address", and assign the MyAddress macro to it.
   **f.** Rename the second button "My Name", and assign the MyName macro to it.
   **g.** Change the second button image to one of your choice.
   **h.** On Sheet3, clear the existing cell data, then test both macro buttons on the My Info toolbar.
   **i.** Use the Toolbars tab of the Customize dialog box to delete the toolbar named My Info.
   **j.** Save and close the workbook, then exit Excel.

## ▶ Independent Challenges

**1.** As a computer-support employee of an accounting firm, you need to develop ways to help your fellow employees work more efficiently. Employees have asked for Excel macros that will do the following:

- Delete the current row and insert a blank row
- Delete the current column and insert a blank column
- Format a selected group of cells with a red pattern, in 12-point Times bold italic

To complete this independent challenge:

**a.** Plan and write the steps necessary for each macro.
**b.** Create a new workbook, then save it as "Excel Utility Macros".
**c.** Create a new toolbar called "Helpers".
**d.** Create a macro for each employee request described above.
**e.** Add descriptive comment lines to each module.
**f.** Add each macro to the Tools menu.
**g.** On the Helpers toolbar, install buttons to run the macros.
**h.** Test each macro by using the Run command, the menu command, and the new buttons.
**i.** Save and then print the module for each macro.
**j.** Delete the new toolbar, and reset the Worksheet menu bar.

**2.** You are an analyst in the finance department of a large bank. Every quarter, you produce a number of single-page quarterly budget worksheets. Your manager has informed you that certain worksheets need to contain a footer stamp indicating that the worksheet was produced in the finance department. The footer also should show the date, the current page number of the total pages, and the worksheet filename. You decide that the stamp should not include a header. It's tedious to add the footer stamp and to clear the existing header and footer for the numerous worksheets you produce. You will record a macro to do this.

To complete this independent challenge:

**a.** Plan and write the steps to create the macro.

**b.** Create a new workbook, then save it as "Header and Footer Stamp".

**c.** Create the macro described above. Make sure it adds the footer with the department name and other information, and also clears the existing header.

**d.** Add descriptive comment lines to the macro code.

**e.** Add the macro to the Tools menu.

**f.** Create a toolbar titled "Stamp", then install a button on the toolbar to run the macro.

**g.** Test the macro to make sure it works from the Run command, menu command, and new button.

**h.** Save and print the module for the macro.

**i.** Delete the new toolbar, then reset the Worksheet menu bar.

**3.** You are an administrative assistant to the marketing vice president at Computers, Inc. A major part of your job is to create spreadsheets that project sales results in different markets. It seems that you are constantly changing the print settings so that workbooks print in landscape orientation and are scaled to fit on one page. You have decided that it is time to create a macro to streamline this process.

To complete this independent challenge:

**a.** Plan and write the steps necessary for the macro.

**b.** Create a new workbook, then save it as "Computers Inc Macro".

**c.** Create a macro that changes the page orientation to landscape and scales the worksheet to fit on a page.

**d.** Test the macro.

**e.** Save and print the module sheet.

**f.** Delete any toolbars you created, and reset the Worksheet menu bar.

**4.** The MediaLoft New York store has recently instituted a budgeting process for its café operation. At the end of every monthly sales report created in Excel, the staff lists the four largest budget items and then fills in what it expects the figures to be for the next month.

    Jim Fernandez at MediaLoft corporate headquarters has asked you to use Excel macros and the MediaLoft intranet site to help automate this task. The New York store staff will then distribute the macro to all stores so they can easily add the budget figures to their monthly reports.

**a.** Connect to the Internet, go to the MediaLoft intranet site at http://www.course.com/illustrated/MediaLoft, click the Accounting link, then click the Cafe Budget link. Examine the information in the NYC Cafe Expenses chart and note the four largest expense categories. Close your browser and disconnect from the Internet.

**b.** To complete this independent challenge, start Excel, create a new workbook, then save it as "Cafe Budget Macro". Create a macro named "CafeBudget" in the current workbook (activated by the [Shift][Ctrl][B] key combination) that does the following:

- Inserts the names of the four largest expense categories in contiguous cells in a column, starting with the current cell.
- Inserts the word "Total" in the cell below the last category.
- Inserts the words "Next Month's Budget" in the cell just above and to the right of the categories. The managers will insert their budget figures in the four cells below this heading, to the right of each category name.
- Totals the four figures the managers will insert and places the sum to the right of the Total label, just below the four figures.
- Inserts a bottom border on the Next Month's Budget cell and on the cell containing the last of the four figures.
- Boldfaces the Total text and the cell to its right that will contain the total.
- Places a thick box border around all the information, fills the area with a light green color, and autofits the column information where necessary.
- Makes the cell to the right of the first category the active cell.

**c.** Clear the worksheet of all contents and formats and test the macro. Edit or rerecord the macro as necessary.

**d.** Make a custom menu item on the Tools menu called "Cafe Budget" that will run the macro you created.

**e.** Create a custom toolbar named "Budgets" with a button containing the image of a calculator on it, and assign the button to your CafeBudget macro.

**f.** Test the custom menu item and the custom toolbar button, clearing the worksheet before running each one.

**g.** Save your workbook, print the results of the macro, then open the macro in the Visual Basic Editor and print the macro code.

**h.** Return to Excel, save and close the workbook, then exit Excel.

# ► Visual Workshop

Create the macro shown in Figure G-22. (*Hint:* Save a blank workbook as "File Utility Macros", then create a macro called SaveClose that saves a previously named workbook. Finally, include the line ActiveWorkbook. Close in the module, as shown in the figure.) Print the module. Test the macro. The line "Macro recorded...by..." will reflect your system date and name.

**FIGURE G-22**

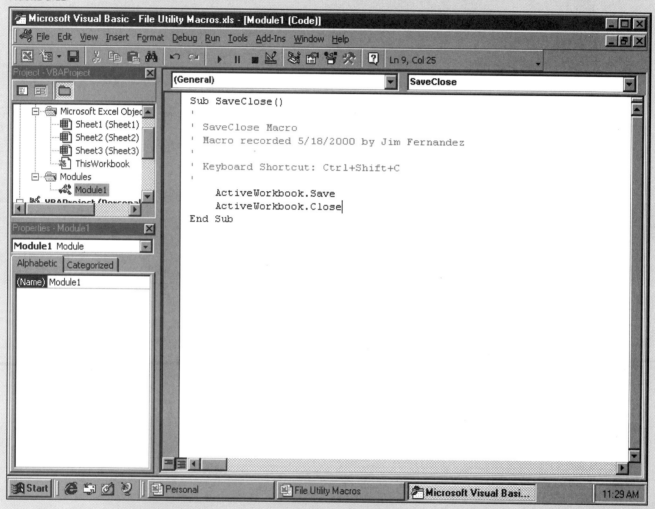

# Using

## Lists

### Objectives

- ► Plan a list
- ► Create a list
- ⌐MOUS⌐ ► Add records with the data form
- ⌐MOUS⌐ ► Find records
- ⌐MOUS⌐ ► Delete records
- ⌐MOUS⌐ ► Sort a list by one field
- ⌐MOUS⌐ ► Sort a list by multiple fields
- ⌐MOUS⌐ ► Print a list

A **database** is an organized collection of related information. Examples of databases include a telephone book, a card catalog, and a roster of company employees. Excel refers to a database as a **list**. Using an Excel list, you can organize and manage worksheet information so that you can quickly find needed data for projects, reports, and charts. In this unit, you'll learn how to plan and create a list; add, change, find, and delete information in a list; and then sort and print a list.

MediaLoft uses lists to analyze new customer information. Jim Fernandez needs to build and manage a list of new customers as part of the ongoing strategy to focus the company's advertising dollars.

# Planning a List

When planning a list, consider what information the list will contain and how you will work with the data now and in the future. Lists are organized into records. A **record** contains data about an object or person. Records, in turn, are divided into fields. **Fields** are columns in the list; each field describes a characteristic about the record, such as a customer's last name or street address. Each field has a **field name**, a column label that describes the field. See Table H-1 for additional planning guidelines. ✐ Jim will compile a list of new customers. Before entering the data into an Excel worksheet, he plans his list using the following guidelines:

## Details

### Identify the purpose of the list
Determine the kind of information the list should contain. Jim will use the list to identify areas of the country in which new customers live.

### Plan the structure of the list
Determine the fields that make up a record. Jim has customer cards that contain information about each new customer. Figure H-1 shows a typical card. Each customer in the list will have a record. The fields in the record correspond to the information on the cards.

### Write down the names of the fields
Field names can be up to 255 characters in length (the maximum column width), although shorter names are easier to see in the cells. Field names appear in the first row of a list. Jim writes down field names that describe each piece of information shown in Figure H-1.

### Determine any special number formatting required in the list
Most lists contain both text and numbers. When planning a list, consider whether any fields require specific number formatting or prefixes. Jim notes that some Zip codes begin with zero. Because Excel automatically drops a leading zero, Jim must type an apostrophe (') when he enters a Zip code that begins with 0 (zero). The apostrophe tells Excel that the cell contains a label rather than a value. If a column contains both numbers and numbers that contain a text character, such as an apostrophe ('), you should format all the numbers as text. Otherwise, the numbers are sorted first, and the numbers that contain text characters are sorted after that; for example, 11542, 60614, 87105, '01810, '02115. To instruct Excel to sort the Zip codes properly, Jim enters all Zip codes with a leading apostrophe.

**FIGURE H-1: Customer record and corresponding field names**

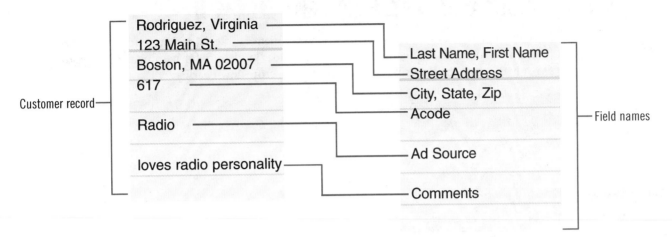

Customer record

- Rodriguez, Virginia ——— Last Name, First Name
- 123 Main St. ——— Street Address
- Boston, MA 02007 ——— City, State, Zip
- 617 ——— Acode
- Radio ——— Ad Source
- loves radio personality ——— Comments

Field names

**TABLE H-1: Guidelines for planning a list**

| size and location guidelines | row and column content guidelines |
|---|---|
| Devote an entire worksheet to your list and list summary information because some list management features can be used on only one list at a time | Plan and design your list so that all rows have similar items in the same column |
| Leave at least one blank column and one blank row between your list and list summary data. Doing this helps Excel select your list when it performs list management tasks such as sorting | Do not insert extra spaces at the beginning of a cell because that can affect sorting and searching |
| Avoid placing critical data to the left or right of the list | Use the same format for all cells in a column |

CLUES TO USE

## Lists versus databases

If your list contains more records than can fit on one worksheet (that is, more than 65,536), you should consider using database software rather than spreadsheet software.

# Creating a List

Once you have planned the list structure, the sequence of fields, and any appropriate formatting, you need to create field names. Table H-2 provides guidelines for naming fields. Jim is ready to create the list using the field names he wrote down earlier.

## Steps

**QuickTip**

To return personalized toolbars and menus to their default state, click Tools on the menu bar, click Customize, click the Options tab in the Customize dialog box, click Reset my usage data to restore the default settings, click Yes, click Close, then close the Drawing toolbar if it is displayed.

1. Start Excel if necessary, open the workbook titled **EX H-1**, save it as **New Customer List**, rename Sheet1 as **Practice**, then if necessary maximize the Excel window
   It is a good idea to devote an entire worksheet to your list.

2. Beginning in cell A1 and moving horizontally, type each field name in a separate cell, as shown in Figure H-2
   Always put field names in the first row of the list. Don't worry if your field names are wider than the cells; you will fix this later.

**Trouble?**

If the Bold button or Borders button does not appear on your Formatting toolbar, click the More Buttons button to view it.

3. Select the field headings in range **A1:I1**, then click the **Bold button** on the Formatting toolbar; with range A1:I1 still selected, click the **Borders list arrow**, then click the **thick bottom border** (second item from left in the second row)

4. Enter the information from Figure H-3 in the rows immediately below the field names, using a leading apostrophe (') for all Zip codes; do not leave any blank rows
   If you don't type an apostrophe, Excel deletes the leading zero (0) in the Zip code. The data appears in columns organized by field name.

**QuickTip**

If the field name you plan to use is wider than the data in the column, you can turn on Wrap Text to stack the heading in the cell. Doing this allows you to use descriptive field names and still keep the columns from being unnecessarily wide. If you prefer a keyboard short-cut, you can press [Alt][Enter] to force a line break while entering field names.

5. Select the range **A1:I4**, click **Format** on the menu bar, point to **Column**, click **AutoFit Selection**, click anywhere in the worksheet to deselect the range, then save the workbook
   Automatically resizing the column widths this way is faster than double-clicking the column divider lines between each pair of columns. Compare your screen with Figure H-4.

**TABLE H-2: Guidelines for naming fields**

| guideline | explanation |
| --- | --- |
| **Use labels to name fields** | Numbers can be interpreted as parts of formulas |
| **Do not use duplicate field names** | Duplicate field names can cause information to be incorrectly entered and sorted |
| **Format the field names to stand out from the list data** | Use a font, alignment, format, pattern, border, or capitalization style for the column labels that are different from the format of your list data |
| **Use descriptive names** | Avoid names that might be confused with cell addresses, such as Q4 |

FIGURE H-2: Field names entered and formatted in row 1

Microsoft Excel - New Customer List
File Edit View Insert Format Tools Data Window Help
Arial 10
A1 = Last Name
Last Name First Name Street Address City State Zip ACode Ad Source Comments

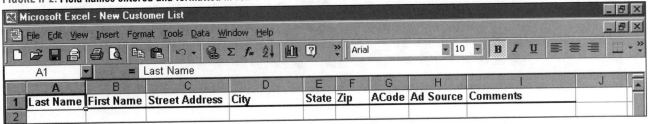

FIGURE H-3: Cards with customer information

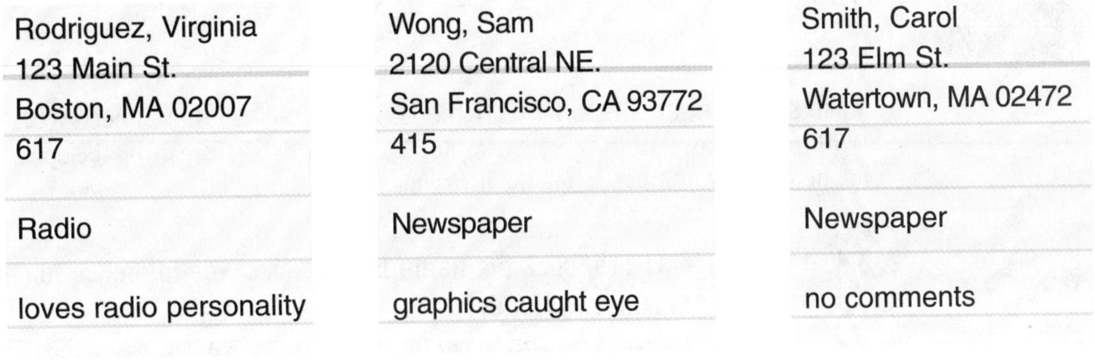

Rodriguez, Virginia
123 Main St.
Boston, MA 02007
617
Radio
loves radio personality
Wong, Sam
2120 Central NE.
San Francisco, CA 93772
415
Newspaper
graphics caught eye
Smith, Carol
123 Elm St.
Watertown, MA 02472
617
Newspaper
no comments

FIGURE H-4: List with three records

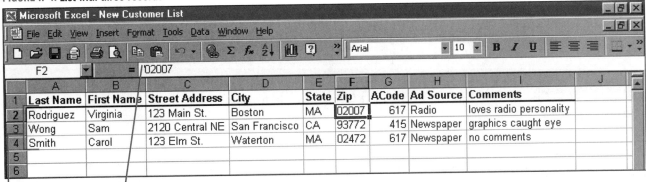

Microsoft Excel - New Customer List
File Edit View Insert Format Tools Data Window Help
Arial 10
F2 = '02007
Last Name First Name Street Address City State Zip ACode Ad Source Comments
Rodriguez Virginia 123 Main St. Boston MA 02007 617 Radio loves radio personality
Wong Sam 2120 Central NE San Francisco CA 93772 415 Newspaper graphics caught eye
Smith Carol 123 Elm St. Waterton MA 02472 617 Newspaper no comments
New records
Leading apostrophe

CLUES TO USE

## Maintaining the quality of information in a list

To protect the list information, make sure the data is entered in the correct field. Stress care and consistency to all those who enter the list data. Haphazardly entered data can yield invalid results later when it is manipulated.

# Adding Records with the Data Form

You can add records to a list by typing data directly into the cells within the list range. Once the field names are created, you also can use the data form as a quick, easy method of data entry. A **data form** is a dialog box that displays one record at a time. By naming a list range in the name box, you can select the list at any time, and all new records you add to the list will be included in the list range. Jim has entered all the customer records he had on his cards, but he receives the names of two more customers. He decides to use the Excel data form to add the new customer information.

## Steps 1 2 3 4

1. **Make sure the New Customer List file is open, then rename Sheet2 Working List**
   Working List contains the nearly complete customer list. Before using the data form to enter the new data, you must define the list range.

2. **Select the range A1:I45, click the name box to select the reference to cell A1 there, type Database, then press [Enter]**
   The Database list range name appears in the name box. When you assign the name Database to the list, the commands on the Excel Data menu apply to the list named "Database".

3. **While the list is still selected, click Data on the menu bar, then click Form**
   A data form containing the first record appears, as shown in Figure H-5.

4. **Click New**
   A blank data form appears with the insertion point in the first field.

5. **Type Chavez in the Last Name box, then press [Tab] to move the insertion point to the next field**

6. **Enter the rest of the information for Jeffrey Chavez, as shown in Figure H-6**
   Press [Tab] to move the insertion point to the next field, or click in the next field's box to move the insertion point there.

7. **Click New to add Jeffrey Chavez's record and open another blank data form, enter the record for Cathy Relman as shown in Figure H-6, then click Close**
   The list records that you add with the data form are placed at the end of the list and are formatted in the same way as the previous records.

8. **Scroll down the worksheet to bring rows 46 and 47 into view, check both new records, return to cell A1, then save the workbook**

**FIGURE H-5:** Data form showing first record in the list

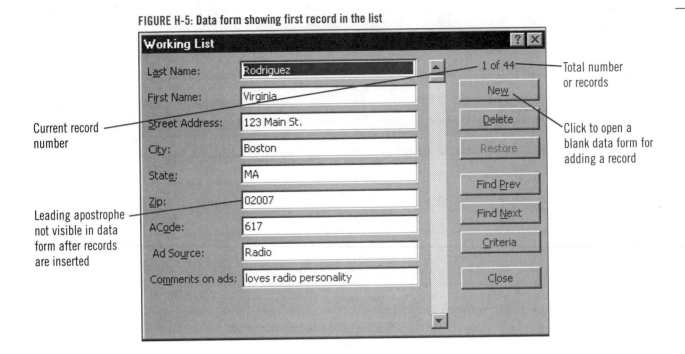

Current record
number

Leading apostrophe
not visible in data
form after records
are inserted

Total number
or records

Click to open a
blank data form for
adding a record

**FIGURE H-6:** Two data forms with information for two new records

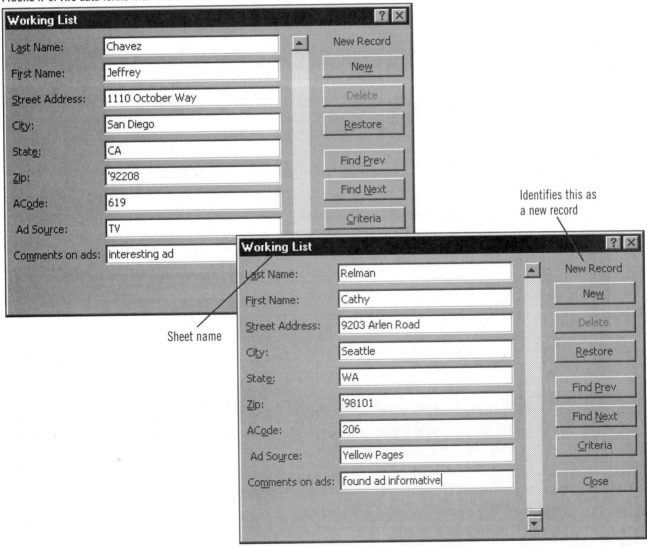

Sheet name

Identifies this as
a new record

# Unit H

## Excel 2000

# Finding Records

From time to time, you need to locate specific records in your list. You can use the Excel Find command on the Edit menu or the data form to search your list. Also, you can use the Replace command on the Edit menu to locate and replace existing entries or portions of entries with specified information. ➤ Jim wants to be more specific about the radio ad source, so he replaces "Radio" with "KWIN Radio." He also wants to know how many of the new customers originated from the company's TV ads. Jim begins by searching for those records with the ad source "TV".

## Steps 1234

### Trouble?
If you receive the message "No list found", select any cell within the list, then repeat Step 1

### QuickTip
You can also use comparison operators when performing a search using the data form. For example, you could specify >50,000 in a Salary field box to return those records in the Salary field with a value greater than $50,000.

1. From any cell within the list, click **Data** on the menu bar, click **Form**, then click **Criteria**
The data form changes so that all fields are blank and "Criteria" appears in the upper-right corner. See Figure H-7. You want to search for records whose Ad Source field contains the label "TV".

2. Press **[Alt][U]** to move to the Ad Source box, type **TV**, then click **Find Next**
Excel displays the first record for a customer who learned about the company through its TV ads. See Figure H-8.

3. Click **Find Next** until there are no more matching records, then click **Close**
There are six customers whose ad source is TV. Next, Jim wants to make the radio ad source more specific.

4. Return to cell A1, click **Edit** on the menu bar, then click **Replace**
The Replace dialog box opens with the insertion point located in the Find what box. See Figure H-9.

5. Type **Radio** in the Find what box, then click the **Replace with box**
Jim wants to search for entries containing "Radio" and replace them with "KWIN Radio".

6. Type **KWIN Radio** in the Replace with box
You are about to perform the search and replace option specified. Because you notice that there are other list entries containing the word "radio" with a lowercase "r" (in the Comments column), you need to make sure that only capitalized instances of the word are replaced.

7. Click the **Match case box** to select it, then click **Find Next**
Excel moves the cell pointer to the first occurrence of "Radio".

8. Click **Replace All**
The dialog box closes, and you complete the replacement and check to make sure all references to "Radio" in the Ad Source column now read "KWIN Radio". Note that in the Comments column, each instance of the word "radio" remains unchanged.

9. Make sure there are no entries in the Ad Source column that read "Radio", then save the workbook

**FIGURE H-7: Criteria data form**

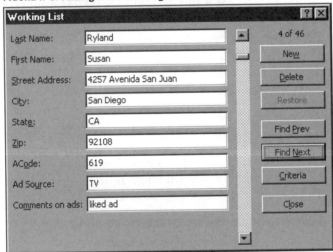

Type TV here ──→ (Ad Source field)

- Identifies this as a Criteria data form
- Click to restore changes you made in the form
- Click to find previous record that matches criterion
- Click to find next record that matches criterion
- Click to return to data form

**FIGURE H-8: Finding a record using the data form**

Working List — 4 of 46

|  |  |
|---|---|
| Last Name: | Ryland |
| First Name: | Susan |
| Street Address: | 4257 Avenida San Juan |
| City: | San Diego |
| State: | CA |
| Zip: | 92108 |
| ACode: | 619 |
| Ad Source: | TV |
| Comments on ads: | liked ad |

Buttons: New, Delete, Restore, Find Prev, Find Next, Criteria, Close

**FIGURE H-9: Replace dialog box**

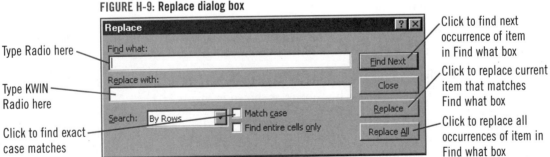

Type Radio here ──→ Find what:

Type KWIN Radio here ──→ Replace with:

Search: By Rows

☐ Match case
☐ Find entire cells only

Click to find exact case matches

- Click to find next occurrence of item in Find what box
- Click to replace current item that matches Find what box
- Click to replace all occurrences of item in Find what box

Buttons: Find Next, Close, Replace, Replace All

---

**CLUES TO USE**

## Using wildcards to fine-tune your search

You can use special symbols called **wildcards** when defining search criteria in the data form or Replace dialog box. The question mark (?) wildcard stands for any single character. For example, if you do not know whether a customer's last name is Paulsen or Paulson, you can specify Pauls?n as the search criteria to locate both options. The asterisk (*) wildcard stands for any group of characters. For example, if you specify Jan* as the search criteria in the First Name field, Excel locates all records with first names beginning with Jan (for instance, Jan, Janet, Janice, and so forth).

# Deleting Records

You need to keep your list up to date by removing obsolete records. One way to remove records is to use the Delete button on the data form. You can also delete all records that meet certain criteria—that is, records that have something in common. For example, you can specify a criterion for Excel to find the next record containing Zip code 01879, then remove the record using the Delete button. If specifying one criterion does not meet your needs, you can set multiple criteria. After he notices two entries for Carolyn Smith, Jim wants to check the database for additional duplicate entries. He uses the data form to delete the duplicate record.

## Steps

**1.** Click **Data** on the menu bar, click **Form**, then click **Criteria**
The Criteria data form appears.

**QuickTip**

You can use the data form to edit records as well as to add, search for, and delete them. Just find the desired record and edit the data directly in the appropriate box.

**2.** Type **Smith** in the **Last Name box**, click the **First Name box**, type **Carolyn**, then click **Find Next**
Excel displays the first record for a customer whose name is Carolyn Smith. You decide to leave the initial entry for Carolyn Smith (record 5 of 46) and delete the second one, once you confirm it is a duplicate.

**3.** Click **Find Next**
The duplicate record for Carolyn Smith, number 40, appears as shown in Figure H-10. You are ready to delete the duplicate entry.

**QuickTip**

Clicking Restore on the data form will not restore deleted record(s).

**4.** Click **Delete**, then click **OK** to confirm the deletion
The duplicate record for Carolyn Smith is deleted, and all the other records move up one row. The data form now shows the record for Manuel Julio.

**5.** Click **Close** to return to the worksheet, scroll down until rows 41–46 are visible, then read the entry in row 41
Notice that the duplicate entry for Carolyn Smith is gone and that Manuel Julio moved up a row and is now in row 41. You also notice a record for K. C. Splint in row 43, which is a duplicate entry.

**6.** Return to cell A1, and read the record information for K. C. Splint in row 8
After confirming the duplicate entry, you decide to delete the row.

**7.** Click cell **A8**, click **Edit** on the menu bar, then click **Delete**
The Delete dialog box opens, as shown in Figure H-11.

**QuickTip**

You can also delete selected cells in a row. Highlight the cells to delete, choose Delete from the Edit menu, and, in the dialog box, indicate if the remaining cells should move up or to the left to replace the selection. Use this command with caution in lists, since with lists you usually delete an entire row.

**8.** Click the **Entire row option button**, then click **OK**
You have deleted the entire row. The duplicate record for K. C. Splint is deleted and the other records move up to fill in the gap.

**9.** Save the workbook
Recall that you can delete a range name by following these steps: click Insert on the menu bar, point to Name, click Define, highlight the range name, and click delete.

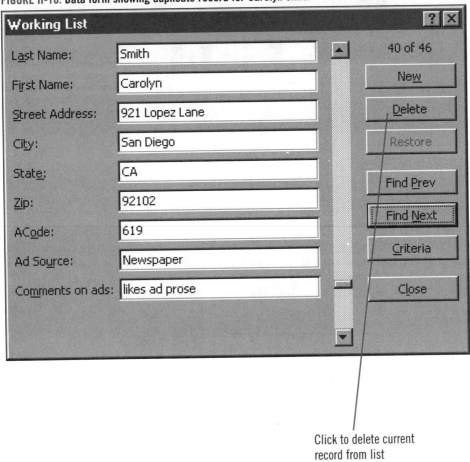

Click to delete current
record from list

FIGURE H-11: Delete dialog box

Click to shift remaining
cells to fill gap created
by deleting cells

Click to delete
current row

Click to delete
current column

## Advantage of deleting records from the worksheet

When you delete a record using the data form, you cannot undo your deletion. When you delete a record by deleting the row in which it resides inside the worksheet area, however, you can immediately restore the record by using the Undo command on the Edit menu, using the Undo button, or pressing [Ctrl][Z].

# Sorting a List by One Field

Usually, you enter records in the order in which they are received, rather than in alphabetical or numerical order. When you add records to a list using the data form, the records are added to the end of the list. Using the Excel sorting feature, you can rearrange the order of the records. You can use the sort buttons on the Standard toolbar to sort records by one field, or you can use the Sort command on the Data menu to perform more complicated sorts. Alternatively, you can sort an entire list or any portion of a list, or you can arrange sorted information in ascending or descending order. In ascending order, the lowest value (the beginning of the alphabet, for instance, or the earliest date) appears at the top of the list. In a field containing labels and numbers, numbers come first. In descending order, the highest value (the end of the alphabet or the latest date) appears at the top of the list. In a field containing labels and numbers, labels come first. Table H-3 provides examples of ascending and descending sorts. ✒️ Because Jim wants to be able to return the records to their original order following any sorts, he begins by creating a new field called Entry Order. Then he will perform several single field sorts on the list.

## Steps

**QuickTip**

Before you sort records, it is a good idea to make a backup copy of your list or create a field that numbers the records so you can return them to their original order, if necessary.

**Trouble?**

If your sort does not perform as intended, press [Ctrl][Z] immediately to undo the sort and repeat the step.

**1.** Enter the text and format in cell J1 shown in Figure H-12, then AutoFit column J

**2.** Type **1** in cell J2, press **[Enter]**, type **2** in cell J3, press **[Enter]**, select cells **J2:J3**, drag the fill handle to cell **J45**

With the Entry Order column complete, as shown in Figure H-12, you are ready to sort the list in ascending order by last name. You must position the cell pointer within the column you want to sort prior to issuing the sort command.

**3.** Return to cell A1, then click the **Sort Ascending button** 🔽 on the Standard toolbar

Excel instantly rearranges the records in ascending order by last name, as shown in Figure H-13. You can easily sort the list in descending order by any field.

**4.** Click cell **G1**, then click the **Sort Descending button** 🔽 on the Standard toolbar

Excel sorts the list, placing those records with higher-digit area codes at the top. Jim wants to update the list range to include original entry order.

**5.** Select the range **A1:J45**, click the **name box**, type **Database**, then press **[Enter]**

You are now ready to return the list to original entry order.

**6.** Click cell **J1**, click the **Sort Ascending button** 🔽 on the Standard toolbar, then save the workbook

The list is back to its original order, and the workbook is saved.

TABLE H-3: Sort order options and examples

| option | alphabetic | numeric | date | alphanumeric |
|---|---|---|---|---|
| **Ascending** | A, B, C | 7, 8, 9 | 1/1, 2/1, 3/1 | 12A, 99B, DX8, QT7 |
| **Descending** | C, B, A | 9, 8, 7 | 3/1, 2/1, 1/1 | QT7, DX8, 99B, 12A |

FIGURE H-12: List with Entry Order field added

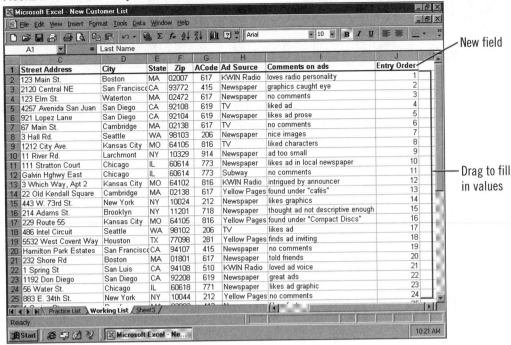

New field

Drag to fill in values

FIGURE H-13: List sorted alphabetically by Last Name

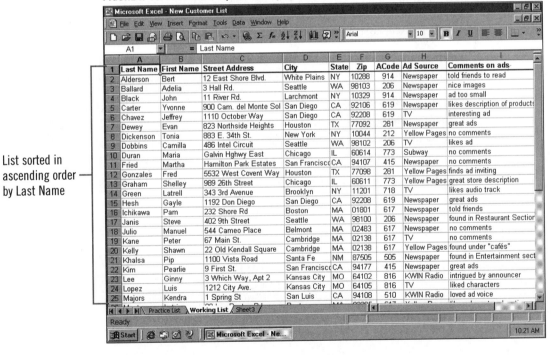

List sorted in ascending order by Last Name

## Rotating and indenting to improve label appearance

The column label you added in cell J1 is considerably wider than the data in the column. In cases like this, you can adjust the format of any label or value: Select the cell, click Format on the menu bar, click Cells, and on the Alignment tab drag the red diamond under Orientation to 90 degrees. You can also add space to the left of any label or value by selecting the cells(s) and clicking the Increase Indent button on the Formatting toolbar.

# Sorting a List by Multiple Fields

You can sort lists by as many as three fields by specifying **sort keys**, the criteria on which the sort is based. To perform sorts on multiple fields, you must use the Sort dialog box, which you access through the Sort command on the Data menu.  Jim wants to sort the records alphabetically by state first, then within the state by Zip code.

## Steps

**1.** Click the **name box list arrow**, then click **Database**

The list is selected. To sort the list by more than one field, you will need to use the Sort command on the Data menu.

**QuickTip**

You can specify a capitalization sort by clicking Options in the Sort dialog box, then clicking the Case sensitive box. When you choose this option, lowercase entries precede uppercase entries.

**2.** Click **Data** on the menu bar, then click **Sort**

The Sort dialog box opens, as shown in Figure H-14. You want to sort the list by state and then by Zip code.

**3.** Click the **Sort by** list arrow, click **State**, then click the **Ascending option button** to select it, if necessary

The list will be sorted alphabetically in ascending order (A-Z) by the State field. A second sort criterion will sort the entries within each state grouping.

**4.** Click the top **Then by list arrow**, click **Zip**, then click the **Descending option button**

You also could sort by a third key by selecting a field in the bottom Then by list box.

**5.** Click **OK** to execute the sort, press **[Ctrl][Home]**, then scroll through the list to see the result of the sort

The list is sorted alphabetically by state in ascending order, then within each state by Zip code in descending order. Compare your results with Figure H-15.

**6.** Return to cell A1, then save the workbook

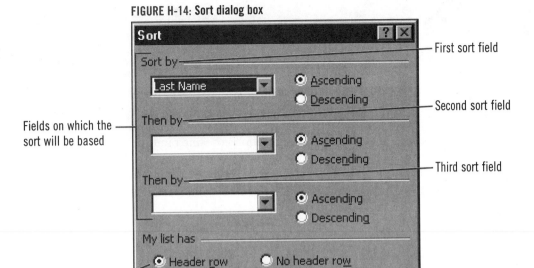

**FIGURE H-14: Sort dialog box**

First sort field

Second sort field

Third sort field

Fields on which the sort will be based

Indicates field name labels will not be included in sort

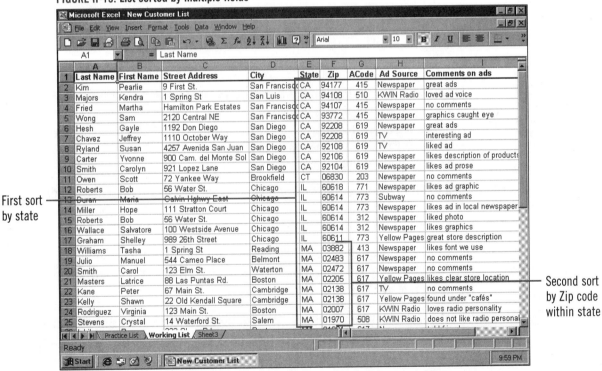

**FIGURE H-15: List sorted by multiple fields**

First sort by state

Second sort by Zip code within state

## Specifying a custom sort order

You can identify a custom sort order for the field selected in the Sort by box. To do this, click Options in the Sort dialog box, click the First key sort order list arrow, then click the desired custom order.

Commonly used custom sort orders are days of the week (Mon, Tues, Wed, etc.) and months (Jan, Feb, Mar, etc.); alphabetic sorts do not sort these items properly.

# Printing a List

If a list is small enough to fit on one page, you can print it as you would any other Excel worksheet. If you have more columns than can fit on a portrait-oriented page, try setting the page orientation to landscape. Because lists often have more rows than can fit on a page, you can define the first row of the list (containing the field names) as the **print title**, which prints at the top of every page. Most lists do not have any descriptive information above the field names on the worksheet. To augment the information contained in the field names, you can use headers and footers to add identifying text, such as the list title or report date. If you want to exclude any fields from your list report, you can hide the desired columns from view so that they do not print. ✎ Jim has finished updating his list and is ready to print it. He begins by previewing the list.

## Steps 1234

**1. Click the Print Preview button** 🔍 **on the Standard toolbar**
Notice that the status bar reads Page 1 of 2. You want all the fields in the list to fit on a single page, but you'll need two pages to fit all the data. The landscape page orientation and the Fit to options will help you do this.

> **QuickTip**
> You can print multiple ranges at the same time by clicking the Print area box in the Sheet tab. Then drag to the select areas you wish to print.

**2. From the Print Preview window, click Setup, click the Page tab, click the Landscape option button** under Orientation, click the **Fit to option button** under Scaling, double-click the **tall box** and type **2**, click **OK**, then click **Next**
The list still does not fit on a single page. Because the records on page 2 appear without column headings, you want to set up the first row of the list, containing the field names, as a repeating print title.

> **QuickTip**
> You can also use the sheet tab to specify whether you want gridlines, high or low print quality, and row and column headings.

**3. Click Close to exit the Print Preview window, click File on the menu bar, click Page Setup, click the Sheet tab, click the Rows to repeat at top box** under Print titles, click any cell in row 1, then click OK
When you select row 1 as a print title, Excel automatically inserts an absolute reference to a beginning row to repeat at the top of each page—in this case, the print title to repeat beginning and ending with row 1. See Figure H-16.

**4. Click Print Preview, click Next to view the second page, then click Zoom**
Setting up a print title to repeat row 1 causes the field names to appear at the top of each printed page. You can use the worksheet header to provide information about the list.

**5. Click Setup, click the Header/Footer tab, click Custom Header, click the Left section box** and type your name, then click the **Center section box** and type **MediaLoft–New Customer List**

**6. Select the header text in the Center section box, click the Font button** 🅰, change the font size to **14** and the style to **Bold**, click **OK**, click **OK** again to return to the Header/Footer tab, then click **OK** to preview the list
Page 2 of the report appears as shown in Figure H-17.

> **QuickTip**
> To print a selected area instead of the entire worksheet, select the area, click File, click Print, and, under Print what, click Selection.

**7. Click Print to print the worksheet, then save and close the workbook**
To print more than one worksheet, select each sheet tab while holding down the [Shift] or [Ctrl] keys, then click the print button on the standard toolbar.

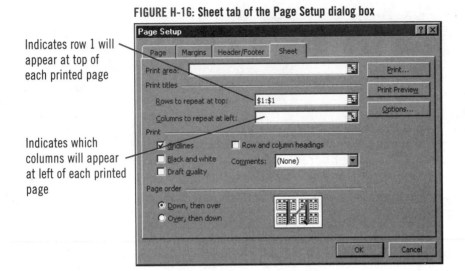

**FIGURE H-16: Sheet tab of the Page Setup dialog box**

Indicates row 1 will appear at top of each printed page

Indicates which columns will appear at left of each printed page

**FIGURE H-17: Print Preview window showing page 2 of completed report**

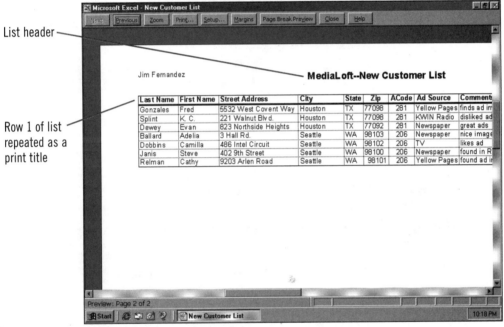

List header

Row 1 of list repeated as a print title

## Setting a print area

There are times when you want to print only part of a worksheet. You can do this in the Print dialog box by choosing Selection under Print what. But if you want to print a selected area repeatedly, it's best to define a **print area**, which will print when you click the Print button on the Standard toolbar. To set a print area, click View on the menu bar, then click Page Break Preview. In the preview window, select the area you want to print. Right-click the area, then select Set Print Area. The print area becomes outlined in a blue border. You can

drag the border to extend the print area (see Figure H-18) or add nonadjacent cells to it by selecting them, right-clicking them, then selecting Add to Print Area. To clear a print area, click File on the menu bar, point to Print Area, then click Clear Print Area.

**FIGURE H-18: Defined print area**

# Practice

## ► Concepts Review

Label each of the elements of the Excel screen shown in Figure H-19.

FIGURE H-19

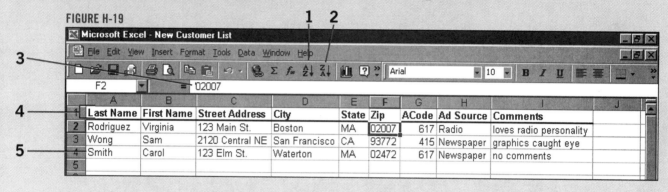

### Match each term with the statement that best describes it.

6. List
7. Record
8. Database
9. Sort
10. Field name

a. Arrange records in a particular sequence
b. Organized collection of related information in Excel
c. Row in an Excel list
d. Type of software used for lists containing more than 65,536 records
e. Label positioned at the top of the column identifying data for that field

**Select the best answer from the list of choices.**

**11. Which of the following Excel sorting options do you use to sort a list of employee names in A-to-Z order?**
  **a.** Ascending
  **b.** Absolute
  **c.** Alphabetic
  **d.** Descending

**12. Which of the following series is in descending order?**
  **a.** 4, 5, 6, A, B, C
  **b.** C, B, A, 6, 5, 4
  **c.** 8, 7, 6, 5, 6, 7
  **d.** 8, 6, 4, C, B, A

**13. Once the _____ is defined, any new records added to the list using the data form are included in the _____.**
  **a.** database, database
  **b.** data form, data form
  **c.** worksheet, worksheet
  **d.** list range, list range

**14. When printing a list on multiple pages, you can define a print title containing repeating row(s) to**
  **a.** Include appropriate fields in the printout.
  **b.** Include field names at the top of each printed page.
  **c.** Include the header in list reports.
  **d.** Exclude from the printout all rows under the first row.

## ▶ Skills Review

**1. Create a list.**
  **a.** Create a new workbook, then save it as "MediaLoft New York Employee List".
  **b.** In cell A1, type the title "MediaLoft New York Employees".
  **c.** Enter the field names and records using the information in Table H-4.
  **d.** Apply bold formatting to the field names.
  **e.** Center the entries in the Years, Full/Part Time, and Training? fields.
  **f.** Adjust the column widths to make the data readable.
  **g.** Save, then print the list.

TABLE H-4

| Last Name | First Name | Years | Position | Full/Part Time | Training? |
|-----------|-----------|-------|----------|----------------|-----------|
| Lustig | Sarah | 3 | Book Sales | F | Y |
| Marino | Donato | 2 | CD Sales | P | N |
| Khederian | Jay | 4 | Video Sales | F | Y |
| Finney | Carol | 1 | Stock | F | N |
| Rabinowicz | Miriam | 2 | Café Sales | P | Y |

### 2. Add records with the data form.

**a.** Select all the records in the list, including the field names, then define the range as "Database".

**b.** Open the data form and add a new record for David Gitano, a one-year employee in Book Sales. David is full time and has not completed the training.

**c.** Add a new record for George Worley, the café manager. George is full time, has worked there two years, and he has completed the training.

**d.** Save the list.

### 3. Find and delete records.

**a.** Find the record for Carol Finney.

**b.** Delete the record.

**c.** Save the list.

### 4. Sort a list by one field.

**a.** Select the Database list range.

**b.** Sort the list alphabetically in ascending order by last name.

**c.** Save the list.

### 5. Sort a list by multiple fields.

**a.** Select the Database list range.

**b.** Sort the list alphabetically in ascending order, first by whether or not the employees have completed training and then by last name.

**c.** Save the list.

### 6. Print a list.

**a.** Add a header that reads "Employee Information" in the center and that includes your name on the right; format both header items in bold.

**b.** Set the print area to include the range A1:F9.

**c.** Delete the database range.

**d.** Print the list, then save and close the workbook.

**e.** Exit Excel.

## ► Independent Challenges

**1.** Your advertising firm, Personalize IT, sells specialty items imprinted with the customer's name and/or logo such as hats, pens, and T-shirts. Plan and build a list of information with a minimum of 10 records using the three items sold. Your list should contain at least five different customers. (Some customers will place more than one order.) Each record should contain the customer's name, item(s) sold, and the individual and extended cost of the item(s). Enter your own data and make sure you include at least the following list fields:

- Item—Describe the item.
- Cost-Ea.—What is the item's individual cost?
- Quantity—How many items did the customer purchase?
- Ext. Cost—What is the total purchase price?
- Customer—Who purchased the item?

To complete this independent challenge:

**a.** Prepare a list plan that states your goal, outlines the data you'll need, and identifies the list elements.

**b.** Sketch a sample list on a piece of paper, indicating how the list should be built. What information should go in the columns? In the rows? Which of the data fields will be formatted as labels? As values?

**c.** Build the list first by entering the field names, then by entering the records. Remember, you will invent your own data. Save the workbook as "Personalize IT".

**d.** Reformat the list, as needed. For example, you might need to adjust the column widths to make the data more readable. Also, remember to check your spelling.

**e.** Sort the list in ascending order by item, then by Customer, then by Quantity.

**f.** Select only the cells with data in the last row. Use the Delete command on the Edit menu to delete those cells, moving the existing cells up to fill the space.

**g.** Type your name in a blank cell and review the worksheet; adjust any items as needed; then print a copy.

**h.** Save your work before closing.

**2.** You are taking a class titled "Television Shows: Past and Present" at a local community college. The instructor has provided you with an Excel list of television programs from the '60s and '70s. She has included fields tracking the following information: the number of years the show was a favorite, favorite character, least favorite character, the show's length in minutes, the show's biggest star, and comments about the show. The instructor has included data for each show in the list. She has asked you to add a field (column label) and two records (shows of your choosing) to the list. Because the list should cover only 30-minute shows, you need to delete any records for shows longer than 30 minutes. Also, your instructor wants you to sort the list by show name and format the list as needed prior to printing. Feel free to change any of the list data to suit your tastes and opinions.

To complete this independent challenge:

**a.** Open the workbook titled EX H-2, then save it as "Television Shows of the Past".

**b.** Using your own data, add a field, then use the data form to add two records to the list. Make sure to enter information in every field.

**c.** Delete any records having show lengths other than 30. (*Hint*: Use the Criteria data form to set the criteria, then find and delete any matching records.)

**d.** Make any formatting changes to the list as needed and save the list.

**e.** Sort the list in ascending order by show name.

**f.** Preview, then print the list. Adjust any items as needed so that the list can be printed on a single page.

**g.** Sort the list again, this time in descending order by number of years the show was a favorite.

**h.** Change the header to read "Television Shows of the Past: '60s and '70s".

**i.** Type your name in a blank cell, then preview and print the list.

**j.** Save the workbook.

**3.** You work as a sales clerk at Nite Owl Video. Your roommate and co-worker, Albert Lee, has put together a list of his favorite movie actors and actresses. He has asked you to add several names to the list so he can determine which artists and what kinds of films you enjoy most. He has recorded information in the following fields: artist's first and last name, life span, birthplace, the genre or type of role the artist plays most (for example, dramatic or comedic), the name of a film for which the artist has received or been nominated for an Academy Award, and, finally, two additional films featuring the artist. Using your own data, add at least two artists known for dramatic roles and two artists known for comedic roles.

To complete this independent challenge:

a. Open the workbook titled EX H-3, then add at least four records using the criteria mentioned above. Remember, you are creating and entering your own movie data for all relevant fields.

b. Save the workbook as "Film Star Favorites". Make formatting changes to the list as needed. Remember to check your spelling.

c. Sort the list alphabetically by Genre. Perform a second sort by Last Name.

d. Preview the list, adjust any items as needed, then print a copy of the list sorted by Genre and Last Name.

e. Sort the list again, this time in descending order by the Life Span field, then by Last Name.

f. Enter your name in a blank cell, then print a copy of the list sorted by Life Span and Last Name.

g. Save your work.

**4.** You work at MediaLoft corporate headquarters, and the Products Department has asked you to create a database to keep track of all CD products that win the People's Choice poll. The poll is new and will be conducted monthly.

To complete this independent challenge:

a. Start Excel, and create a new file with the following list headings: Artist LN, Artist FN, Title, Category, and In Stock, and save the file as "People's Choice". Format the title row with formats of your choice.

b. Connect to the Internet, and go to the MediaLoft intranet site at http://www.course.com/Illustrated/MediaLoft. Click the Products link, and print the page, which contains a table entitled "Results of People's Choice Poll". Disconnect from the Internet.

c. Use the information from the table to create the first six records of your list. For the In Stock column, show the first three products as in stock (Y) and the second three as not in stock (N). AutoFit the columns and save the file.

d. Open the file EX H-4, copy the records, and paste them into your database.

e. Find the CD by Jim Brickman.

f. Find the CD with the title "Mellow".

g. Use the Replace command to find all the records in the Rock category and change the category name to Rock N Roll. Adjust the column widths as necessary.

h. Sort the list by category.

i. Add a new field for Month, indicating the month each recording won the award. Assign a month (January, February, or March) to each winner so that each category has one winner per month.

j. Sort the list by month.

k. Sort the list by category and the artist's last name.

l. Sort by stock status, category, and the artist's last name.

m. Print the list, then save and close the file.

# ▶ Visual Workshop

Create the worksheet shown in Figure H-20. Save the workbook as "Famous Jazz Performers". Once you've entered the field names and records, sort the list by Contribution to Jazz and then by Last Name. Change the page setup so that the list is centered on the page horizontally and the header reads "Famous Jazz Performers". Preview and print the list, then save the workbook.

**FIGURE H-20**

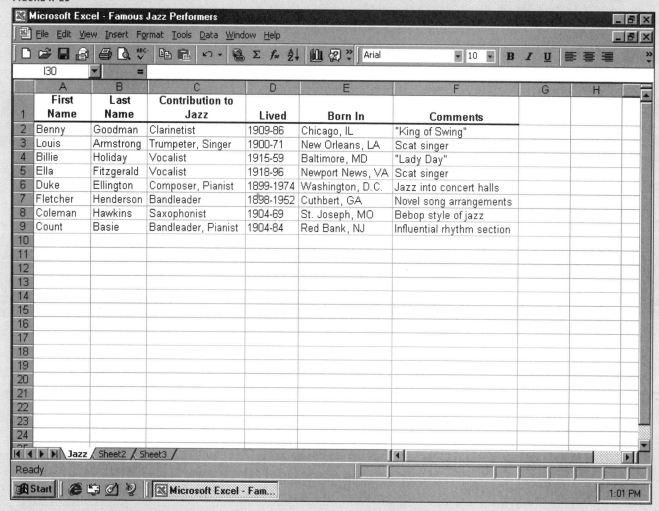

# Excel 2000 MOUS Certification Objectives

Below is a list of the Microsoft™ Office User Specialist program objectives for Core Excel 2000 skills showing where each MOUS objective is covered in the Lessons and Practice. This table lists the Core MOUS certification skills covered in the units in this book (Units A-H). For more information on which Illustrated titles meet MOUS certification, please see the inside cover of this book.

| MOUS standardized coding number | Activity | Lesson page where skill is covered | Location in lesson where skill is covered | Practice |
|---|---|---|---|---|
| **XL2000.1** | **Working with cells** | | | |
| XL2000.1.1 | Use Undo and Redo | Excel B-4 | Steps 7–8, QuickTip | |
| XL2000.1.2 | Clear cell content | Excel A-10 | Trouble, Step 2 | Skills Review |
| XL2000.1.3 | Enter text, dates, and numbers | Excel A-10<br>Excel B-4 | Steps 2–7<br>Step 7 | Skills Review,<br>Independent Challenges 2–4<br>Skills Review |
| XL2000.1.4 | Edit cell content | Excel B-4 | Steps 3–10 | Skills Review,<br>Independent Challenges 2–3 |
| XL2000.1.5 | Go to a specific cell | Excel E-2 | Step 3 | Skills Review |
| XL2000.1.6 | Insert and delete selected cells | Excel E-11 | Clues to Use | Skills Review |
| XL2000.1.7 | Cut, copy, paste, paste special and move selected cells, use the Office Clipboard | Excel B-10<br>Excel B-11<br>Excel B-14 | Steps 2–4<br>Clues to Use<br>QuickTip | Skills Review,<br>Independent Challenges 1–4 |
| | Paste Special | Excel B-11<br>Excel E-3 | Clues to Use<br>Clues to Use | Skills Review<br>Skills Review |
| XL2000.1.8 | Use Find and Replace | Excel F-2 | QuickTip | |
| XL2000.1.9 | Clear cell formats | Excel C-6 | QuickTip | Skills Review |

| MOUS standardized coding number | Activity | Lesson page where skill is covered | Location in lesson where skill is covered | Practice |
| --- | --- | --- | --- | --- |
| XL2000.1.10 | Work with series (AutoFill) | Excel B-14<br>Excel B-15 | Step 3<br>Clues to Use | Skills Review |
| XL2000.1.11 | Create hyperlinks | Excel F-14 | Steps 1–7 | |
| **XL2000.2** | **Working with files** | | | |
| XL2000.2.1 | Use Save | Excel A-10 | Step 8 | Skills Review |
| XL2000.2.2 | Use Save As (different name, location, format) | Excel A-8<br>Excel F-16 | Steps 5–6<br>Steps 1–8 | Skills Review<br>Skills Review |
| XL2000.2.3 | Locate and open an existing workbook | Excel A-8 | Steps 1–4 | Skills Review |
| XL2000.2.4 | Create a folder | Excel F-16 | QuickTip | |
| XL2000.2.5 | Use templates to create a new workbook | Excel G-5 | Clues to Use | |
| XL2000.2.6 | Save a worksheet/workbook as a Web page | Excel F-16 | Steps 1–7 | Skills Review |
| XL2000.2.7 | Send a workbook via e-mail | Excel F-17 | Clues to Use | |
| XL2000.2.8 | Use the Office Assistant | Excel A-14 | Steps 1–6, Clues to Use | Independent Challenge 1 |
| **XL2000.3** | **Formatting worksheets** | | | |
| XL2000.3.1 | Apply font styles (typeface, size, color and styles) | Excel C-4<br><br>Excel C-6 | Steps 2–5, Clues to Use<br>Steps 2–7 | Skills Review<br>Independent Challenges 1–4, Visual Workshop |
| XL2000.3.2 | Apply number formats (currency, percent, dates, comma) | Excel C-2 | Steps 3–5 | Skills Review, Independent Challenges 1–4, Visual Workshop |

| MOUS standardized coding number | Activity | Lesson page where skill is covered | Location in lesson where skill is covered | Practice |
|---|---|---|---|---|
| XL2000.3.3 | Modify size of rows and columns | Excel C-8<br>Excel C-9 | Steps 1–7<br>Clues to Use | Skills Review,<br>Independent Challenges 1–4 |
| XL2000.3.4 | Modify alignment of cell content | Excel C-6 | Step 7 | Skills Review,<br>Independent Challenges 1–4 |
| XL2000.3.5 | Adjust the decimal place | Excel C-1 | Step 5 | Skills Review |
| XL2000.3.6 | Use the Format Painter | Excel C-3<br>Excel C-14 | Clues to Use<br>Step 6 | Skills Review,<br>Independent Challenges 1–4 |
| XL2000.3.7 | Apply autoformat | Excel C-7 | Clues to Use | |
| XL2000.3.8 | Apply cell borders and shading | Excel C-12 | Steps 2–8 | Skills Review,<br>Independent Challenges 1–4 |
| XL2000.3.9 | Merging cells | Excel C-6 | Step 6 | Skills Review,<br>Independent Challenge 2 |
| XL2000.3.10 | Rotate text and change indents | Excel H-13 | Clues to Use | |
| XL2000.3.11 | Define, apply, and remove a style | Excel E-4 | Step 4 | |
| **XL2000.4** | **Page setup and printing** | | | |
| XL2000.4.1 | Preview and print worksheets & workbooks | Excel A-12<br><br>Excel B-18<br><br>Excel F-6 | Steps 1–5<br><br>Step 7<br><br>Step 6 | Skills Review,<br>Independent Challenges 2–4<br>Skills Review,<br>Visual Workshop<br>Skills Review,<br>Independent Challenge 1 |
| XL2000.4.2 | Use Web Page Preview | Excel F-16 | Step 7 | |
| XL2000.4.3 | Print a selection | Excel H-16 | QuickTip | |
| XL2000.4.4 | Change page orientation and scaling | Excel D-16<br>Excel E-16 | Steps 2–5<br>Step 6 | Skills Review |

| MOUS standardized coding number | Activity | Lesson page where skill is covered | Location in lesson where skill is covered | Practice |
|---|---|---|---|---|
| XL2000.4.5 | Set page margins and centering | Excel E-17 | Clues to Use | Skills Review |
| XL2000.4.6 | Insert and remove a page break | Excel F-12 | Steps 1–6 Clues to Use | |
| XL2000.4.7 | Set print, and clear a print area | Excel H-17 | Clues to Use | Skills Review |
| XL2000.4.8 | Set up headers and footers | Excel F-5 | Clues to Use | Skills Review |
| XL2000.4.9 | Set print titles and options (gridlines, print quality, row & column headings) | Excel H-16 | QuickTip | |
| **XL2000.5** | **Working with worksheets & workbooks** | | | |
| XL2000.5.1 | Insert and delete rows and columns | Excel C-10 | Steps 1–6 | Skills Review |
| XL2000.5.2 | Hide and unhide rows and columns | Excel F-8 Excel F-8 | Step 3 Table F-1 | |
| XL2000.5.3 | Freeze and unfreeze rows and columns | Excel F-2 | Steps 2–7 | Skills Review |
| XL2000.5.4 | Change the zoom setting | Excel F-10 | Step 1 | Skills Review |
| XL2000.5.5 | Move between worksheets in a workbook | Excel B-18 | Steps 1–2 | Skills Review, Independent Challenges 1–4 |
| XL2000.5.6 | Check spelling | Excel C-16 | Steps 1–5 | |
| XL2000.5.7 | Rename a worksheet | Excel B-18 | Steps 3–4 | Skills Review, Independent Challenges 1–4 |
| XL2000.5.8 | Insert and delete worksheets | Excel B-18 | QuickTip | Skills Review |
| XL2000.5.9 | Move and copy worksheets | Excel B-18 Excel B-19 | Step 6 Clues to Use | |

| MOUS standardized coding number | Activity | Lesson page where skill is covered | Location in lesson where skill is covered | Practice |
|---|---|---|---|---|
| XL2000.5.10 | Link worksheets & consolidate data using 3D References | Excel F-6 | Steps 1–8<br>Clues to Use | Skills Review |
| **XL2000.6** | **Working with formulas & functions** | | | |
| XL2000.6.1 | Enter a range within a formula by dragging | Excel B-8 | Steps 4–6 | |
| XL2000.6.2 | Enter formulas in a cell and using the formula bar | Excel B-6 | Steps 1–4 | Skills Review,<br>Independent Challenges 1–4 |
| XL2000.6.3 | Revise formulas | Excel B-16 | Steps 6–7 | Skills Review,<br>Independent Challenges 1–4 |
| XL2000.6.4 | Use references (absolute and relative) | Excel B-12<br>Excel B-14<br>Excel B-16 | Details<br>Steps 1–8<br>Steps 1–8 | Skills Review,<br>Independent Challenges 1, 4 |
| XL2000.6.5 | Use AutoSum | Excel B-8 | Steps 2–4 | Skills Review |
| XL2000.6.6 | Use Paste Function to insert a function | Excel B-8 | Steps 7–9 | |
| XL2000.6.7 | Use basic functions (AVERAGE, SUM, COUNT, MIN, MAX) | Excel B-8<br>Excel B-9 | Steps 8–9<br>Clues to Use | Skills Review |
| XL2000.6.8 | Enter functions using the formula palette | Excel E-12 | Steps 6–7 | Skills Review |
| XL2000.6.9 | Use date functions (NOW and DATE) | Excel E-8 | Clues to Use | Skills Review |
| XL2000.6.10 | Use financial functions (FV and PMT) | PMT Excel E-14<br>FV Excel E-15 | Steps 2–5<br>Clues to Use | Skills Review<br>Skills Review |
| XL2000.6.11 | Use logical functions (IF) | E-10 | Steps 1–5 | Skills Review |

| MOUS standardized coding number | Activity | Lesson page where skill is covered | Location in lesson where skill is covered | Practice |
|---|---|---|---|---|
| **XL2000.7** | **Using charts and objects** | | | |
| XL2000.7.1 | Preview and print charts | Excel D-16 | Steps 2–8 | Skills Review, Independent Challenges 1–4, Visual Workshop |
| XL2000.7.2 | Use chart wizard to create a chart | Excel D-4 | Steps 2–7 | Skills Review, Independent Challenges 1–4, Visual Workshop |
| XL2000.7.3 | Modify charts | Excel D-6<br>Excel D-8<br>Excel D-10 | Steps 2–8<br>Steps 2–6<br>Steps 2–6 | Skills Review, Independent Challenges 1–4, Visual Workshop |
| XL2000.7.4 | Insert, move, and delete an object (picture) | Excel F-15 | Clues to Use | Skills Review |
| XL2000.7.5 | Create and modify lines and objects | Excel D-12<br>Excel D-14 | Steps 4–8<br>Steps 2–8 | |

# Project Files List

To complete many of the lessons and practice exercises in this book, students need to use a Project File that is supplied by Course Technology and stored on a Project Disk. Below is a list of the files that are supplied, and the unit or practice exercise to which the files correspond. For information on how to obtain Project Files, please see the inside cover of this book. The following list only includes Project Files that are supplied; it does not include the files students create from scratch or the files students create by revising the supplied files.

| Unit | File supplied on Project Disk | Location file is used in unit |
|---|---|---|
| Excel Unit A | EX A-1.xls | Lessons |
| | EX A-2.xls | Skills Review |
| Excel Unit B | EX B-1.xls | Lessons |
| | EX B-2.xls | Skills Review |
| | EX B-3.xls | Independent Challenge 3 |
| Excel Unit C | EX C-1.xls | Lessons |
| | EX C-2.xls | Skills Review |
| | EX C-3.xls | Independent Challenge 1 |
| | EX C-4.xls | Independent Challenge 2 |
| | EX C-5.xls | Visual Workshop |
| Excel Unit D | EX D-1.xls | Lessons |
| | EX D-2.xls | Independent Challenge 1 |
| | EX D-3.xls | Independent Challenge 2 |
| | EX D-4.xls | Independent Challenge 3 |
| | EX D-5.xls | Visual Workshop |
| Excel Unit E | EX E-1.xls | Lessons |
| | EX E-2.xls | |
| | EX E-3.xls | |
| | EX E-4.xls | |
| | EX E-5.xls | Skills Review |
| | EX E-6.xls | Independent Challenge 1 |
| | EX E-7.xls | Independent Challenge 2 |
| | EX E-8.xls | Independent Challenge 4 |
| Excel Unit F | EX F-1.xls | Lessons |
| | Pay Rate Classifications | |
| | EX F-2.xls | Skills Review |
| | Expense Details | |
| | EX F-3.xls | Independent Challenge 1 |

| Unit | File supplied on Project Disk | Location file is used in unit |
|------|-------------------------------|-------------------------------|
| **Excel Unit G** | No files supplied | |
| **Excel Unit H** | EX H-1.xls | Lessons |
| | EX H-2.xls | Independent Challenge 2 |
| | EX H-3.xls | Independent Challenge 3 |
| | EX H-4.xls | Independent Challenge 4 |

Excel 2000

# Glossary

**3-D references** A reference that uses values on other sheets or workbooks, effectively creating another dimension to a workbook.

**Absolute reference** A cell reference that contains a dollar sign before the column letter and/or row number to indicate the absolute, or fixed, contents of specific cells. For example, the formula $A$1+$B$1 calculates only the sum of these specific cells no matter where the formula is copied in the workbook.

**Active cell** The current location of the cell pointer.

**Address** The location of a specific cell or range expressed by the coordinates of column and row; for example, A1.

**Alignment** The horizontal placement of cell contents; for example, left, center, or right.

**Anchors** Cells listed in a range address. For example, in the formula =SUM(A1:A15), A1 and A15 are anchors.

**Area chart** A line chart in which each area is given a solid color or pattern to emphasize the relationship between the pieces of charted information.

**Arguments** Information a function needs to create the answer. In an expression, multiple arguments are separated by commas. All of the arguments are enclosed in parentheses; for example, =SUM(A1:B1).

**Arithmetic operator** A symbol used in a formula, such as + or -, / or *, to perform mathematical operations.

**Attribute** The styling features such as bold, italics, and underlining that can be applied to cell contents.

**AutoComplete** A feature that automatically completes labels entered in adjoining cells in a column.

**AutoFill** A feature that creates a series of text or numbers when a range is selected using the fill handle.

**AutoFit** A feature that automatically adjusts the width of a column to accommodate its widest entry when the boundary to the right of the column selector is double-clicked.

**AutoFormat** Preset schemes that can be applied to format a range instantly. Excel comes with 16 AutoFormats that include colors, fonts, and numeric formatting.

**AutoSum** A feature that automatically creates totals using the AutoSum button.

**Background color** The color applied to the background of a cell.

**Bar chart** A chart that shows information as a series of (horizontal) bars.

**Border** The edge of a selected area of a worksheet. Lines and color can be applied to borders.

**Cancel button** The X in the formula bar; it removes information from the formula bar and restores the previous cell entry.

**Cell** The intersection of a column and row in a worksheet.

**Cell address** The unique location identified by intersecting column and row coordinates.

**Cell pointer** A highlighted rectangle around a cell that indicates the active cell.

**Cell reference** The address or name that identifies a cell's position in a worksheet; it consists of a letter that identifies the cell's column and a number that identifies its row; for example, cell B3. Cell references in worksheets can be used in formulas and are relative or absolute.

**Chart** A graphic representation of information from a worksheet. Types include 2-D and 3-D column, bar, pie, area, and line charts.

**Chart sheet** A separate sheet that contains a chart linked to worksheet data.

**Chart title** The name assigned to a chart.

**Chart Wizard** A series of dialog boxes that helps create or modify a chart.

**Check box** A square box in a dialog box that can be clicked to turn an option on or off.

**Clear** A command on the Edit menu used to erase a cell's contents, formatting, or both.

**Clipboard** A temporary storage area for cut or copied items that are available for pasting. See *Office Clipboard*.

**Clipboard toolbar** A toolbar that shows the contents of the Office Clipboard; contains buttons for copying and pasting items to and from the Office Clipboard.

**Close** A command that closes the file so you can no longer work with it, but keeps Excel open so that you can continue to work on other workbooks.

**Column chart** The default chart type in Excel that displays information as a series of (vertical) columns.

**Column selector button** The gray box containing the letter above the column.

**Conditional format** The format of a cell based on its value or the outcome of a formula.

**Conditional formula** A formula that makes calculations based on stated conditions, such as calculating a rebate based on a purchase amount.

**Consolidate** To add together values on multiple worksheets and display the result on another worksheet.

**Control menu box** A box in the upper-left corner of a window used to resize or close a window.

**Copy** A command that copies the content of selected cells and places it on the Clipboard.

**Cut** A command that removes the cell contents from the selected area of a worksheet and places them on the Clipboard.

**Data entry area** The unlocked portion of a worksheet where users are able to enter and change data.

**Data form** In an Excel list (or database), a dialog box that displays one record at a time.

**Data marker** A graphical representation of a data point, such as a bar or column.

**Data point** Individual piece of data plotted in a chart.

**Data series** The selected range in a worksheet that Excel converts into a graphic and displays as a chart.

**Database** An organized collection of related information. In Excel, a database is called a list.

**Delete** A command that removes cell contents from a worksheet.

**Dialog box** A window that opens when more information is needed to carry out a command.

**Dummy column/row** Blank column or row included at the end of a range that enables a formula to adjust when columns or rows are added or deleted.

**Dynamic page breaks** In a larger workbook, horizontal or vertical dashed lines that represent the place where pages print separately. They also adjust automatically when you insert or delete rows or columns, or change column widths or row heights.

**Edit** A change made to the contents of a cell or worksheet.

**Electronic spreadsheet** A computer program that performs calculations on data and organizes information into worksheets. A worksheet is divided into columns and rows, which form individual cells.

**Enter button** The check mark in the formula bar used to confirm an entry.

**Exploding pie slice** A slice of a pie chart that has been pulled away from the whole pie to add emphasis.

**External reference indicator** The exclamation point (!) used in a formula to indicate that a referenced cell is outside the active sheet.

**Field** In a list (an Excel database), a column that describes a characteristic about records, such as first name or city.

**Field name** A column label that describes a field.

**Fill color** Cell background color.

**Fill Down** A command that duplicates the contents of the selected cells in the range selected below the cell pointer.

**Fill handle** A small square in the lower-right corner of the active cell used to copy cell contents.

**Fill Right** A command that duplicates the contents of the selected cells in the range selected to the right of the cell pointer.

**Find** A command used to locate information the user specifies.

**Floating toolbar** A toolbar within its own window that is not anchored along an edge of the worksheet.

**Font** The typeface or design of a set of characters (letters, numbers, symbols, and punctuation marks).

**Footer** Information that prints at the bottom of each printed page; on screen, a footer is visible only in Print Preview. To add a footer, use the Header and Footer command on the View menu.

**Format** The appearance of text and numbers, including color, font, attributes, borders, and shading. See also *Number format*.

**Format Painter** A feature used to copy the formatting applied to one set of text or in one cell to another.

**Formula** A set of instructions used to perform numeric calculations (adding, multiplying, averaging, etc.).

**Formula bar** The area below the menu bar and above the Excel workspace where you enter and edit data in a worksheet cell. The formula bar becomes active when you start typing or editing cell data. It includes the Enter button and the Cancel button.

**Freeze** To hold in place selected columns or rows when scrolling in a worksheet that is divided in panes. See also *panes*.

**Function** A special, predefined formula that provides a shortcut for a commonly used calculation; for example, AVERAGE.

**Gridlines** Horizontal and/or vertical lines within a chart that make the chart easier to read.

**Header** Information that prints at the top of each printed page; on screen, a header is visible only in Print Preview. To add a header, use the Header and Footer command on the View menu.

**Hide** To make rows, columns, formulas, or sheets invisible to workbook users.

**HTML** Hypertext Markup Language, the format of pages that a Web browser such as Internet Explorer or Netscape Navigator can read.

**Hyperlink** An object (a filename, a word, a phrase, or a graphic) in a worksheet that, when you click it, will display another worksheet, called the target.

**Input** Information that produces desired results in a worksheet.

**Insertion point** Blinking I-beam that appears in the formula bar during entry and editing.

**Internet** A large computer network made up of smaller networks and computers.

**Intranet** An internal network site used by a particular group of people who work together.

**Label** Descriptive text or other information that identifies the rows and columns of a worksheet. Labels are not included in calculations.

**Label prefix**   A character that identifies an entry as a label and controls the way it appears in the cell.

**Landscape orientation**   A print setting that positions the worksheet on the page so the page is wider than it is tall.

**Legend**   A key explaining how information is represented by colors or patterns in a chart.

**Line chart**   A graph of data that is mapped by a series of lines. Line charts show changes in data or categories of data over time and can be used to document trends.

**Linking**   The dynamic referencing of data in other workbooks, so that when data in the other workbooks is changed, the references in the current workbook are automatically updated.

**List**   The Excel term for a database, an organized collection of related information.

**Lock**   To secure a row, column, or sheet so that data there cannot be changed.

**Logical test**   The first part of an IF function; if the logical test is true, then the second part of the function is applied, and if it is false, then the third part of the function is applied. In the function IF(Balance>1,000,Rate*0.05,0), the 5% rate is applied to balances over $1,000.

**Macro**   A set of instructions, or code, that performs tasks in the order you specify.

**Mixed reference**   Formula containing both a relative and an absolute reference.

**Mode indicator**   A box located at the lower-left corner of the status bar that informs you of the program's status. For example, when Excel is performing a task, the word "Wait" appears.

**More Buttons button**   A button you click on a toolbar to view toolbar buttons that are not currently visible.

**Mouse pointer**   A symbol that indicates the current location of the mouse on the desktop. The mouse pointer changes its shape at times; for example, when you insert data, select a range, position a chart, change the size of a window, or select a topic in Help.

**Moving border**   The dashed line that appears around a cell or range that is copied to the Clipboard.

**Name box**   The left-most area in the formula bar that shows the cell reference or name of the active cell. For example, A1 refers to cell A1 of the active worksheet. You can also get a list of names in a workbook using the Name list arrow.

**Named range**   A range of cells given a meaningful name; it retains its name when moved and can be referenced in a formula.

**Number format**   A format applied to values to express numeric concepts, such as currency, date, and percentage.

**Object**   A chart or graphic image that can be moved and resized and contains handles when selected.

**Office Assistant**   An animated character that appears to offer tips, answer questions, and provide access to the program's Help system.

**Office Clipboard**   A temporary storage area shared by all Office programs that can be used to cut, copy, and paste multiple items within and between Office programs. The Office Clipboard can hold up to 12 items collected from any Office program. See also *Clipboard toolbar.*

**Open**   A command that retrieves a workbook from a disk and displays it on the screen.

**Order of precedence**   The order in which Excel calculates parts of a formula: (1) exponents, (2) multiplication and division, and (3) addition and subtraction.

**Output**   The end result of a worksheet.

**Panes**   Sections into which you can divide a worksheet when you want to work on separate parts of the worksheet at the same time; one pane freezes, or remains in place, while you scroll in another pane until you see the desired information.

**Paste**   A command that moves information on the Clipboard to a new location. Excel pastes the formula, rather than the result, unless the Paste Special command is used.

**Paste Function**   A series of dialog boxes that lists and describes all Excel functions and assists the user in function creation.

**Pie chart**   A circular chart that represents data as slices of pie. A pie chart is useful for showing the relationship of parts to a whole; pie slices can be extracted for emphasis. See also *Exploding pie slice.*

**Point**   A unit of measure used for fonts and row height. One inch equals 72 points.

**Pointing method**   Specifying formula cell references by selecting the desired cell with your mouse instead of typing its cell reference; this eliminates typing errors.

**Portrait orientation**   A print setting that positions the worksheet on the page so the page is taller than it is wide.

**Precedence**   Algebraic rules that Excel uses to determine the order of calculations in a formula with more than one operator.

**Print Preview**   A command you can use to view the worksheet as it will look when printed.

**Print title**   In a list that spans more than one page, the field names that print at the top of every printed page.

**Program**   Task-oriented software (such as Excel or Word) that enables you to perform a certain type of task, such as data calculation or word processing.

**Programs menu**   The Windows 95/98 Start menu that lists all available programs on your computer.

**Range**   A selected group of adjacent cells.

**Range format**   A format applied to a selected range in a worksheet.

**Record**   In a list (an Excel database), data about an object or a person.

**Relative cell reference** A type of cell reference used to indicate a relative position in the worksheet. It allows you to copy and move formulas from one area to another of the same dimensions. Excel automatically changes the column and row numbers to reflect the new position.

**Replace** A command used to find one set of criteria and replace it with new information.

**Reset usage data** An option that returns personalized toolbars and menus to their default settings.

**Row height** The vertical dimension of a cell.

**Row selector button** The gray box containing the number to the left of the row.

**Save** A command used to permanently store your workbook and any changes you make to a file on a disk. The first time you save a workbook you must give it a filename.

**Save As** A command used to create a duplicate of the current workbook with a new filename. Used the first time you save a workbook.

**Selection handles** Small boxes appearing along the corners and sides of charts and graphic images that are used for moving and resizing.

**Series of labels** Pre-programmed series, such as days of the week and months of the year. They are formed by typing the first word of the series, then dragging the fill handle to the desired cell.

**Sheet** Another term used for a *worksheet*.

**Sheet tab** A description at the bottom of each worksheet that identifies it in a workbook. In an open workbook, move to a worksheet by clicking its sheet tab. Also known as *Worksheet tab*.

**Sheet tab scrolling buttons** Buttons that enable you to move among sheets within a workbook.

**Sort keys** Criteria on which a sort, or a reordering of data, is based.

**Spell check** A command that attempts to match all text in a worksheet with the words in the dictionary.

**Start** To open a software program so you can use it.

**Status bar** The bar at the bottom of the Excel window that provides information about various keys, commands, and processes.

**Target** The location that a hyperlink displays after you click it.

**Text annotations** Labels added to a chart to draw attention to a particular area.

**Text color** The color applied to the text within a cell.

**Tick marks** Notations of a scale of measure on a chart axis.

**Title bar** The bar at the top of the window that indicates the program name and the name of the current worksheet.

**Toggle button** A button that turns a feature on and off.

**Toolbar** A bar that contains buttons that give you quick access to the most frequently used commands.

**Truncate** To shorten the display of a cell based on the width of a cell.

**Values** Numbers, formulas, or functions used in calculations.

**View** A set of display or print settings that you can name and save for access at another time. You can save multiple views of a worksheet.

**What-if analysis** A decision-making feature in which data is changed and automatically recalculated.

**Wildcard** A special symbol you use in defining search criteria in the data form or Replace dialog box. The most common types of wildcards are the question mark (?), which stands for any single character, and the asterisk (*), which represents any group of characters.

**Window** A rectangular area of a screen where you view and work on a worksheet.

**Workbook** A collection of related worksheets contained within a single file.

**Worksheet** An electronic spreadsheet containing 256 columns by 65,536 rows.

**Worksheet tab** See *Sheet tab*.

**Worksheet window** The worksheet area in which data is entered.

**World Wide Web** A structure of documents, called pages, connected electronically over a large computer network called the Internet.

**X-axis** The horizontal line in a chart.

**X-axis label** A label describing the x-axis of a chart.

**Y-axis** The vertical line in a chart.

**Y-axis label** A label describing the y-axis of a chart.

**Zoom** A feature that enables you to focus on a larger or smaller part of the worksheet in Print Preview.

# Index

## special characters

' (apostrophe)
    indicating numbers as text with, EXCEL H-2, EXCEL H-4
    prefacing code comments with, EXCEL G-9
$ (dollar sign)
    identifying absolute cell references with, EXCEL B-16
= (equal sign)
    indicating formulas, EXCEL B-6, EXCEL E-2
! (exclamation point)
    external reference indicator, EXCEL F-6
? (question mark) wildcard, EXCEL H-9
###### symbols
    column width and, EXCEL C-8

## ▶A

absolute cell references, EXCEL E-8
    copying formulas with, EXCEL B-16–17
    defined, EXCEL B-12
    identifying, EXCEL B-16
    for named ranges, EXCEL B-17
    using, EXCEL B-12–13
active cell, EXCEL A-6
Active Sheet(s) option button, EXCEL A-12
alignment
    defined, EXCEL C-6
    of labels, EXCEL A-10, EXCEL C-6–7
    setting, EXCEL E-17
    of text in charts, EXCEL D-12
    of values, EXCEL A-10
annotating charts, EXCEL D-14–15
apostrophe (')
    indicating numbers as text with, EXCEL H-2, EXCEL H-4
    prefacing code comments with, EXCEL G-9
area charts, EXCEL D-3, EXCEL D-9
arguments
    defined, EXCEL E-6
    in functions, EXCEL B-8–9
arithmetic operators, EXCEL B-6
Arrow button, EXCEL D-14
arrow keys
    navigating worksheet with, EXCEL A-11
arrows
    adding to charts, EXCEL D-14
ascending order sorts, EXCEL H-12–13, EXCEL H-14
Assign Macro dialog box, EXCEL G-14
attachments
    e-mailing workbooks as, EXCEL F-17
attributes
    conditional formatting, EXCEL C-14–15
    defined, EXCEL C-6
    of labels, EXCEL C-6–7
AutoCalculate, EXCEL E-7
AutoFit, EXCEL C-8
AutoFit Selection, EXCEL C-9, EXCEL H-4
AutoFormat, EXCEL C-7
AutoShape, EXCEL D-14
AutoSum function, EXCEL B-8, EXCEL E-6–7
AVERAGE function, EXCEL B-8, EXCEL B-9, EXCEL E-13

## ▶B

[Backspace] key
    correcting errors with, EXCEL A-10
bar charts, EXCEL D-3, EXCEL D-8–9
Between conditional formatting option, EXCEL C-15
blank lines
    inserting in macro code, EXCEL G-9
Bold button, EXCEL C-6
border buttons, EXCEL C-12, EXCEL C-13
borders
    for field names, EXCEL H-4
    in worksheets, EXCEL C-12–13

## ▶C

calculations
    with AutoCalculate, EXCEL E-7
    dates in, EXCEL E-8–9
    future value, with FV function, EXCEL E-15
    generating multiple totals with AutoSum, EXCEL E-6–7
    payment, with PMT function, EXCEL E-14–15
Cancel button, EXCEL B-4
case
    matching, in searches, EXCEL H-8–9
Category Axis Title, EXCEL D-12
cell address, EXCEL A-6
cell entries
    copying, EXCEL B-10–11
    editing, EXCEL B-4–5
    moving, EXCEL B-10–11
cell names. See named cells
cell pointer, EXCEL A-6
    returning to cell A1, EXCEL F-2
cell references
    absolute, EXCEL B-12–13, EXCEL E-8
    copied formulas and, EXCEL E-8
    defined, EXCEL B-6, EXCEL B-12
    mixed, EXCEL B-12
    relative, EXCEL B-12–13, EXCEL B-14–15
cells
    active, EXCEL A-6
    applying colors, patterns, and borders to, EXCEL C-12–13
    defined, EXCEL A-6
    deleting, EXCEL E-11
    deleting contents of, EXCEL G-6
    deleting formatting of, EXCEL G-6
    filling with sequential text, EXCEL B-15
    formatting, EXCEL C-2–3
    hiding, EXCEL F-8–9
    inserting, EXCEL E-11
    locking, EXCEL F-8–9
    moving border, EXCEL B-6
    protecting, EXCEL F-8–9
    ranges of, EXCEL A-10, EXCEL B-4–5
    unlocking/relocking, EXCEL F-9
Center button, EXCEL C-6
Chart Objects list box, EXCEL D-6, EXCEL D-7
Chart Options dialog box, EXCEL D-10–11, EXCEL D-12–13
charts, EXCEL A-2, EXCEL D-1–17
    annotating, EXCEL D-14–15
    creating, EXCEL D-4–5
    drawing on, EXCEL D-14–15
    editing, EXCEL D-8–9
    enhancing, EXCEL D-12–13
    formatting, EXCEL D-10–11
    identifying objects in, EXCEL D-7
    moving, EXCEL D-6–7
    planning, EXCEL D-2–3
    previewing, EXCEL D-16–17
    printing, EXCEL D-16–17
    resizing, EXCEL D-6–7
    rotating, EXCEL D-8
    uses of, EXCEL D-1
chart sheets, EXCEL D-4
Chart Source Data dialog box, EXCEL D-4
Chart toolbar, EXCEL D-6–7
    buttons, EXCEL D-10
    docking, EXCEL D-6
chart type buttons, EXCEL D-9
chart types
    area, EXCEL D-3, EXCEL D-9
    bar, EXCEL D-3, EXCEL D-8–9, EXCEL D-9
    changing, EXCEL D-8–9
    column, EXCEL D-3, EXCEL D-8–9
    commonly used, EXCEL D-3
    doughnut, EXCEL D-9
    line, EXCEL D-3, EXCEL D-9
    pie, EXCEL D-3, EXCEL D-9, EXCEL D-15
    radar, EXCEL D-9
    selecting, EXCEL D-2

3-D, EXCEL D-8, EXCEL D-9
    3-D area, EXCEL D-9
    3-D bar, EXCEL D-9
    3-D column, EXCEL D-9
    3-D cone, EXCEL D-9
    3-D cylinder, EXCEL D-9
    3-D line, EXCEL D-9
    3-D pie, EXCEL D-9
    3-D surface, EXCEL D-9
    XY (scatter), EXCEL D-3, EXCEL D-9
Chart Wizard button, EXCEL D-4
Clipboard, EXCEL B-10–11
Clippit, EXCEL A-14
Collapse dialog box, EXCEL B-8, EXCEL B-9, EXCEL E-12
Collapse Dialog Box button, EXCEL E-12
color
    using in worksheets, EXCEL C-12–13
column charts, EXCEL D-3, EXCEL D-8–9, EXCEL D-9
    three-dimensional, EXCEL D-8
Column command, EXCEL C-8
column headings
    printing, EXCEL H-16
Column Hide command, EXCEL C-9
column labels
    improving appearance of, EXCEL H-12
    sorting and, EXCEL H-12
columns
    deleting, EXCEL C-10–11
    dummy, EXCEL C-11
    freezing, EXCEL F-2–3
    hiding/unhiding, EXCEL F-9
    inserting, EXCEL C-10–11
Column Standard Width command, EXCEL C-8, EXCEL C-9
Column Unhide command, EXCEL C-9
column width
    adjusting, EXCEL C-8–9
    adjusting for field names, EXCEL H-4
    restoring defaults, EXCEL C-8, EXCEL C-9
Column Width command, EXCEL C-8–9
Column Width dialog box, EXCEL C-8
combination charts, EXCEL D-3
Comma style, EXCEL C-2
comments
    adding to macro code, EXCEL G-9
comparison operators, EXCEL E-11
conditional formatting, EXCEL C-14–15
    deleting, EXCEL C-15
    options, EXCEL C-15
Conditional Formatting dialog box, EXCEL C-14–15
conditional formulas
    building with IF function, EXCEL E-10–11
    defined, EXCEL E-10
consolidating data
    with 3-D references, EXCEL F-6–7
    with linking, EXCEL F-7
Copy button, EXCEL B-10, EXCEL B-14
copying
    active worksheet, EXCEL F-4
    cell entries, EXCEL B-10–11
    formulas, EXCEL E-2–3, EXCEL E-8–9
    formulas, with absolute cell references, EXCEL B-16–17
    formulas, with relative cell references, EXCEL B-14–15
    named ranges, EXCEL B-17
    with Paste Special command, EXCEL E-3
    worksheets, EXCEL B-19
copy pointer, EXCEL B-3
COUNTA function, EXCEL E-12–13
COUNT function, EXCEL B-9, EXCEL E-12–13
criteria
    for deleting records, EXCEL H-10–11
    for finding records, EXCEL H-8–9
Criteria data form, EXCEL H-8–9
cross (normal) pointer, EXCEL B-3
Currency style, EXCEL C-2–3
Custom Buttons
    for Macros toolbar, EXCEL G-16–17

# Index

custom formats
    for numbers and dates, EXCEL E-9
Customize dialog box, EXCEL G-16–17
    restoring defaults with, EXCEL A-7, EXCEL A-8
custom sort order, EXCEL H-15
custom views
    saving, EXCEL F-10–11
Custom Views dialog box, EXCEL F-10–11

## ▶ D
data
    consolidating, with 3-D references, EXCEL F-6–7
    illustrating in charts, EXCEL D-2
    recalculation of, EXCEL A-2
    sharing with others, EXCEL A-2
databases
    defined, EXCEL H-1 (See also lists)
    vs. lists, EXCEL H-3
data entry
    computer vs. manual systems, EXCEL A-2
data entry area
    locking cells outside of, EXCEL F-8
data form
    adding records to lists with, EXCEL H-6–7
data format, EXCEL C-2
data markers, on charts, EXCEL D-2
data points, on charts, EXCEL D-2
data series
    formatting, for charts, EXCEL D-10–11
DATE function, EXCEL E-8
dates
    in calculations, EXCEL E-8–9
    custom formats, EXCEL E-9
    functions, EXCEL E-8–9
DD-MM-YY format, EXCEL C-2
defaults
    column width, EXCEL C-8, EXCEL C-9
    macros names, EXCEL G-4
    menus, EXCEL A-7, EXCEL E-2
    restoring with Customize dialog box, EXCEL A-7, EXCEL A-8
    toolbars, EXCEL A-7, EXCEL D-4, EXCEL E-2
Define Name dialog box, EXCEL B-5
Delete button, EXCEL H-10–11
Delete Conditional Format dialog box, EXCEL C-15
Delete dialog box, EXCEL E-11
[Delete] key
    correcting errors with, EXCEL A-10
deleting
    cells, EXCEL E-11
    conditional formatting, EXCEL C-15
    macros, EXCEL G-6
    ranges, EXCEL H-10
    records, EXCEL H-10–11
    rows and columns, EXCEL C-10–11
    worksheets, EXCEL B-18, EXCEL F-4–5
descending order sorts, EXCEL H-12, EXCEL H-14
diagonal resizing pointer, EXCEL D-7
dictionary (spell checker)
    modifying, EXCEL C-16
displaying
    formula contents, EXCEL E-16–17
dollar sign ($)
    identifying absolute cell references with, EXCEL B-16
doughnut charts, EXCEL D-9
drag-and-drop
    copying information with, EXCEL B-10–11
drawing
    on charts, EXCEL D-14–15
Drawing toolbar, EXCEL D-14
drawn objects
    charts as, EXCEL D-6
draw pointer, EXCEL D-7
drop shadows
    surrounding chart titles, EXCEL D-12
dummy columns, EXCEL C-11
dummy rows, EXCEL C-11
dynamic page breaks, EXCEL F-12

## ▶ E
editing
    cell entries, EXCEL B-4–5
    charts, EXCEL D-8–9

Edit mode
    changing to, EXCEL B-4
    correcting errors in, EXCEL A-10
electronic spreadsheets. See also worksheets
    defined, EXCEL A-2
e-mail
    sending workbooks via, EXCEL F-17
embedding objects
    in worksheets, EXCEL B-11
Entire workbook option button, EXCEL B-18
entry order sorts, EXCEL H-12
equal sign (=)
    indicating formulas, EXCEL B-6, EXCEL E-2
Equal to conditional formatting option, EXCEL C-15
Excel 2000
    advantages of, EXCEL A-2
    exiting, EXCEL A-16–17
    Help system, EXCEL A-14–15
    starting, EXCEL A-4–5
Excel Chart Wizard, EXCEL D-4–5
Excel Macro Recorder
    recording macros with, EXCEL G-4–5, EXCEL G-8
Excel window. See worksheet window
exclamation point (!)
    external reference indicator, EXCEL F-6
exiting
    Excel 2000, EXCEL A-16–17
Expand dialog box, EXCEL B-8
exploded pie charts, EXCEL D-15
external reference indicator, EXCEL F-6

## ▶ F
field names
    adjusting column widths for, EXCEL H-4
    borders for, EXCEL H-4
    defined, EXCEL H-2
    guidelines for, EXCEL H-5
    planning, EXCEL H-2
fields
    defined, EXCEL H-2
    planning, EXCEL H-2
    sorting lists by, EXCEL H-12–13
fill handle pointer, EXCEL B-3
fill handles
    copying formulas with, EXCEL B-14–15
Fill Right method, EXCEL B-14
Fill Series command, EXCEL B-15
finding
    records in lists, EXCEL H-8–9
    with wildcards, EXCEL H-9
finding text, EXCEL F-2
folders
    creating, in Save As dialog box, EXCEL F-16
fonts
    in charts, EXCEL D-12
    conditional formatting, EXCEL C-14–15
    defined, EXCEL C-4
    formatting, EXCEL C-4–5
    types of, EXCEL C-5
font size
    defined, EXCEL C-4
    formatting, EXCEL C-4–5
    row height and, EXCEL C-8
footers
    specifying, EXCEL F-5
Format button, EXCEL D-12
Format Cells dialog box, EXCEL C-2–3, EXCEL C-4–5,
    EXCEL C-12–13, EXCEL C-14, EXCEL E-9
Format Chart Title dialog box, EXCEL D-12
Format Column commands, EXCEL C-8–9
Format Data Series dialog box, EXCEL D-10–11
Format Painter, EXCEL C-3, EXCEL C-14
formatting
    charts, EXCEL D-10–11
    chart titles, EXCEL D-12
    clearing, EXCEL C-6
    conditional, EXCEL C-14–15
    custom, for numbers and dates, EXCEL E-9
    defined, EXCEL C-2
    deleting, EXCEL G-6
    fonts and font sizes, EXCEL C-4–5
    numbers, EXCEL C-2–3, EXCEL H-2

    predefined, EXCEL C-7
    shortcuts, EXCEL C-6
    values, EXCEL C-2–3
    worksheets, EXCEL C-1–17
Formatting toolbar, EXCEL H-4
    changing fonts and font sizes with, EXCEL C-4
    defined, EXCEL A-6
    restoring defaults, EXCEL A-7
formula bar
    defined, EXCEL A-6
    editing cell entries in, EXCEL B-4–5
    formulas with names in, EXCEL E-4–5
Formula Palette, EXCEL E-13
formula prefix (equal sign), EXCEL B-8
formulas
    absolute cell references in, EXCEL B-12
    conditional, EXCEL E-10–11
    copying, EXCEL E-2–3, EXCEL E-8–9
    copying, with absolute cell references, EXCEL B-16–17
    copying, with relative cell references, EXCEL B-14–15
    defined, EXCEL B-6
    displaying contents of, EXCEL E-16–17
    editing with Formula Palette, EXCEL E-13
    entering, EXCEL B-6–7
    entering with Formula Palette, EXCEL E-13
    hiding/unhiding, EXCEL F-8–9
    inserting and deleting rows and columns and, EXCEL C-10
    order of precedence in, EXCEL B-6
    pointing method for, EXCEL B-6
    precedence rules, EXCEL E-2
    printing contents of, EXCEL E-16–17
    relative cell references in, EXCEL B-12
    with several operators, EXCEL E-2–3
    using names in, EXCEL E-4–5
Freeze panes command, EXCEL F-2
freezing
    rows and columns, EXCEL F-2–3
functions, EXCEL B-7–8
    arguments for, EXCEL B-8
    date, EXCEL E-8–9
    defined, EXCEL B-7
    entering, EXCEL E-6
    frequently used, EXCEL B-9
    most recently used, EXCEL B-8
    statistical, EXCEL E-12–13
future value, EXCEL E-15
FV function, EXCEL E-15

## ▶ G
Go To command, EXCEL E-2
Greater than conditional formatting option, EXCEL C-15
Greater than or equal to conditional formatting option, EXCEL C-15
gridlines
    on charts, EXCEL D-10
    printing, EXCEL H-16

## ▶ H
headers
    specifying, EXCEL F-5
Help, EXCEL A-14–15
hiding
    formulas, EXCEL F-8–9
    worksheets areas, EXCEL F-7–8
horizontal resizing pointer, EXCEL D-7
HTML files
    saving Excel files as, EXCEL F-16–17
hyperlinks
    creating between Excel files, EXCEL F-14–15
Hypertext Markup Language. See HTML files

## ▶ I
I-beam pointer, EXCEL B-3, EXCEL D-7
IF function
    building conditional formulas with, EXCEL E-10–11
Increase Decimal button, EXCEL C-2
indenting
    labels, EXCEL H-12
Insert ClipArt window, EXCEL F-15
Insert dialog box, EXCEL C-10–11, EXCEL E-11

Insert Hyperlink dialog box, EXCEL F-14–15
inserting
    blank lines, in macro code, EXCEL G-9
    cells, EXCEL E-11
    columns, EXCEL C-10–11
    pictures, EXCEL F-15
    rows, EXCEL C-10–11
    worksheets, EXCEL F-4–5
insertion point, EXCEL B-4
Internet, EXCEL F-16
intranets, EXCEL F-16
Italics button, EXCEL C-6

▶ L

Label Ranges dialog box, EXCEL E-4
labels. *See also* column labels
    alignment of, EXCEL A-10, EXCEL C-6–7
    attributes of, EXCEL C-6–7
    defined, EXCEL A-10
    entering, EXCEL A-10–11
    entering numbers as, EXCEL A-10
    truncated, EXCEL A-10
landscape orientation, EXCEL E-16–17
    printing charts in, EXCEL D-16–17
    printing worksheets in, EXCEL H-16
Less than conditional formatting option, EXCEL C-15
Less than or equal to conditional formatting option, EXCEL C-15
line charts, EXCEL D-3, EXCEL D-9
linking
    consolidating data with, EXCEL F-7
lists, EXCEL H-1–17
    adding records with data form, EXCEL H-6–7
    creating, EXCEL H-4–5
    databases *vs.*, EXCEL H-3
    defined, EXCEL H-1
    finding records in, EXCEL H-8–9
    maintaining quality of information in, EXCEL H-5
    number formatting for, EXCEL H-2
    planning, EXCEL H-2–3
    printing, EXCEL H-16–17
    row and column content guidelines, EXCEL H-3
    size and location guidelines, EXCEL H-3
    sorting, by multiple fields, EXCEL H-14–15
    sorting by one field, EXCEL H-12–13
Locked check box, EXCEL F-8
locking selected cells, EXCEL F-8–9
logical operators
    conditional formatting and, EXCEL C-14–15
logical tests, EXCEL E-10

▶ M

macros, EXCEL G-1–17
    adding as menu items, EXCEL G-14–15
    adding blank lines to, EXCEL G-9
    adding comments to code, EXCEL G-9
    creating toolbars for, EXCEL G-16–17
    default names for, EXCEL G-4
    defined, EXCEL G-1
    deleting, EXCEL G-6
    descriptions of, EXCEL G-2–3
    disabling, EXCEL G-3
    editing, EXCEL G-8–9
    enabling, EXCEL G-3
    naming, EXCEL G-2
    Personal Macro Workbook, EXCEL G-12–13
    planning, EXCEL G-2–3
    recording, EXCEL G-4–5
    running, EXCEL G-6–7
    shortcut keys for, EXCEL G-10–11
    stopping, while running, EXCEL G-6
    storing, EXCEL G-2
    storing in modules, EXCEL G-8
    uses of, EXCEL G-1
    viruses and, EXCEL G-3
Major Gridlines checkbox, EXCEL D-10
margin lines
    displaying in Print Preview window, EXCEL D-16
margins
    setting, EXCEL E-17
Match case box, EXCEL H-8–9

MAX function, EXCEL B-9, EXCEL E-12–13
menu bar, EXCEL A-6
menus
    adding macros to, EXCEL G-14–15
    restoring defaults, EXCEL E-2
    restoring defaults to, EXCEL A-7
Merge and Center button, EXCEL C-6
Microsoft Clip Gallery, EXCEL F-15
MIN function, EXCEL B-9, EXCEL E-12–13
Minor Gridlines checkbox, EXCEL D-10
mixed cell references, EXCEL B-12
mode indicator, EXCEL B-4
modules
    storing macros in, EXCEL G-8
More Buttons button, EXCEL A-6, EXCEL A-7
mouse pointers. *See* pointers
move chart pointer, EXCEL D-7
move pointer, EXCEL B-3
moving
    cell entries, EXCEL B-10–11
    charts, EXCEL D-6–7
    named ranges, EXCEL B-17
    worksheets, EXCEL B-18–19
moving border, EXCEL B-6

▶ N

name box, EXCEL A-6
named cells
    in formulas, EXCEL E-4–5
named ranges
    absolute references for, EXCEL B-17
    copying, EXCEL B-17
    in formulas, EXCEL E-4–5
    moving, EXCEL B-17
    range names, EXCEL B-5
named worksheets, EXCEL B-18–19
names
    producing list of, EXCEL E-5
navigating worksheets, EXCEL A-11
    with hyperlinks, EXCEL F-14
New Toolbar dialog box, EXCEL G-16–17
normal (cross) pointer, EXCEL B-3
Not between conditional formatting option, EXCEL C-15
Not equal to conditional formatting option, EXCEL C-15
NOW function, EXCEL E-8
numbers
    custom formats, EXCEL E-9
    entering as labels, EXCEL A-10
    formatting, EXCEL C-2–3, EXCEL H-2

▶ O

objects
    charts as, EXCEL D-6
    embedding, EXCEL B-11
    identifying in charts, EXCEL D-7
    moving, EXCEL D-6
    resizing, EXCEL D-6
Office Assistant, EXCEL A-14–15
    changing, EXCEL A-14
Office Assistant dialog box, EXCEL A-14
Office Clipboard, EXCEL B-10–11
Open dialog box, EXCEL A-8–9
operators
    multiple, in formulas, EXCEL E-2–3
    precedence and, EXCEL E-2
order of precedence, EXCEL E-2
    in formulas, EXCEL B-6

▶ P

Page Break command, EXCEL F-12
Page Break Preview, EXCEL F-13, EXCEL H-17
page breaks, EXCEL F-12–13
    dynamic, EXCEL F-12
    horizontal, EXCEL F-12–13
    vertical, EXCEL F-12
page numbering, EXCEL F-12–13
Page Setup dialog box, EXCEL D-16–17
    Sheet tab, EXCEL H-16–17
Page Setup options, EXCEL E-16–17

panes
    defined, EXCEL F-2
    splitting worksheets in, EXCEL F-3
parentheses
    formulas using, EXCEL E-2
Paste button, EXCEL B-14
Paste command, EXCEL B-10
Paste Function dialog box, EXCEL B-8, EXCEL B-9
Paste Special command, EXCEL B-11, EXCEL E-3
patterns
    using in worksheets, EXCEL C-12–13
payments
    calculating with PMT function, EXCEL E-14–15
Percent style, EXCEL C-2, EXCEL E-4
Personal Macro Workbook, EXCEL G-1, EXCEL G-12–13
pictures
    inserting, EXCEL F-15
pie charts, EXCEL D-3, EXCEL D-9
    exploding slice, EXCEL D-15
PMT function, EXCEL E-14–15
pointers
    cell, EXCEL A-6, EXCEL F-2
    commonly used, EXCEL B-3, EXCEL D-7
    copy, EXCEL B-3
    cross (normal), EXCEL B-3
    diagonal resizing, EXCEL D-7
    draw, EXCEL D-7
    fill handle, EXCEL B-3
    horizontal resizing, EXCEL D-7
    I-beam, EXCEL B-3, EXCEL D-7
    move, EXCEL B-3
    move chart, EXCEL D-7
    vertical resizing, EXCEL D-7
    Zoom, EXCEL E-16
pointing method
    for entering formulas, EXCEL B-6
points
    defined, EXCEL C-4
    row height in, EXCEL C-8
Portrait option, EXCEL E-16–17
posting files to the Web, EXCEL F-16
precedence, order of, EXCEL E-2
previewing
    charts, EXCEL D-16–17
    worksheets, EXCEL A-12–13, EXCEL B-18
print areas
    clearing, EXCEL H-17
    setting, EXCEL H-17
Print dialog box, EXCEL A-12–13, EXCEL H-17
printing
    charts, EXCEL D-16–17
    formula contents, EXCEL E-16–17
    landscape orientation, EXCEL D-16–17
    lists, EXCEL H-16–17
    more than one worksheet, EXCEL H-16
    multiple ranges, EXCEL H-16
    selected areas of worksheets, EXCEL H-16–17
    setting margins and alignment for, EXCEL E-17
    worksheets, EXCEL A-12–13
Print Preview, EXCEL E-16–17, EXCEL G-14, EXCEL H-16–17
    for charts, EXCEL D-16–17
    for page breaks, EXCEL F-13
    for worksheets, EXCEL A-12–13
    Zoom in, EXCEL A-12
print title, EXCEL H-16
Programs list, EXCEL A-4–5
protection, of worksheets areas, EXCEL F-8–9
Protection tab, EXCEL F-8–9

▶ Q

question mark (?) wildcard, EXCEL H-9

▶ R

radar charts, EXCEL D-9
range address, EXCEL B-5
range finder, EXCEL B-16
range names. *See* named ranges
ranges
    defined, EXCEL A-10, EXCEL B-5
    deleting, EXCEL H-10

# Index

formatting, EXCEL C-2–3
  printing multiple, EXCEL H-16
  working with, EXCEL B-4–5
recalculation
  computer *vs.* manual systems, EXCEL A-2
recording macros, EXCEL G-4–5
Record Macro dialog box, EXCEL G-4–5, EXCEL G-10–11,
  EXCEL G-12–13
records
  defined, EXCEL H-2
  deleting, EXCEL H-10–11
  finding in lists, EXCEL H-8–9
  restoring, EXCEL H-11
Redisplay Dialog Box button, EXCEL E-12
references
  creating, EXCEL F-6
  external reference indicators, EXCEL F-6
  3-D, EXCEL F-6–7
relative cell references
  copying formulas with, EXCEL B-14–15
  defined, EXCEL B-12
  using, EXCEL B-12–13
Relative Reference button, EXCEL G-10–11
Replace All option, EXCEL H-8–9
Replace dialog box, EXCEL H-8–9
Replace option, EXCEL H-8–9
Report Manager, EXCEL F-10
resizing charts, EXCEL D-6–7
restoring records, EXCEL H-11
rotating charts, EXCEL D-8
rotating labels, EXCEL H-12
row headings
  printing, EXCEL H-16
Row Height command, EXCEL C-8
rows
  deleting, EXCEL C-10–11
  dummy, EXCEL C-11
  freezing, EXCEL F-2–3
  hiding/unhiding, EXCEL F-9
  inserting, EXCEL C-10–11
  specifying height of, EXCEL C-8
running macros, EXCEL G-6–7

## ▶S

Save As command
  creating new workbook with, EXCEL A-8–9
Save As dialog box, EXCEL F-16–17
  creating folder in, EXCEL F-16
Save command, EXCEL A-8
saving
  custom views, EXCEL F-10–11
  as HTML files, EXCEL F-16–17
  workbooks, EXCEL A-8–9
scatter (XY) charts, EXCEL D-3, EXCEL D-9
ScreenTips, EXCEL A-14
searches. *See* finding
section handles
  for charts, EXCEL D-4
selections, of worksheets
  printing, EXCEL E-17
sequential text
  filling cells with, EXCEL B-15
sheet tabs, EXCEL A-6
sheet tab scrolling buttons, EXCEL A-6, EXCEL B-18
shortcut keys
  for macros, EXCEL G-10–11
shortcuts
  formatting, EXCEL C-6
sort buttons, EXCEL H-12
Sort command, EXCEL H-12
Sort dialog box, EXCEL H-14–15
sorting
  ascending order, EXCEL H-12–13, EXCEL H-14
  custom sort order, EXCEL H-15
  descending order, EXCEL H-12, EXCEL H-14
  entry order, EXCEL H-12
  lists, by multiple fields, EXCEL H-14–15
  lists, by one field, EXCEL H-12–13
sort keys, EXCEL H-14–15

spell checking, EXCEL C-16–17
Spelling dialog box, EXCEL C-16–17
splitting worksheets, EXCEL F-3
spreadsheets. *See* worksheets
Standard toolbar
  defined, EXCEL A-6
  restoring defaults, EXCEL A-7
Start button, EXCEL A-4
Start menu, EXCEL A-5
statistical functions, EXCEL E-12–13
status bar, EXCEL A-6
Stop Recording button, EXCEL G-4–5
Stop Recording toolbar, EXCEL G-4–5, EXCEL G-10–11
Style dialog box, EXCEL E-4
styles
  applying, EXCEL E-4
  defined, EXCEL E-4
  defining own, EXCEL E-4
SUM function, EXCEL B-8, EXCEL B-9, EXCEL E-13
  entering with AutoSum button, EXCEL E-6–7

## ▶T

targets
  hyperlinks to, EXCEL F-14–15
templates
  creating workbooks with, EXCEL G-5
text
  alignment in charts, EXCEL D-12
  color of, EXCEL C-12–13
  sequential, filling cells with, EXCEL B-15
text annotations
  adding to charts, EXCEL D-14–15
  repositioning, EXCEL D-15
Text box button, EXCEL D-14
three-dimensional charts
  rotating, EXCEL D-8
  types of, EXCEL D-9
3-D references, EXCEL F-6–7
tick marks, EXCEL D-2
title bar, EXCEL A-6
titles
  for charts, EXCEL D-12–13
  printing, EXCEL H-16
  for x- and y-axis, EXCEL D-12–13
TODAY function, EXCEL E-8
toolbars
  creating for macros, EXCEL G-16–17
  defined, EXCEL A-6
  Drawing, EXCEL D-14
  Formatting, EXCEL A-6, EXCEL A-7, EXCEL C-4
  restoring defaults, EXCEL A-7, EXCEL D-4, EXCEL E-2
  Standard, EXCEL A-6, EXCEL A-7
truncated labels, EXCEL A-10

## ▶U

Underline button, EXCEL C-6
Undo button, EXCEL B-4
Undo command
  restoring deleted records with, EXCEL H-11
Unfreeze panes command, EXCEL F-2

## ▶V

Value Axis Title, EXCEL D-12
values
  alignment of, EXCEL A-10
  defined, EXCEL A-10
  entering, EXCEL A-10–11
  formatting, EXCEL C-2–3
vertical resizing pointer, EXCEL D-7
views
  custom, saving, EXCEL F-10–11
viruses
  macros and, EXCEL G-3

## ▶W

Web
  preparing workbooks for publishing on, EXCEL F-14–17
Web Page Preview, EXCEL F-16–17

what-if analysis
  copying formulas with absolute cell references for,
    EXCEL B-16–17
  defined, EXCEL A-2
wildcards
  for searches, EXCEL H-8–9
workbooks, EXCEL F-1–17
  closing, EXCEL A-16–17
  consolidating data from, with linking, EXCEL F-7
  creating, by modifying existing workbook, EXCEL A-8–9
  creating hyperlinks between, EXCEL F-14–15
  creating with templates, EXCEL G-5
  defined, EXCEL A-6
  deleting worksheets from, EXCEL F-4–5
  inserting pictures in, EXCEL F-15
  inserting worksheets in, EXCEL F-4–5
  opening, EXCEL A-8–9
  protecting, EXCEL F-9
  saving, EXCEL A-8–9
  saving as HTML documents, EXCEL F-16–17
  sending via e-mail, EXCEL F-17
  specifying headers and footers for, EXCEL F-5
  using range names in, EXCEL B-5
Worksheet menu bar
  adding macros to, EXCEL G-14–15
worksheets
  borders in, EXCEL C-12–13
  calculations for, EXCEL B-2
  color in, EXCEL C-12–13
  common business uses for, EXCEL A-3
  computer *vs.* manual systems, EXCEL A-2–3
  conditional formatting, EXCEL C-14–15
  copying, EXCEL B-19, EXCEL F-4
  creating, EXCEL A-2, EXCEL B-2–3
  defined, EXCEL A-2
  deleting, EXCEL B-18, EXCEL F-4–5
  embedding objects in, EXCEL B-11
  formatting, EXCEL C-1–17
  hiding areas of, EXCEL F-8–9
  inserting, EXCEL F-4–5
  moving, EXCEL B-18–19
  moving among, EXCEL B-18
  naming, EXCEL B-18–19
  navigating, EXCEL A-11
  navigating with hyperlinks, EXCEL F-14
  page breaks and page numbering, EXCEL F-12–13
  patterns in, EXCEL C-12–13
  planning and designing, EXCEL B-2–3
  predefined formats, EXCEL C-7
  previewing, EXCEL A-12–13, EXCEL B-18
  printing, EXCEL A-12–13, EXCEL H-16–17
  printing more than one, EXCEL H-16
  printing selected areas of, EXCEL E-17, EXCEL H-16–17
  protecting areas of, EXCEL F-8–9
  saving as HTML documents, EXCEL F-16–17
  spell checking, EXCEL C-16–17
  splitting into multiple panes, EXCEL F-3
  title for, EXCEL B-2
worksheet window
  defined, EXCEL A-6
  viewing, EXCEL A-6–7
workspaces, EXCEL F-11
Wrap Text, EXCEL H-4

## ▶X

x-axis, EXCEL D-2
  creating titles for, EXCEL D-12–13
XY (scatter) charts, EXCEL D-3, EXCEL D-9

## ▶Y

y-axis, EXCEL D-2
  creating titles for, EXCEL D-12–13

## ▶Z

Zoom
  in Print Preview, EXCEL A-12
Zoom box, EXCEL F-10
Zoom pointer, EXCEL E-16